Tourism and Hospitality Industry

Manoranjan Pandey

NAMAN PUBLISHER & DISTRIBUTORS
NEW DELHI

Published by
Sangeeta Jain for Naman Publisher & Distributors
7360-B, Prem Nagar,
Gali No.1, Shakti Nagar,
Delhi-110007
PH: 23823642, MOB.: 09013478302
E-mail: rajivjain72@ymail.com

First Published – 2011

ISBN–978-81–920935–3-6

SOLE DISTRIBUTOR
JINDAL BOOK SERVICES
LG-4A, Ganpati Bhawan,
4675-B/21, Ansari Road,
Darya Ganj, Delhi - 110002

Jacket Designed by :
S.M. Graphics

Printed by:
Sachin Printers, Delhi, India

Preface

As per the Travel and Tourism Competitiveness Report 2009 by the World Economic Forum, India is ranked 11th in the Asia Pacific region and 62nd overall, moving up three places on the list of the world's attractive destinations. It is ranked the 14th best tourist destination for its natural resources and 24th for its cultural resources, with many World Heritage sites, both natural and cultural, rich fauna, and strong creative industries in the country. India also bagged 37th rank for its air transport network. The India travel and tourism industry ranked 5th in the long-term (10-year) growth and is expected to be the second largest employer in the world by 2019. India's hotel pipeline is the second largest in the Asia-Pacific region. The Indian hospitality industry is projected to grow at a rate of 8.8 per cent during 2007-16, placing India as the second-fastest growing tourism market in the world. Initiatives like massive investment in hotel infrastructure and open-sky policies made by the government are all aimed at propelling growth in the hospitality sector.zz

Commencing with a slow growth at the start of the millennium, the Indian tourism industry has performed quite well in the last couple of years. The Indian tourism industry has out performed the global tourism industry in terms of growth in the volume of international tourists as well as in terms of revenue. The World Travel and Tourism Council (WTTC) has named India along with China as one of the most fastest growing tourism industries for the next 10 to 15 years. According to WTTC the Travel and Tourism Industry contributes 2.1 per cent to India's GDP. The industry employed an estimated 24,349,000 people in 2006 (5.4% of total employment, or 1 in every 18.4 jobs). The key driver for this growth in the Indian tourism industry has been a fast growing economy for the last 3-4 years. Despite lagging in the basic infrastructure that supports the tourism industry, Indian tourism industry has been showing an impressive double-digit growth. In order to sustain this growth and meet the expectations, it is essential for the Government of India to invest in infrastructure such as transport and accommodations.

This book is designed and presented in an easy to read and easy to understand format. It will be beneficial to both aspiring professionals and those already in the industry.

We hope this text book meets its intended purpose as a practical resource, and serve as a vehicle for promoting the professionalism of this important segment of the Hospitality Industry.

MANORANJAN PANDEY

Contents

	Preface	*iii*
1.	Development of Tourism Industry	1
2.	Lodging Services	36
3.	Food Service Facilities	74
4.	Marketing of Tourism and Hospitality	112
5.	Tourism Planning and Operations	141
6.	Development of Health Tourism	176
7.	Modern Trends in Tourism and Hospitality Services	210
8.	Sustainable Tourism Development	248
	Bibliography	286
	Index	288

1

Development of Tourism Industry

Reasons for tourism growth are numerous, but six predominate. First, the move to shorter working hours and, second, the dynamic development of the "right" to holidays and vacations both mean that more people have more leisure time. Third, the high level of private transport promotes mobility. Next, improvements in real income have created a "new middle class." Initially, this phrase was used to describe an emerging, affluent blue-collar group.

Today it frequently describes two-income families. Fifth, a tendency to saturation in the consumer sector frees up more personal consumption resources for travel. And finally, new mediums of communication have made once exotic destinations familiar and less intimidating than before. These same communication advances have greatly facilitated the business of keeping in touch with home when traveling to remote destinations.

The result of the above dynamics has been substantial growth in employment in the tourism sector. To illustrate this growth, we can examine data that describe standard industrial classification : hotels, motels, and tourist courts. This industry is selected to represent tourism because it is one of the few that is more-or-less purely touristic. Data on employment change in SIC 701 were collected for the years 1967 to 1987 for the thirteen western states.

A measure of the health of tourism in a state is the performance of the hotel sector against the larger group of service activities of which tourism is a part. Of the five states tourism grow in relative importance, Nevada is certainly the standout. In 1967, one-third of its service workers were in hotels and motels; in 1987, the share is almost one-half. It should be noted that most of Nevada's hotels have casinos and casino employees are counted as hotel workers.

Despite the fact that Nevada's hotel employment data are in one sense inflated, they speak to the fact that tourism is a major industry. Other states that show well in terms of relative growth are Wyoming and Hawaii. Wyoming is a small state - its relative growth is more impressive than its absolute growth.

Hawaii, on the other hand, is impressive in both absolute and relative terms. Between 1967 and 1987, Hawaii's service employment grew from 48,000 to 132,000, and hotel employment jumped from 17 percent to 24 percent of the service total. It is interesting to note that in all western states, the share of total service employment in hotels is larger in nonmetropolitan than in metropolitan areas. This finding is consistent with settlement system theory, but it is interesting nonetheless.

Perhaps the experiences of Hawaii and Nevada help to emphasize the significance of this measure since over one-half of all nonmetropolitan service workers in these states are employed in the hotel industry. However, even in the states at the bottom of the list, hotel employment is both relatively and absolutely important in rural areas. In short, the tourism industry has grown substantially in recent years, and conditions fostering additional growth appear to be in place. Nonmetropolitan areas already have benefited from this growth. Tourism is a significant component in the nonmetropolitan economies of most western states, and it is likely that tourism's position in nonmetropolitan areas will become stronger as metropolitan areas grow and become more affluent.

Development Strategy

Despite an abundance of scholarly and professional literature to the contrary, the terms economic development and recruitment of manufacturing plants are often thought of as describing identical callings. Slowly, and probably in part because so much attention has been given to the "decline-of-manufacturing-growth-of-services" topic, other industries are gaining the attention of development professionals and citizen groups concerned with economic development issues.

Tourism is currently at or at least near the top of the list of popular alternatives. The benefits of tourism can be substantial, but the industry also has a downside. There is no escaping the fact that economic gains will come with costs; both physical and human environments will be affected. Much of the literature suggests that the benefits of tourism outweigh the liabilities, although some studies, especially those dealing with tourism in Third and Fourth World settings, indicate that the net effects of tourism can be negative.

Benefits of Tourism

Many of the benefits of tourism are easily appreciated whereas others are more obscure. The more frequently mentioned of these potential direct benefits include:

— Tourism is, by definition, an export industry. As such, it has the potential to improve the regional balance of payments by increasing the demand for goods and services in a number of different sectors. This can be significant in nonmetropolitan areas where the export base is limited.

— Diversification is a frequent goal of local and regional development planning efforts. In nonmetropolitan areas especially, tourism offers a means of diversifying the economic base and reducing the seasonality in employment at the same time. For example, farmers or forestry workers may find winter employment when a ski complex is developed.

— Public officials are generally supportive of tourism development efforts because they hold the potential for increasing public revenue. Both because of the direct investment in a region and personal income growth, local and state governments can expect increased property and personal tax revenues.

— Finally, Patton suggests that tourism has the potential to use idle or excess capacity in declining regions. As a result, unemployment can be reduced and the fixed cost of infrastructure and institutional capacity can be spread over more consuming units.

In addition to the above direct effects, there are significant indirect economic benefits. The principal indirect benefit is the multiplier type impacts initiated by tourist spending. In addition, Gearing, Swart, and Var identified six impacts that can be considered to be positive externalities or spin-off benefits.

— The tourist industry leads to the development of an infrastructure for visitors as well as local residents.

— Jobs are made available for the relatively unskilled workers of the region.

— Tourism can be the main component of a regional policy aimed at achieving an equitable balance between uhe industrialized and nonindustrialized areas in a region.

— The tourist industry may contribute to the development of other industries, such as leather goods, handicrafts, watchmaking, jewelry, textiles, glassware, food and beverage, specialty confectionery, recreational equipment and supplies, and any other items consumed by tourists or by tourist-serving firms.

— Development of the tourist industry may promote a better image of the region in the eyes of the nation and thereby enable it to achieve other objectives such as business recruitment and retention.

— Tourism can build local self-esteem by demonstrating that the area is, indeed, desirable.

When potential direct benefits are taken together with indirect or spin-off benefits, an extensive list is created. Moreover, most regions will find the list seductive. Nonmetropolitan regions with limited options for growth and development are particularly likely to find the tourism option difficult to resist.

Liabilities

Tourism does have a down side-at least a potential down side. As seductive as the tourism option may be, the intelligent development planner will weigh the benefits and liabilities, and he or she will base programmatic decisions on the estimated net benefits associated with alternative strategies.

The list of potential liabilities or costs is long. Several economic items under the single heading of "leakage effects":

— Imported goods, particularly food and drink. These are frequently mentioned in the literature. Nonmetropolitan areas typically are importers of most manufactured food items. Inasmuch as these items are a major portion of most tourist budgets, the local region gains relatively little. Belisle found that in Jamaica, 54 percent of the food used in resort hotels is imported. In nonmetropolitan portions of the United States, the percentages will likely be even higher in a great many cases.

— Remittances of profits abroad by foreign companies that own hotels and other tourist facilities. This once was a problem for "the other guy," but not for us in the United States. The case of Japanese investment in Hawaii, California, and several other states suggests that the impacts of this leakage variable are no longer exotic. Investments by nonlocals, even those with substantial leakage, may indeed be better than no investment at all. On the other hand, it is equally clear from a local development standpoint that an investment with minimal leakage is preferable to one with massive leakage. The challenge for local officials is to determine what taxation policies should be enacted to capture funds for additional economic development programs and infrastructure investments while maintaining a positive environment for future investments.

— Remittances of wages by expatriate workers also has become a local concern. Ten or twenty years ago, this item would be illustrated by reference to a European guest worker program. Now a United States example might appropriately reference workers from Mexico or Central America who hold jobs in the United States but send much of their paychecks home.

— Fees and royalties for franchised businesses. These are frequently transferred out of the region.

— Payments to nonlocal airlines, tour companies, and travel agents. These also typically leave the region - especially if the region is rural.

— Nonlocal or out-of-region promotion costs. Items include advertising costs, trade show cases, and business development or prospecting trips.
— Local residents may increase expenditures on imports due to the demonstration effects of tourism.

In addition to economic leakages, cultural conflicts are a recurring theme in studies of tourism in relatively isolated parts of the United States or in Third and Fourth World settings. Gray offers a fairly colorful description of this potential problem. Tourists "irritate their hosts through sheer arrogant display of wealth and/or brazen disregard of their hosts' sensitivities and values." The effects of tourism on the communal and ethnic conflicts that may exist in the host society and the effects of the moral and religious attitudes toward tourism are themes explored by Wu in his study of Pacific Rim tourism.

Closer to home, it is easy to imagine conflicts arising on southwestern Indian reservations like the Hopi or Navajo or in virtually any other culturally distinctive community separated from mainstream America along racial, ethnic, or religious lines. Changing tastes and preferences also can bring problems - especially for communities overly dependent on only one or two tourism products. Rademan in his paper on skiing and ski towns in the United States notes that demographics are working against the ski industry as the pool of prime-age skiers moves from the 18- to 34-year-old age group to the 35- to 54-year-old age group. He notes that older skiers favor less-taxing skiing conditions than younger skiers; resorts must adjust.

They also must adjust to the mini baby boom that is coming as some older skiers leave the ranks of the DINKS. Ski areas will have to develop promotional strategies to draw this group away from Disney-style theme parks. Three additional potential liabilities are environmental damage, seasonality of activity, and low-wage structure.

Environmental issues include the impacts of mass tourism on fragile natural environments, microenvironment issues such as the ethics of a swim-with-the-dolphins attraction at the Hyatt Regency Waikoloa, and the negative impacts of the handful of tourists who now visit Antarctica.

Seasonality also may be a problem. Investment in both the tourism project itself and in infrastructure and other overhead capital is usually seasonally stranded; that is, underutilized. Local labor and merchants may find pronounced swings in income. Influxes of transient, seasonal workers can add a sense of instability to the tourist-based community.

Finally, tourism tends to be a low-wage industry. In fact, it shows some of the characteristics of the hightech type industries discussed by Markusen: a large number of relatively poorly paid workers and a handful of relatively well-paid owners and managers. Given this wage structure, opportunities for upward mobility are limited, at least in the short term. In the long run, however, appropriate taxing policy should enhance educational infrastructure and other human capital building institutions. An increase in human capital would, through time, increase incomes of local residents.

In sum, it is interesting to note that tourism has its greatest impact on rural areas and on the less industrialized states. Put another way, tourism is most impressive when the competition is not very stiff. The several reasons for this are discussed below, but clearly the fact that tourism is a relatively low-wage pursuit is a key ingredient in the explanation. In his article on tourism in Australia, Cooper states that "the mass tourism industry has been widely seen as an important countervailing force to the problem of rural-urban drift." It seems fair to say that proponents of tourism in the United States have reached a similar conclusion although the basis of their assertions is not always clear.

Planning for Tourism Development

Now tourism is one of the largest industries in the world and has incredible potential for economic growth, it potentially carries with it significant negative social and environmental impacts. With growing international interest in community-based tourism, the task of maintaining cultural and environmental integrity in small, fragile communities has never been more critical. With potential for quick economic gain, such integrity may be sacrificed by shortsighted and harmful development schemes, with both communities and tourists ultimately losing.

Klong Khwang in Thailand is an example of a village where tourism development is being actively planned and developed with a strong emphasis on community involvement. Throughout Southeast Asia there is considerable pressure on communities to seek alternative forms of economic development. In many instances tourism has been identified as a substantial source of employment and income generation.

There are a number of sustainable development issues related to tourism and one of the challenges of sustainable urban tourism destination management is to help communities make effective decisions relating to tourism development. The art of the tourism development and management process is to balance the opportunities and costs for the community, the environment and the tourists. As a tourism destination, Klong Khwang is still very much at the formative stage. However, as tourism development progresses, efforts are being made to help the community identify and achieve tourism objectives by emphasizing principles that support community participation, environmental sustainability and cultural integrity.

Sustainable urban tourism destination management is based on the need to move from the rhetoric of sustainable development to locally-grounded tourism and management practices. Specifically, sustainable urban tourism destination management explores the challenges of achieving economic benefits from sustainable community tourism while mitigating negative social, cultural, and environmental influences. The goal is not to simply create more opportunities for the hotel and hospitality industry. Rather it is to recognize tourism as a major forçe in community development, a force that must be carefully planned and managed taking into account the principle of sustainability.

Klong Khwang is very much a "work in progress" with respect to its development as a tourism destination. Currently, the village receives small groups of international tourists (approximately 10 people each) that book in advance with the Tourism Authority of Thailand (TAT). These groups are international press representatives and who receive assistance from the TAT in the form of English-speaking guides and transportation. Other visitors to Klong Khwang are primarily locals from neighboring communities who wish to pay respect to the reclining Buddha and the 'Sema Thammachak' (stone wheel of Thamma), as well as visit the archeological site. Typically, visitors spend upwards of one hour visiting Klong Khwang and contribute approximately 10,000 baht/month through Wat (Temple) donations.

The local District Director of Sung Nern and the Poo Yai Baan (community headman) are strongly committed to a tourism development plan based on community development objectives. These include:

(a) developing and implementing a tourism program for which "community life" will be central and that include, as core pieces, Thailand's largest stone reclining Buddha and an as yet unexcavated archaeological city;

(b) developing income generating activities for community members through handicrafts, food preparation and community tours; and

(c) at a later stage excavating the archaeological city and moat under the direction of the Fine Arts Department of Thailand.

The development of Klong Khwang, specifically in terms of planning and process, has been aided by a Training and Technology Transfer Program (TTTP) involving the Asian Institute of Technology (Bangkok) and a consortium of Canadian universities. At the local government level, TTTP team members are assisting officials in a capacity-building process of critical reflection focusing on factors such as carrying capacity, marketing, and social and environmental impacts, and specifically in terms of how these relate to the community-defined tourism objectives. To facilitate this process, TTTP has undertaken the following:

— preparing visual representations of strategic community sites as a guide for the physical development of the village and to encourage community participation;

— designing marketing and promotional materials, including brochures and postcards where local officials are responsible for supplying data such as the key points of interest in Klong Khwang and wording for the print materials;

— developing and describing the various components for the master development plan.

Through these activities, TTTP members provide technical assistance, but they do not design the community tourism plan. Appropriately, this task is left to those who have stakes in the outcome. At the community level, a very strategic approach to tourism planning and development is being implemented, one which reinforces stakeholders' roles in the decision-making process by ensuring community participation. Although effective community participation is an essential principle of sustainable development, it is often one of the most difficult to carry out in practice. Responding to this challenge, and in an effort to build community readiness and capacity to embrace tourism, the Klong Khwang villagers, with help from the TTTP team, conducted a full-scale "mock tourism day."

The tourism day had a series of objectives. Specifically, it was designed to provide the villagers with an opportunity to experience a significant flow of visitors into their community, thereby creating the opportunity for residents to experience tourists, and tourism-related issues, first hand. It also provided the opportunity to test the community's infrastructure from a visitation perspective, and to evaluate the attractiveness of the site as a tourism destination. Finally, it provided the residents with the opportunity to make an experiential decision as to whether or not they were eager to accept and develop tourism as a village activity over a longer period of time. In the mock tourism exercise, a team of students, friends, and family from the TTTP posed as "tourists for a day" in Klong Khwang (the group numbered over 40 and represented ages ranging from mid-teens to early 50s, with an equal representation of males and females).

The village headman and community developed the program and specific tourism activities members. From providing English-speaking tour guides and planning an interesting sightseeing itinerary, through to a large buffet lunch, the community proved to be extremely well organized. Evaluations confirmed that the "tourists" had an enjoyable and educational day, and, more importantly, the community experienced the demands and opportunities associated with hosting a large group of tourists. This tourism day proved to be very effective at providing a basis for experienced-based community discussions of basic tourism issues.

Topics included the desirability of large tour groups, the timing of visits, the adequacy of present facilities and infrastructure including waste management, the location of toilet facilities, the time commitment required of a local women's group for preparing tour group lunches, the distribution of economic benefits, and the influence on daily community life.

Destination Management

Destination management seeks, through an integrated approach to ensure viable and sustainable development. Experience has shown that tourism destinations must develop appropriate organizational structures, carry out a range of planning and design activities, be deeply and directly involved in marketing the destination, and view product development as an essential element of the overall tourism development process. In addition, it is critical that economic and environmental goals are met. At the present time, Klong Khwang's economy is based almost entirely on agriculture, with rice being the main crop.

In conjunction with the community's objective to increase tourism based on community life, a Klong Khwang tourism brochure and various postcards have been designed and produced. Local officials provided input on brochure wording and identified key points of interest, while local Chulalongkorn University graduates afforded artistic input and desktop publishing expertise. The results of this joint effort included not only tangible products for marketing purposes but also an increased capacity for local officials to engage in marketing and design activities.

The Klong Khwang women's collective is a key contributor to the community's tourism development program. In the future, this will likely involve handicrafts, such as woven reed mats, as a potential income generating activity. Other activities could include hosting buffet lunches such as the one that took place during the mock tourism day and that highlighted authentic Thai village cuisine of the type not found in the cities. However, the issue of available time is critical as these activities are inevitably in addition to the heavy workload of village life. The potential benefits for protecting and enhancing cultural heritage through tourism activities are significant.

These include developing village identity, creating and enhancing community pride, building or re-building cultural amenities within a region, stabilizing the community, giving purpose to community development, and broadening community horizons. All these have the potential to influence Klong Khwang, and are key drivers with respect to encouraging tourism development within the village.

Just as importantly, there are potentially negative effects associated with tourism development, even on a small scale. These include increased cost of living, displacement of traditional residents, increased crime, undermining local traditions & ways of life, pollution and environmental degradation, pressure on services and facilities, creation of regional disparities and the commodification of culture. In fact, local Klong Khwang officials are already facing challenges relating to architectural controls.

One year into the process of developing Klong Khwang as a sustainable tourism destination, it is apparent that a cautious and thoughtful approach is required. Indisputably a fragile community, large tour groups in Klong Khwang will be detrimental to both the environment and the patterns associated with community life. Indeed, as an example of the latter, during the mock tourism day a villager removed her hat while working, explaining that this made her more "presentable." Tourists and tourism affect the local environment, and seemingly small changes are cumulative in nature. Changes to villagers' dress and lifestyles in order to accommodate correct or incorrect notions of tourists' expectations run counter to the basic precepts of sustainable, community-based tourism. The viability of tourism in Klong Khwang will continue to be a significant issue.

A clear understanding of the nature of both product and visitor, realistic expectations of tourism revenues, and appropriate interpretive strategies and guide training are all factors that must be considered prior to the implementation of any tourism program. If, for example, the tourism product is to be traditional community life, then the community must address the difficult challenge of maintaining its traditional, authentic character. Further, if community members are expected to share in the costs associated with tourism, such as decreased freedom to renovate housing, then it is important that financial benefits be broadly distributed. The task of maintaining the traditional and authentic character of the community's buildings and layout will be interesting.

If tourism proves to be successful, and the economic gains benefit the community holistically, there will be resources for improving public and private buildings. In fact, some homes have already been renovated with much of the traditional character now hidden by modern improvements. The irony is that as the community gets more money to spend on improvements, it will have to withstand pressures to modernize outside the construct of traditional village architecture. The tourism product is based in large measure on the community, as it now exists. Community agreement and persuasion, rather than regulation, will be necessary.

Interestingly, the community is satisfied with a very modest level of financial returns from tourism, at least at the present time. Donations left by tourists are used for the maintenance and expansion of the temple, to augment the revenues from the store run by the women's cooperative, and for community projects. Through the planning process, the community has chosen to proceed with a model for tourism development that will produce modest numbers of visitors. This level of development will position tourism as a seasonal activity, separate from and for the most part not disrupting the existing agricultural base of the community.

Villagers believe this will prove to be the least intrusive on the community while providing for much-needed income at specific times of the year. This modest approach necessitates a much lower level of involvement on the part of residents and a smaller financial investment. Also, such tourism development recognizes the fragility of the community, limited carrying capacity, restricted budgets, economic goals, and the desire to protect the agricultural base. This is not to say that tourism is lacking in value and importance, but rather that it simply reflects one component of the community's overall development objectives.

Concept of Sustainable Development

The concept of sustainable development emerged in the mid-80's, out of the Brundtland Report, as it is known, written at the request of the United Nations, by the Commission for Development and the Environment. The sustainable development option is based on the idea that conserving our natural and cultural capital is possible without compromising the future and that this is compatible with development in the present. The global strategy for sustainable development was finally coined in 1992, at the United Nations Conference on the Environment and Development (UNCED), also known as the Earth Summit and the Rio Conference. Item three of the Rio Declaration states that the right to development must be fulfilled so as to equitably meet developmental and environmental needs of present and future generations.

Of the many definitions of, and approaches to sustainable development, we would like to mention the definition put forward by H. Daly, economist of the World Bank: "for a society to be physically sustainable, its global material and energy inputs must meet three conditions:

1 The rate at which renewable resources are used must not exceed the rate at which they are regenerated.
2 The rate at which non renewable resources are used must not exceed the rate at which renewable substitutes are developed.
3 The rate of emissions of polluting agents must be in accordance with the environment's capacity to assimilate them".

Sustainable Tourism

This concept is the consequence of the industry adapting the strategy of Sustainable Development to the world of tourism. On an international scale, it was formulated at the World Conference on Sustainable Tourism, held on the island of Lanzarote in 1995. It is generally accepted that sustainability in tourism means being ecologically acceptable in the long term and financially viable and fair from a social and ethical viewpoint, for local communities. Thus, tourism must become part of the natural, cultural and human environment, respecting the fragile balance that is characteristic of many holiday destinations, particularly on small islands and in environmentally sensitive areas.

Sustainable tourism will place special emphasis on conserving the cultural heritage and traditions of local communities, enabling destinations to enhance their social and cultural heritage and improve the quality of life of their people. Within a strategy of environmental quality as a means of conserving destinations and satisfying customer needs, top priority has been given to promoting the participation of everyone involved in the tourist industry and opting for cultural, technological and professional innovation.

Special priority will be given to covering environmental costs through a system of setting fairer prices and by paying special attention to ecologically sensitive and degraded areas; the role of transport, energy and waste management policies.

Responsible Tourism

The very term places the emphasis squarely on assuming and recognising the responsibilities both the tourist industry and tourists themselves have to the environment and to the cultural heritage of each tourist destination, whilst maintaining the concept of sustainable development as the final goal.

Rural Tourism

Rural tourism covers all tourism activities involving natural, social and cultural elements that operate in a rural environment. It is characterised by: integration in the local environment, complementarity to the main economical activities of the area, utilisation of local products and participation in local activities.

The concept of rural tourism often encompasses a whole range of specialist market segments that are available in the countryside, such as agro-tourism, eco-tourism, green tourism, adventure tourism, cultural tourism and sports tourism.

Eco-tourism

Eco-tourism is tourism that operates in natural protected areas. It is, therefore, a highly specialised form of tourism, in which priority is given to conservation, over any other variable. This kind of tourism attracts people who travel to unspoilt wilderness areas for the specific purpose of learning about and admiring the ecosystems and their components, and the cultural features of the region by observing and studying them. This is an aesthetic, scientific and even philosophical rather than a merely recreational approach to tourism.

In eco-tourism, priority is given to conserving natural areas, so eco-tourism planning must be subordinated to conservationist interests. In fact, in most cases it is considered as a means of making the protected area in question economically sustainable and providing development for local communities. The positive aspects of eco-tourism do not eliminate the possibility of generating negative effects, such as the very fact of bringing visitors to virgin or extremely fragile areas.

Green Tourism

This is a form of tourism in which the landscape plays the leading role, as a meeting point where human and natural variables converge. It is a kind of tourism that is linked to a rural or natural setting, where the aim is to integrate visitors and the local population. In fact, the local population plays a vital role in receiving tourists. It is a term that is half way between rural tourism and eco-tourism, mentioned above. In fact, it is term that is being increasingly ignored because of its vagueness in the face of the progressive segmentation of the tourism market.

Other Forms of Tourism

The growth of the tourist industry has led to the appearance of new kinds of tourist activity, in response to very specific segments of demand. We could mention agro-environmental, cultural, adventure and sports tourism for their environmental influence.

Agro-environmental tourism is a specialised form of rural tourism, in which visitors stay at farms and take part in agricultural activities, thus playing an integral part in the everyday life of the farm.

Cultural tourism is based on using the area's cultural heritage as a means of conserving and promoting it. Thematic routes, site museums, traditional fiestas and festivals are just some aspects of this kind of tourism, which can be found both in town and in the most out-of-the-way hamlet.

Adventure tourism has proliferated recently as a way of generating a sense of discovery by using largely unspoilt areas with very little man-made infrastructure or facilities.

Sports tourism is based on using rural or natural areas for practising open-air sports. It started out with traditional activities like sailing, cycling and skiing, but the range of activities has now increased to include high risk sports such as white water rafting, mountain biking, orienteering and survival.

Eco-labels

These are the tourism version of green labels, which can be defined as instruments for informing consumers about goods or services that are environmentally friendlier than their competitors. The objective of green labels is to improve sales and the image of the product bearing the label; gradually increase consumer awareness; provide true and accurate information; force businessmen to accept responsibility for the effect their products have on the environment and, last but by no means least, to protect the environment. These same characteristics are also valid for tourist "eco-labels". The basic qualities of tourist eco-labels are:

— Reliable environmental information for the consumer to facilitate his decision making process when acquiring tourist goods or services.

— Improvements in supplier relations and management by reducing the environmental impact of establishments by adopting the necessary measures to meet the criteria of the label and gain a marketing advantage by enhancing supplier confidence.

— Innovation in the industry, through joint commitment to continuous improvement and motivation for introducing technological innovation.

As instruments of self-regulation, the tourist "eco-labels" should become attractive to both suppliers and consumers of tourist products and should become accepted as valid information instruments in the market.

Environmental Management System (EMAS)

An appropriate business strategy requires equally appropriate implementation and integration of an Environmental Management System (EMAS), whose objective is to define and implement the environmental policy that is best suited to the activity, goods or services supplied by the company. It should prevent and minimise environmental impact, ensuring the system's aptitude for controlling said impact and of being able to demonstrate this aptitude to those concerned. An EMAS provides a framework for each company to constantly manage its environmental actions in an active and systematic manner, in order to:

— Contribute to the development of an active approach in environmental matters.

— Enable companies to set specific environmental objectives and targets.

EMAS are developed in four major steps:

1. Planning, which leads to objectives and targets being set and defines the strategies for achieving them.
2. Organisation, which seeks to establish an organisational structure with defined functions and responsibilities.
3. Application, which determines the results that will be obtained with varying environmental behaviour.
4. Monitoring, which is the necessary framework for assessing the results obtained, diagnose the whole process and improve it.

Eco-audit

An audit is a review and verification of different aspects of a company or activity. Depending on the area under review, there are different kinds of audits; accounting, special and functional audits. An environmental audit, or eco-audit, comes into the category of special audits, like other management, safety or hygiene type audits. The eco-audit is a process carried out by a company with a view to finding out its environmental status at a given moment in time, encompassing a broad range of situations. There are different types of audit, depending on the subject to be audited and on its objectives.

Eco-audits can be internal or external, depending on who does them and what the objectives of the audit are. In the world of tourism, they are usually used as part of the Environmental Management System. Here, there are two types: Initial Environmental Review, which is an audit that tells us the company's environmental situation and lays the foundations for an EMAS, and the Environmental Review, which is a periodic audit that is carried out to monitor progress and fulfilment of EMAS goals and objectives.

Tourism Development in Manyallaluk

Manyallaluk (Man-yalla-look) is an Aboriginal community with a population of 150 people situated on two thousand square kilometres of land, one hundred kilometres east of the town of Katherine, in the Northern Territory, Australia.

The land borders Arnhem Land, and Nitmiluk and Kakadu National Parks. Much of it is rugged and stony. Tourism in Manyallaluk is promoted by a community-owned-and-operated Aboriginal, cultural tour organization that runs one and two day tours throughout the year. The enterprise also manages an onsite camping ground and a 16-unit, powered-site, caravan park.

In addition, the community-owned shop sells artifacts made by the local people, as well as basic goods to the tourists. Most visitors to Manyallaluk come via Darwin. From Darwin south to Katherine by car takes a little more than three hours, over a distance of 310 kilometers. Tour companies arrange for transport from Katherine to Manyallaluk, or you may drive your own vehicle.

In 1985 the Jawoyn Association was formed to represent the interests of the Jawoyn people. The Association was keen to establish business enterprises on Jawoyn owned land in order to provide employment for local Aboriginal people and minimize their dependency on government funding. In 1990, the year before tourism actually started, there were fewer than 50 people living in the community, and there was no formal work.

The quality of the housing was poor and there was no electricity or telephones. In fact, the people had to travel

35 kilometres to Barunga, or even further to Katherine, for shopping and health care. At that time all funding for Eva Valley was administered through the Barunga Community Council, and a 1990 Northern Building Consultant's report described the community as "typical of a remote area 'minor' Community, where the provision of services, facilities, housing and infrastructure are provided on an adhoc annual funding basis with little knowledge of the intentions and aspirations of local people and little evidence of forward planning."

Tourist Experience

The one-day tour is the core tourist experience at Manyallaluk. It also provides the platform for the first day of the two-day tour. The tour is run by a group of men and women guides and provides tourists with plenty of opportunity for informal interaction. During the morning of the one-day tour, tourists are taken on a bush walk where they are shown bush tucker and bush medicines, told about the cultural significance of the local plants, taught their Aboriginal language names, and given details on how the plants are collected, prepared and used.

After a barbecue lunch of kangaroo and beef, along with salads and home-made damper, tourists are given a 'hands on' introduction to traditional skills, including spear throwing, basket making, fire making, painting, and playing the didgeridoo. At the end of the day, tourists on the two day tour travel in a four-wheel drive vehicle to a bush camp, in a picturesque setting next to a large waterhole. They spend the second day in the company of an Aboriginal guide walking in the bush and viewing rock art sites in the area. These sites connect with the large number of rock art sites located along the rocky escarpments throughout Kakadu National Park and Arnhem Land.

Manyallaluk is accessible all year with an ordinary two-wheel drive vehicle. This gives it a great advantage since most remotely-situated Aboriginal tour enterprises in the Northern Territory are not accessible by self-drive vehicles. Approximately 1,750 tourists visit Manyallaluk each year, with more than 80 percent of them taking the one-day tour. Over 65 per cent are international tourists with the three main markets being the United Kingdom, the United States, and Germany. More than 85 per cent of the visitors travel independently, while just 14 per cent are part of an organized tour group.

Participation Community

The tour enterprise is the focus of the Manyallaluk CDEP program. Often as many as 20 people are working as guides and up to 50 are employed full or part-time through CDEP. Other CDEP jobs include mechanical, building and maintenance work, horticultural jobs, and work in the office and shop. Those who do not work directly with tourists support the enterprise by keeping equipment maintained and making Manyallaluk an attractive place to visit.

The community has a 'no work, no pay' policy, and the pay structure rewards commitment and seniority through the top-up of wages from tourism income. Manuel Pamkal, one of the guides at Manyallaluk, links tourism and work opportunities to an improved lifestyle at Manyallaluk. "People want to stay here and work. Manyallaluk has a restricted area for alcohol. In other places they're drinking much and fighting too much. They have got lots of jobs.....garbage run, creche, multi-purpose centre, buffalo catching, mud brick machine to make own house, fencing. Tourism is a really big one for us." Women have played a major role in the development of the Manyallaluk tour enterprise and CDEP wages mean that some families now enjoy two incomes.

There is a creche for women with young children, and older children now attend school each day at Barunga. Several women have completed child care courses, and some women have passed their driving tests, something that significantly affects their opportunities. There are new opportunities for young people as well, and several young men and women have become trainee guides. Though some young people may still experience difficulties, this future does hold potential for paid employment and parents are active role models in this regard. All this represents a major change in less than a decade.

Economic Benefits

Visitor numbers continue to grow, though income from tourism has risen more rapidly because Manyallaluk is less dependent on outside tour operators. Currently, 75 percent of all tourists visiting Manyallaluk make direct bookings. This has drastically reduced commissions paid to external operators.. Before the growth of tourism, there was no local store at Manyallaluk. Consequently any money local people had was spent outside the community.

Now residents shop at the community-owned store, and profits have been used to build a cool room and purchase other equipment for the community. Income from the sale of artifacts produced by residents has also increased dramatically since tourists started coming to Manyallaluk. In 1995 the shop earned AU$13,000 gross on the sale of artifacts alone.

Only permanent residents of the community are eligible for membership in the Manyallaluk Aboriginal Corporation and to participate in community decision-making. This means that all benefits from the tourism business accrue directly to the local community. Also, no individuals, inside or outside the community, are paid dividends from the profits of the tourism enterprise.

Local Culture and Traditional Heritage

The development of tourism at Manyallaluk has provided new opportunities for the promotion and practice of aboriginal culture and generated new interest in the display and interpretation of heritage. Specifically, tourism has helped strengthen regional identity. Typically tourists know very little about the regional differences of the native peoples, and international tourists, in particular, think that all Aboriginal people have boomerangs, or didgeridoos. The tours at Manyallaluk teach tourists about the distinctive regional culture shared by the people of Arnhem land. Tourism has also strengthened traditional skills. Before the development of tourism, people lived at Manyallaluk in order to access the plentiful supply of natural resources.

The residents were keen hunters and foragers, and at least one of the older men reportedly still used a spear, as well as a gun. When tourism began to develop, many of these men and women became guides and began teaching their skills to tourists. Now, the older people are passing their skills on to the young people, some of whom have spent most of their lives living in towns rather than the bush.

Tourism has enabled community members to practice their skills to the point where several of the guides have recently won art and spear throwing competitions at the annual Barunga festival, one of the largest indigenous festivals in Australia. Tourism has also had a direct effect on language and art. Often, tourists are keen to hear Aboriginal languages and learn a few words. The guides at Manyallaluk teach the tourists about the community languages and also about Kriol, the local Aboriginal English.

Younger members of the community who knew very little of the language are now learning it so they can work with the tourists. There are 200 art sites on Manyallaluk, many of them not yet recorded. Since tourism started, guides have a greater opportunity to visit country away from the community and take an active custodial role over the sites. In addition to this, several of the guides are skilled story tellers and their role includes telling tourists some of the regional stories from the "Dreaming". Younger guides are now learning to tell those stories.

Sustainability in Environment

The Manyallaluk area is quite large, and tourists are only permitted to visit a very small portion. That means with careful management and by regularly changing routes and sites, the community is able to minimize environmental impact. Also, tourists must always be accompanied by a guide when away from the tourist area.

This reduces the possibility of damage to sites of specific significance, and to the landscape more generally. Several of the guides have lived at Manyallaluk all of their lives and are always on the lookout for the smallest changes. The guides are careful to monitor the use of natural resources. The pandanus used for weaving, and other raw materials growing near the community, are used with tourists, while community members travel further away to collect raw materials for their own use.

Similarly, kangaroo meat for the tourists' lunch is bought at the butcher shop in Katherine, while community members hunt for themselves on Manyallaluk land. Consistent efforts are made to manage the community and tourist areas from an environmental perspective. Since 1991 many trees have been planted and the area has been generally cleaned up. Hot water is heated using solar panels and, where possible, materials are recycled. Even the cardboard boxes from the shop are used as mulch under trees.

Social Sustainability

The Manyallaluk community is developing a tourist enterprise to provide long-term economic independence and self-determination for its people. Each stage in the development of the tourist enterprise is discussed by the community as a whole. The tourism manager is responsible for the day-to-day operation, but strategic decisions are made through the elected council.

As a result, the pace and style of development is controlled, ensuring its overall sustainability. The community area is separate and out of sight from the tourist area, and tourists are not permitted to visit it. This ensures community privacy and allows guides to go home and relax at the end of the day without being permanently on display. The community council has also decided there will be no photography of the community homes.

Manyallaluk has developed an innovative work structure which has been one of the keys to the success of the enterprise. Guides work in two groups, which are basically two extended families. Each group works seven days on and then has seven days off. This gives the guides time to maintain family responsibilities and engage in other activities, such as shopping, hunting and artifact production.

These groups are also large enough to allow the guides to adhere to the cultural rules governing kin relationships and speech avoidance, where, in some instances, family members are not permitted to name each other, speak directly to each other, or be alone together. The development and operation of tourism at Manyallaluk is, of course, not without challenges.

Two of the Manyallaluk tour products were withdrawn from the market. Determining what tourists want, and what the community is able to provide while retaining its internal priorities is always challenging. In addition, it is difficult to fill all management positions because numeracy and literacy skills are generally low. At this stage Manyallaluk continues to employ non-Aboriginals in certain training and management roles.

Tourism in Sai Kung

Sai Kung is located at the eastern end of Kowloon Peninsula, it comprises 12,680 hectares, including 70 outlying islands. Sai Kung is the second largest administrative district in Hong Kong, China. Recently, It has developed from what was once a quiet and sleepy fishing village into a burgeoning tourist destination, both for local Hong Kong residents and, more recently, for international visitors.

Often described as the "back garden" of Hong Kong, Sai Kung is famous for its picturesque scenery, excellent seafood, great hiking trails, a perfect harbour, and Hong Kong's only public golf course. Sai Kung is a scenic 20-30 minute drive from downtown Kowloon via Clearwater Bay Road and Hirma's Highway. From the other direction, the Sai Sha Road links the district with Ma On Shan and Shatin. Administratively, Sai Kung includes Clearwater Bay which, among other attractions, is home to Hong Kong's University of Science and Technology.

In the 1950s and 1960s, Sai Kung was a small fishing village and home to just a few basic industries such as ship breaking. By the early 1980s, however, commercial fishing had declined in economic importance for a number of reasons including the size of catches and increasing regional competition. Fortunately, the natural beauty of the area, including its beaches and the small, easily-accessible islands, began to attract tourists from other districts in Hong Kong and beyond.

This development began to flower, particularly when the transportation system within Hong Kong became better developed. Initially, this shift developed without planning or overt intention. Fishing simply declined, while tourism expanded. Although there was no overt development policy or philosophy for Sai Kung in the 1970s, the development which did take place during this period did not overpower the area. As a result, Sai Kung has retained much of its earlier charm. It is very much a natural, rather than a constructed, or sanitized, tourism destination.

It was during the 1980s that the central Hong Kong Government began to take an active role in the development of the Sai Kung area. This included creating parks, opening a public golf course, and developing and promoting science camps for children, all within the district. During this period the economy was strong, and these factors in combination created jobs and fuelled further development.

The increase in tourists encouraged the development of more restaurants and retail stores, and this, in turn, created more job opportunities particularly for the unemployed and underemployed. By the 1990s, a very active District Council was working hand-in-hand with the central Government to take advantage of and expand the potential associated with the burgeoning tourism industry. In 1992, Sai Kung established a local tourism development working group. This group organized the first Kai Sung Seafood Fair, an event which married Sai Kung's fishing heritage with tourism potential.

Now, just a few years later, this event is well established and attracts thousands of local and international visitors. In 1996, a major report was commissioned with a view to taking tourism to new heights in Sai Kung. This vision includes a major waterfront development based on a large platform that will stretch out to an island where there will be a restaurant and spectator seating for boat races. This plan is under review.

The core attraction in Sai Kung is the seafood restaurants. Visitors select fresh seafood directly from the enormous variety available from the dozen or more pier-side vendors. It's then taken directly to a restaurant of the visitor's choosing, where the chef prepares and serves the selection in a matter of minutes. The seafood vendors and restaurants overlook the harbour area and many visitors take advantage of this to tour the harbour in one of the many boats available for hire.

The Dragon Boat Festival, held each year in Sai Kung on the fifth day of the fifth month of the Chinese lunar calendar, celebrates the life of the famous poet Qu Yuen. When Yuen drowned himself to protest against government corruption, villagers rowed their boats out to save him, all the while throwing dumplings into the water in the hope that fish would eat these rather than the body of the patriot. Sai Kung was the first Hong Kong district with overseas participation in its dragon boat racing. The Tin Hau Festival also attracts thousands of tourists, most of whom are from nearby Kowloon and Hong Kong Island.

Held on the third day of the third month in the lunar calendar, this festival celebrates the birthday of Tin Hau, the Taoist goddess of the sea who, according to legend, saved her brothers from a storm at sea. Many of the tourists are fisherfolk who pray at the temple for safety from storms and for plentiful catches. After burning paper offerings and incense at the temple, the worshippers go to Tin Hau's bedroom to touch her mattress. Lucky ones who find a peanut under the mattress may have a baby. The Kau Sai Chau public golf course is located just offshore from Sai Kung Town on Kau Sai Island.

It attracts local and overseas players, as well as many tourists who simply "walk" the island and watch the players. There are two 18 hole courses, a driving range and a club house. Golf instruction is available. Future plans include hosting international tournaments. The Sai Kung Country Park attracts many visitors to the District. In fact, most of the Sai Kung Peninsula is parkland of various types. Popular places within the park system include Wong Chuk Wan, Tsai Pak Tam Chung and Wong Shek Pier.

Within the park system, numerous barbecue sites are available for families who come for a few hours to get away from the bustle of the New Territories, Kowloon and Hong Kong Island. For hikers, there are several walking trails which range in degree of difficulty. Following the seashore, the Pak Tam Chung trail is one of the least arduous. It is a nice 30 minute stroll. By contrast, the Luk Wu hiking trail takes three to four hours of serious walking as it follows a high ridge giving an excellent view of Clearwater Peninsula, Sharp Peak and the High Island Reservoir. Sai Kung is well know for its public beaches.

Three of the most popular are the Clearwater Bay 1 and 2 beaches, and the Silverstrand Bay beach. Good water quality, excellent scenery and easy access are three of the most attractive features associated with these beaches. Shower facilities, change rooms and food stalls are available at all of them. Several of the islands also have enticing beaches, the best known being Kiu Tsui and Hap Mun. The first of these is served by a small ferry, and has a restaurant, food stalls and public restrooms.

Compared to the south side of Hong Kong Island, these beaches are quiet. Not surprisingly, Sai Kung District is the centre for pleasure boating in the New Territories. Hebe Heaven, just a short distance south of Sai Kung Town, is home to four marinas, including the Hebe Heaven Yacht Club, the Shelter Cove branch of the Royal Hong Kong Yacht Club, the Hong Kong Marina and Marina Cove. The latter is a large residential and shopping complex. Visiting sailors are lured to both the safe shelter and the attractions of the area, adding to the tourism numbers.

Other attractions that draw tourists to the Sai Kung District include the Che Kung Temple at Ho Chung, the Sheung Yiu Folk Museum, Tung Lung Island, and the Catholic Church that draws as many as 10,000 from Kowloon and Hong Kong Island for Sunday services. Sai Kung District attracts 1.5 million tourists each year. Most are day visitors, with 80 per cent being from Hong Kong. Gradually, however, the percentage and number of international visitors is increasing. For the most part, local visitors are attracted to the parks, temples, golf course and the church, while international visitors come mainly for the seafood and the sights and sounds of the harbour.

The Sai Kung community benefits directly from increased tourism, and through the District Board and other committees is a key constituent in the development and management of attractions and programming designed to enhance tourism. The District Board includes 17 members, and this group is chartered with the key responsibility of working with the Central Government to plan and implement development schemes. This has, for example, included both activity-planning, such as the dragon boat racing and the Seafood Festival, as well as long-range master planning.

It is also the District Board which has hired tourism and planning experts to help guide the development process for Sai Kung. Appointment to the District Board is for four years, and residency within the area is required. The Hong Kong Tourist Association (HKTA) also plays an important role in supporting the District Board. As the transformation from fishing village to tourism centre took place during the 1970s and 1980s, and Sai Kung Town began to attract more tourists. Many of the families who had made their living spending days or weeks at sea, moved to the land.

Men, who for generations had captained fishing boats, began taking employment as masters of private recreational vessels, many of which are semi-permanently moored in the marinas around Hebe Heaven. This meant more time was spent in port and on day trips, with fewer overnight trips away from town. Whereas in the past it was common for the family to spend days at sea fishing, husband and wife working side by side, it now became common for the family to remain in port. This change had its greatest influence on women and youth. In particular, women began to look for other work, just as tourism was expanding.

Many found opportunities owning and operating small boats catering to tourists. Others began working in, and in many cases co-owning, restaurants, and still others found opportunities in the retail trade which expanded dramatically with the increased number of tourists. For the most part, it is the women who own and operate the small boats which ferry people around the harbour for an hour or so to see the islands and other points of interest. Not so long ago, these same women worked alongside their husbands, as a family unit, on the fishing boats. Now they have their own small businesses and their own income streams.

2

Lodging Services

Hospitality has a very vast market. All those who have stayed in hotels or have plans to stay in hotels or any other lodging establishment can be put under hospitality market. Hence all travelers including tourists, visitors, businessmen, leisure travelers, pilgrims and company executive's etc—can be the hospitality market. Depending upon the purpose of travel people can be classified under either commercial hospitality market or leisure hospitality market.

Common Law states that a "Hotel is a place where all who conduct themselves properly, and who being able to pay and ready to pay for their entertainment, are received, if there be accommodation for them, and who without any stipulated engagement as to the duration of their, stay or as to the rate of compensation, are while there, supplied at a reasonable cost with their meals, lodging and other services and attention as are necessarily incident to the use as a temporary home."

A hotel may be called as an establishment where primary business is to provide to the general public lodging facilities and which may also furnish one or more of the various services such as food: beverage, laundry, uniformed services etc. Hence, hotel can also be called as home multiplied by commercial activities. The term 'Hotel' refers to 'a house of entertainment of travelers'. The word

'Hotel' is of ancient origin, but its use in English for a house offering lodging and food for travelers is recent. The Hostlers of London took the name of Inn keeping in 1473. The world Hostler' or 'Ostler' having come to mean an inn servant.

The term 'Hotel' was used in England in about 1760. British law as a "place where a bonafide traveler can receive food and shelter, provided he is in a position to pay for and is in a fit condition to be received" defines hotel or inn. In legal terminology a: hotel is an inn and is required under common law to offer to its visitors lodging, food and protection, 10 their baggage. Hotel service is generally based on these three fundamental necessities of life. In addition to these a modem hotel provides its visitors many luxuries of modem urban city living, all under one roof.

History of Lodging

Early history of accommodation for travelers can be traced back to the Greek word 'Xenia', which not only meant hospitality but also the protection given to a traveler from discomforts. The city was bound to offer hospitality. In Sparta city, although due to rigorous customs visitors were not encouraged, yet goddess Athena was considered as protector of strangers and hence her name was 'Xenia Athena'. In this period travelers were mainly diplomats, philosophers; intellectuals arid researchers. Guests were invited to stay with noblemen.

In ancient Olympia, buildings constructed with the aim to accommodate strangers can be seen. They were called 'Leonidio' and were, built in 4th century B.C. The concept of hospitality can also be drawn back to ancient times. Homer finds mention of it in 'Iliad' and 'The Odyssey'. Hotel keeping can also be traced back to many centuries and its evolution through the, ages has been brought about by Britain's economical and industrial changes and developments.

During the seventh and eighth centuries, it was thee monasteries that applied hospitality to strangers and, as no charge was made for the accommodation, a travelers were expected to contribute according to their means to the Abeey funds. As more people began to travel they grouped themselves together not only for company but for mutual protection from highway and robbers.

Consequently travelers arrived in groups at a monastery and it was often difficult to accommodate them all. To overcome this, separate lodging houses, called 'Inns' were built. The word 'inn' came to mean a 'Lodging House' and until the passing of the Hotel proprietors Act in 1956, it was the legal term for 'Hotel' and hotel proprietors were legally referred to as 'Common innkeepers'. 'Common' in this sense referred to Common Law. In the thirteenth and fourteenth centuries, manor houses, being hospitable places; willingly gave accommodation to travelers. As no payment was expected, travelers tipped the servants as a 'thank you' for the generous hospitality received—thus the practice of tipping was born.

When high taxes crippled the generosity and hospitality of the owners of the manor houses, many became commercial inns. During Elizabeth the First's reign, posting houses were established and travelers, in addition to getting refreshment were able to change horses before continuing their journey. The turn of the century saw an era that was called the 'Belle Epoch' when the grand and luxurious hotels flourished. A few hotels are still operating today. In London and some other cites attempts have been made to recapture some of the grandeur of the past era in the making of modem hotels, and bring back the memories the grand hotels of olden days.

The next stage in the cycle of evolution of the hotel industry was the coming of the motorcar. It enabled people to visit those parts of the country not reached by railways. This gave birth to inland resorts and the hotel Industry began to flourish. International air, travel has helped create the modem 'stop-over' hotel. With the increase in this form of travel, the number of hotels built close to airports has multiplied. Another trend in hotel keeping is the motel, which is the twentieth-century version of the old 'Coach Inn'.

People traveling the country by car, stopping overnight here and there, require not only refreshment for themselves, but also safe parking for their cars. Post Houses, developed by the Trust House Forte Group are in fact the modern version of the old coaching inns.

Hotel Industry

In India too the development of hotel industry is closely linked to travel. In India travel was mainly on animals(mule, horse and camel) and for rest during their travel at strategic points Dharmashalas, Sarais, Chaupals of Panchayats, Chowthry (in South India) and temples and religious places were provided by rich People such as Rajas, Kings, Zamindars etc. Usually free accommodation and food for travelers was given. During medieval period it was mandatory for the state authorities to provide food and shelter to the wayside traveler. These developed during the Muslim period.

Many famous and well known musafir khanas and sarais were made in the Sindh province during the Arab invasion, and also at Peshawar and Lahore. Mohammad Tughlak and Feroz Shah Tugalak made inns in the northern part of India. Later, Sher Shah Suri, Akbar, Jahangir and Shah Jahan made inns in different parts of India. Jahanara Begum built a very beautiful sarai at

Sahibabad (Begamabad) and its beautiful garden is still there and is called Queens Garden or Azad Park The fountain in the upper garden has the inscription "Gar Firdaus Bar Rui Zaminast-Haminhastu, Haminhastu, Haminastu".

Delhi has always been traditionally hospitable, and we find overwhelming evidence of this in the innumerable sarais and rest houses of this ancient city. Delhi has been built seven times in the area spanning from Mehrauli to Shahjahanabad. Delhi is belived to be the oldest living capital of the world. During their reigns rulers of Delhi built sarais throughout their kingdom for the comforts of travelers.

The sarais afforded a baoli or a talab (a bathing tank), a stable, a dargah for prayer and sometimes a bimarkhana—a place for sick and ill travelers. A sufi or saint also lilved often in the sarai. Many rulers such as Allauddin Khilji banned the selling, consumption and drinking of spirits in sarais. Most of the sarais in Delhi belong ot the Slave Period. As per Shiab-al-din Alumrai there were 2000 Khangabs and sarais in Delhi and its suburbs. Most of these have not survived. Some of the famous sarais in Delhi are mentioned below:

— *Qutub Sarai*: At the entrance of the tomb of Kamali Jamali, it had a 50 feet deep baoli in its courtyard.

— *Ladha Sarai*: Also called as Baghi-Nazir, it is 300 yards south of the tomb of Jamali. It was built in 1748.

— *Lado Sarai*: Also in the same vicinity, it was originallyl a caravan sarai.

— *Sarban Sarai*: It is in Kamlapati Garden, very close to Delhi-Qutub Road.

— *Daud Sarai*: It is situated about 500 yards south of the tomb of Maulana Quli Khan in Qutub area.

— *Kallu Sarai*: Built during Tughlaq period, it is in the vicinity of Sarvpriya Vihar area. Its main feature, a rubble masonary building, is called as Bijay Mandal.

— *Arab ki Sarai*: It was built in 1560-61 by Hamida Banu Begam, wife of Humayun, as a settlement of 300 Arabs (whom she had brought with her while returning from a pilgrimage to Mecca)

— *Sheikh Sarai*: It was named after a popular saint Sheikh Allauddin who lived there and had his tomb during his own lifetime.

Some more popular sarais of Delhi are Sarai Shahji built in Mughal period, Gur Ki Sarai on the eastern side of Karnal Road with its mosque of Hyrewali_ Sarai Bangash near Fatehpuri mosque, Sarai Topkhana, the Dargha Shah Sabi Baksh with its musafir khana on Faiz Bazar road, fai Sarai on southeast of Hauzkhas village, Katwarig Sarai in the centre of the village, Phus ki Sarai, Ghatu_Sarai, Nepa Sarai and the famous Yusuf Sarai, etc. Many small and big Indian hotel groups are operating in various parts of India. Apart from India, some international hotel chains such as Sheratan, Hilton, Ramada, Sofitel, Meridien, Hyatt and Mariott are either operating or planning to operate in India on franchise basis.

Welcome Group: It is the hotel division of I.T.C. Ltd. ITC entered into hotel business in 1975 with the opening of Hotel Chola Madras. The logo represents a traditional Indian welcome in the form of Namaste in an open doorway with the slogan "Nobody gives you India like we do". The motto of Welcome Group is "We enjoy people" Welcome Group has hotels in various cities) India such as Agra, Delhi, Aurangabad, Jaipur, Goa, Gwalior etc.

Oberoi Hotels: Rai Bahadfur M.S. Oberoi started his hotel career as a clerk in 1922 at Faletti's Cecil Hotel in Simla. Later Mr. Ernest Clarke sold his share to Mr M.S. Oberoi, who under the deed of dissolution dated August

14, 1934, became, the sole, absolute, and exclusive owner of Clarke's Hotel, Simla and Delhi. Mr. Oberoi later took over the Grand Hotel at Calcutta on lease and by the end of World War II, the Grand Hotel became a byword for good service and elegant comfort in hotels. He established Oberoi Hotel Pvt. Ltd. in 1946 and later, an 26th May 1949, established East India Hotel Ltd. (EIHL) at Calcutta. Many hotels were added to EIHL during the period.

Later two very important hotels were added -Oberoi Intercontinental in August 1965 in New Delhi and Oberoi Sheraton in 1973 in Bombay. EIHL is now one of the largest and one of the most reputed hotel chains of India with hotels not only in India but also abroad. Oberoi has a hotel training institute at Delhi and future plans of expansion.

Hotel Ambassador, New Delhi: 0ne of the flagship hotel belonging to Lala Ram Parshad who is considered as one of the pioneers of the Hotel Industry in India (now managed by Taj Hotel in Delhi). In 1946, he purchased two hotels in Mussoorie, UP. and operated one hotel in Bokaro. Lala Ram Parshad was appointed Technical Director of Hotel Ashok, New Delhi during its constructian stage and was the first Asian to be se1ected as an executive member of International Hotel Association, (I.H.A) in 1969. He was amongst the first few hoteliers to realise the importance of trained manpower in hotel industry and was associated with various Hotel Management Institutes and Food Craft Institute in India.

U.P. Hotels and Restaurants Ltd: Famous as Clarke's Group of Hotels, it was established on 13th February, 1961. It started with its flagship hotel Clarke Shiraz Agra. Later hotels—Clarke's Awadh, Clarke's Amer, and Clarke's Varanasi at Lucknow, Jaipur and Varanasi, respectively, were added to this chain.

Ritz Chain: A chain belonging to R.N. Kapoor family with hotels at Mumbai, Hyderabad, Kolkata and Coonoor (in South India). Specialised in Italian cuisine.

Spencers: Started hotel business in I 912 in Calcutta. Purchased Connamera Hotel in Madras and opened West End in Bangalore, Malabar at cochin and Trivandrum, Blue Mountains at Kotagiri in 1942 and Savoy in Ooty in 1943. Vegetarian hotels in Madras (Geetha, Ashoka and Ajanta) and Hotel Arakua in Banagalore.

Sinclairs: A chain of hotel operating in eastern part of the country with hotels at Darjeeling and Takadah.

Hotel Corporation of India(HCI): A corporation set up in 1971. It started with its first hotel at Bombay in 1974. Later hotels in Delhi, Srinagar, Rajgir etc. were added to this group.

International Corporate Hotels

These are large chains, which are almost household words in the industry, such as Hilton, Inter-Continental, Hyatt. Some of the groups are a combination of company owned, franchise and management contract operations while others are entirely owned by an individual or a company. Their main features include standardisation of service, facilities and price, and many chains endeavor to operate a hotel in most major capitals throughout the world. Some countries have national hotel companies, which operate hotels at home and abroad, such as, the Taj and Oberoi hotel groups. These are both Indian companies which are well known outside India.

Not all groups of hotels are large or widely dispersed. Some companies own a group, which may consist of no more than four to five hotels, and they may be confined to a particular area such as the beach resorts. These are hotels which are privately owned or independent of any company. Many guests enjoy staying at an establishment of this type because of the individuality of the operation.

Hotel Consortium

Independently owned hotels form a liaison which provides them with the advantages of shared advertising costs, bulk purchasing and referral of bookings. The guest has the advantage of knowing each hotel in the consortium will be of similar standard and price. Best Western Hotels is an example of! worldwide network of independently owned hotels. Development in the field of transportation, communication and increase in population had effect on the growth, type and location of hotels and supplementary accommodation.

The classification of these hotels and supplementary units with in the industry is a complicated task. Hotels are of various types depending on number of factors like the nature and facilities offered, size, location etc. Classification in the real sense separates accommodation into different categories or class on the basis of objective criteria, for example, by the type of accommodation, such as hotels, motels, tourist lodges, holiday camps etc. It seeks to present information about tourist accommodation units in a form, which enable the user to find information he requires. Information thus obtained will help to compare like with like.

Star Category Hotels

In addition to the approval of a hotel project at the planning stage from the point of view of its suitability for foreign tourists, the hotel on completion is inspected as a functioning establishment or approval and placement in the appropriate "Star" category. There are five such categories ranging from 5 star for hotels which offer luxury features, to one star for hotels which offer adequate standard of comfort and cleanliness. For the guidance of entrepreneurs in planning a hotel to qualify for a particular category, the government dearly lays down the facilities expected of establishments in each category.

There are no uniform criteria at international level for grading and classification of hotels. When inquired the reaction of the tourists, it was pointed out that it is more important to list facilities alone with the rates fixed, thereby giving them the choice to select. Quality is more important to them than the physical aspects of a hotel. Many hoteliers pointed out that the star system creates an impression of luxury and waste—an artificial label with unwanted connotations. Material criteria's are unsatisfactory. These criteria's 30 not contain any built in guarantees.

Facility wise, a luxury hotel will not merit any consideration of, for instance, it does not employ sufficient personnel. Quality of service is very important consideration. After all, hotels constitute a service industry. The standard for gradation of hotels in India are laid down by the government of India from the points of view of the suitability of the hotel for foreign tourists. All hotels which are approved get worldwide publicity through tourist literature published by the government and distributed in India as well as abroad/overseas and are eligible for foreign exchange for their essential imports of equipment and provision and for their advertising, publicity and promotion abroad, from the government's special quota of foreign exchange for tourist promotion.

In addition to the approval of a hotel project at the planning stage from the point of view of suitability for foreign tourists, the hotel on completion is inspected 25 functioning establishment for approval and placement in the appropriate star category. There are certain general features, facilities and services expected of establishments in each category. For example, hotels in the category of four, five star, and five star deluxe should be completely air-conditioned, three star hotels need have airconditioning in only 50% of rooms; two star hotels need not serve continental cuisine and one star hotels need have only 25 attached baths.

According to the regulatory conditions for approved hotels, the officials of the government or any other officer deputed by it to inspect hotel premises from time to time will be allowed free access with or without prior notice. In the event of breach of any of the conditions by the hotels, the government shall have the right to withdraw the approval. Complaints regarding luggage having been rifled, valuable stolen and impolite treatment of the staff are common from the guests.

In most of the hotels left the message in the guest rooms requesting them to deposit their valuables and jewellery with the management. Similarly, in some of the hotels the air-conditioned plants have not worked effectively. The guests also make many other complaints. The government, who forwards it to the representatives of the region concern, also receives many of these complaints. These representatives find it impossible to complain and take the action against them because of their friendship with the hotel management. Not only this, these representatives are well known to the staff of the local hotels and therefore, are not in a position to carry out a surprise check of the hotel's facilities and services.

A satisfied tourist will help in the development of tourist traffic. A dissatisfied tourist will be injurious to the tourist industry and spoil the reputation of hotels and the tourist region. Official registration approval and grading requirements provide valuable guidelines in planning hotels and other accommodation, indicating the standard of space and facilities needed to satisfy a particular marketing criteria, conditions for grants of subsidies, loan facilities, agreement for subsequent management, are also generally linked to these facilities.

One Star Category Hotels

The general construction of the building of one star category hotels should be good and the locality and environs including immediate approach should be suitable. The hotel should have at least 10 lettable bedrooms of which at least 25% should have attached bathroom with a bathroom for every 4 of the remaining rooms. At least 25% of the bathrooms should have western style WCs. All bathrooms should have modern sanitation and running cold water with adequate supply of hot water, soap and toilet paper. The rooms should be properly ventilated and should have clean and comfortable beds and furniture.

There should be a reception counter with a telephone and a telephone for the use of guests and visitors. There should be a clean and moderately well equipped dining room/restaurant serving clean wholesome food, and there should be a clean, wellequipped kitchen and pantry. There should be experienced, courteous and efficient staff in smart and clean uniforms and the senior staff coming in contact with guests should possess a. working knowledge of English Housekeeping at the hotel should be of a good standard and clean and good quality linen, blankets towels etc. should be supplied. Similarly crockery, cutlery and glassware should be of good quality

Two Star Category Hotels

The building of two star category hotel should be well constructed and the locality and environs including the approach should be suitable for a good hotel. The hotel should have at least 10 lettable bed room of which at least 75% should have attached bath rooms with showers and a bath room for every four of the remaining rooms and should be with modern sanitation and running cold water with an adequate supply of hot water, soap and toilet paper. 25% of the rooms should be air-conditioned,and all rooms must be properly ventilated, clean and comfortable, with all the necessary items of furniture. There should be a well-furnished lounge.

There should be a reception counter with a telephone. There should be a telephone or call ball in each room and there should be a telephone on each floor unless each room has a separate telephone. There should be a well-maintained and well-equipped dining room I restaurant serving good clean wholesome food, and a clean, hygienic and wellequipped kitchen and pantry.

There should be experienced, courteous and efficient staff in smart and clean uniforms. The supervisory staff coming in contact with guests should understand English. There should be provision for laundry and dry cleaning services. Housekeeping at the hotel should be of a good standard and clean and good quality linen, blankets, towels etc. should be provided. Similarly crockery, cutlery and glassware should be of a good quality.

Three Star Category Hotels

The architectural features and general construction of the building of three star category hotels should be of a very good standard and the locality including the immediate approach and environs should be suitable for a very good hotel and there should be adequate parking facilities for cars. The hotel should have at least 20 lettable bed rooms, all with attached bath room with bath tubs and/or showers and should be modem in design and equipped with fittings of a good standard, with hot and cold running water.

At least 50 per cent of the rooms should be airconditioned (except in hill stations where there should be heating arrangements in all the bed rooms, dining rooms, restaurant and lounge) and the furniture and furnishings such as carpets, curtains etc., should be of a very good standard and design. There should be adequate number of lifts in buildings with more than two stories including the ground floor. There should be a well appointed lounge and separate ladies' and gentlemen's cloak rooms equipped with fittings of a good standard.

There should be a reception and information counter attended by qualified and experienced staff, and a bookstall, recognised Travel agency, money changing and safe deposit facilities 01} the premises. There should be a telephone in each room (except in seasonal hotels where there should be a call bell in each room and a telephone on each floor for the use of hotel guests) and a telephone for the use of guests and visitors to the hotel. There should be a well equipped and well maintained air-conditioned dining room I restaurant and wherever permissible by law there should be a bar permit room. The kitchen, pantry and cold storage should be clean and organised for orderliness and efficiency.

The hotel should offer good quality cuisine Indian as well as continental and the food and beverage service should be of a good standard. There should be qualified, trained, experienced, efficient and courteous staff in the smart and clean uniforms and the supervisory staff coming in contact with the guests should understand English and the Senior staff should possess a good knowledge of English.

There should be provision for laundry and dry cleaning service. Housekeeping at the hotel should be of a very good standard and there should be adequate supply of linen, blankets, towels etc. of good quality. Similarly, cutlery, crockery, glassware should be of good quality. Each bedroom should be provided with a vacuum jug / thermos flask with cold, boiled drinking water. The hotel should provide orchestra and ball room facilities and should attempt to present specially choreographed Indian cabaret.

Four Star Category Hotels

The facade, architectural feature and general construction of the building of four-star category hotel should be distinctive and the locality including the immediate approach and the environs should be suitable for a hotel of this category. There should be adequate parking facilities for cars. The hotel should have at least 25 lettable bedrooms, all with attached bathrooms. At least 50% of the bathrooms must have long baths or the most modern shower chambers, with 24 hours service of hot and cold running water.

All public rooms and private rooms should be fully airconditioned (except in hill stations where there should. be heating arrangements) and should be well furnished with carpets, curtains, furniture, fittings, etc. in good taste. It would be advisable to employ the services of professionally qualified and experienced interior designers of repute for this purpose. There should be an adequate number of efficient lifts in buildings of more than 2 storeys including the ground floor. There should be a well-appointed lobby and ladies' and gentleman's cloaks room equipped with fittings of a standard befitting a hotel of this category.

There should be a reception, cash and information counter attended by trained and experienced personnel. There should be a special room for conference/banquet purposes. There should a bookstall, recognised travel agency, money changing and safe deposit facilities and a left luggage room on the premises. There should be a telephone in each room and telephone for the use of guests and visitors and provisions for a radio or relayed music in each room.

There should be well equipped, welt furnished and well maintained dining rooms/restaurants on the premises, and wherever permissible 'by law, there should be an elegant, well-equipped bar/permit room. The kitchen pantry and cold storage' should be professionally designed to ensure efficiency of operation and should be well equipped. The hotel should offer both international and Indian cuisine and the food and beverage service should be of the highest standards. There should be professionally qualified, highly trained, experienced, efficient and courteous staff in smart, clean uniforms, and the staff coming in contact with guests should understand English.

The supervisory and senior staff should possess a good knowledge of English. It will be desirable for some of the staff to have a knowledge of foreign languages and staff knowing at least one continental language should be rotated on duty at all times. There should be 24 hours service for reception information and Telephones. There should be provision for reliable laundry and dry cleaning services. Housekeeping at the hotel should be of the highest possible standard and there should be a plentiful supply of linen, blankets, towels etc. that should be of the highest quality available.

Similarly, the crockery, cutlery and glassware should be provided with a vacuum jug / thermos flask with ice cold, boiled drinking water except where centrally chilled purified drinking water is provided. There should be special restaurant/dining room where facilities for dancing and an orchestra are provided.

Five Star Category Hotels

The facade, architectural features and general construction of the building of five star and five star deluxe hotels should have the distinctive qualities of a luxury hotel of this category. Five star deluxe category hotels are a qualitative extension of the five star categories, while quantitatively, the basic features are as of a five star category. In a five star deluxe hotel, the comparative all around standard of service and amenities are of very superior quality and high standard. The locality including the immediate approach and environs should be suitable for a luxury hotel this category, and there should be adequate parking space for cars.

The hotel should have at least 25 lettable bedrooms, all with well appointed, attached bathrooms with long baths or the most modern shower chambers, with 24 hours service of hot and cold running water. All public rooms and private rooms should be fully air-conditioned (except in hill stations where there should be heating arrangements) and should be well appointed with superior quality carpets, curtains, furniture, fittings, etc. in good taste.

It would be advisable to employ the services of professionally and experienced interior designers of repute for this purpose. There should be an adequate number of efficient lifts in builuing of more than 2 storeys including the ground floor, with 24 hours service. There should be a well-designed and properly equipped swimming pool (except in hill stations). There should be a well-appointed lobby and ladies and gentleman cloakrooms equipped with fittings and furniture of highest standard. There should be a reception, cash and information counter attended by highly qualified, trained and experienced personnel, and conference facilities in the form of one each or more of conference rooms /banquet halls and private dining rooms.

There should be a bookstall, beauty parlor, barber shop, recognised travel agency, money changing and safe deposit facilities, left luggage room, florist and a shop for toilet requisites and medicines on the premises. There should be a telephone in each room and telephone for the use of guests and visitors and provision for a radio or relayed music in each room. There should be a well equipped, well furnished and well maintained dining room/ restaurant on the premises; and wherever permissible by law there should be an elegant, well equipped bar/permit room.

The kitchen pantry and cold storage should be professionally designed to ensure efficiency of operation and should be well equipped. The hotel should offer both international and Indian cuisine and the food and beverage service should be of the highest standards. There should be professionally qualified highly trained experienced, efficient and courteous staff ins mart, clean uniforms, and the staff coming in contact with guests should understand English. The supervisory and senior staff should possess a good knowledge of English.

It will be desirable for some of the staff to have a knowledge of foreign languages and staff knowing at least one continental language should be rotated on duty at all times. There should be 24 hours service for reception, information and telephones. There should be provision for reliable laundry and dry-cleaning services. Housekeeping at the hotel should be of the highest possible standard and there should be a plentiful supply of all lines, blankets, towels, etc. which should be of the highest quality available.

Hotel Boom in Asian Countries

In Asian countries, tourism has posted double-digit increases in recent years even with the reduced annual growth rates since 1995. Vietnam reported an increase of 18.9 percent between 1995 and 1996, while the Philippines posted a 16.4 percent rise. Tourist arrivals in Hong Kong and Japan have been near 14.7 percent. Not all countries, however, showed record gains. Thailand's arrivals lagged with only a 3.5 percent increase, while Malaysian visitor arrivals actually declined by more than 4 percent in 1996. Just as significant, tourism receipts for the region rose at a faster rate than arrivals in 1996, demonstrating the positive economic impact of tourism in Asia.

Tourism receipts climbed a healthy 12.8 percent for Asia / Pacific from 1995 to 1996.[2] It is indeed very encouraging to see China, for instance, registering a 20 percent growth in tourism receipts, totaling almost US$10 billion. Singapore (14.6 percent), the Philippines (13.9 percent) and Hong Kong (12.8 percent) all experienced a significant increase in tourism receipts. Yet Malaysia and Thailand again suffered, showing a mere 0.4 percent and 1.2 percent improvement respectively.

Regional markets in Asia / Pacific offer dramatically different profiles when it comes to new hotel development. East Asia and the Pacific registered the fastest increase in hotel accommodation measured by bed-places, adding 2.9 million beds between 1980 and 1995. This represents a compound annual growth rate of 10.9 percent. This trend will continue especially with China becoming the major source for supply growth in north Asia. South Asia - India, Myanmar and Nepal, among others has seen only minimal growth in hotel supply given both inadequate economic and political policies in recent years. This is likely to change as we enter the 21st century, with these three countries showing exceptional opportunities for hotel development.

Hotel Markets

A profile of the hotel boom in Asia also reveals that the region's primary cities - including Bangkok, Kuala Lumpur, Manila and Hong Kong are at different stages in the development cycle. In many cases, these differences are dramatic, reflecting a wide range of supply - and - demand characteristics.

Bangkok

In the past five years, the Bangkok hotel room supply nearly doubled from 10,608 in 1992 to 19,323 in 19%. Given only modest demand growth over the same period, this has led to an oversupply of rooms with occupancy rates at about 65 percent. The occupancy rate in 1995 and 1996 showed only slight improvements, and this occurred only because room rates were eased. Bangkok had become one of the most affordable destinations in Asia even before the currency devaluation of the Thai baht. The daily room rate of luxury hotel rooms has averaged US$75, and demand is not likely to increase as prices are already rock-bottom. It is anticipated that room rates will decrease slightly in 1997 with occupancy unchanged. Furthermore, additional supply during the next two years will reduce the bottom line even more in an already depressed market.

Kuala Lumpur

Malaysia, along with its capital city, Kuala Lumpur, have suffered from minimal increases in tourist arrivals during recent years compared to other Asian destinations, with slower growth straining the hotel and tourism industry. To prepare for the 1998 Cornrnonwealth Games, the government has initiated a tax incentive scheme, which has led to a "development frenzy" in Kuala Lumpur. New supply in the firstclass and luxury segment is projected at more than 3,400 rooms by 1999. This additional supply, primarily in the up-market segment, is likely to further depress occupancy and room rate growth during the next three to five years. Hotel occupancy rates fell from the mid-80s to high 70s between 1995 and 1996, as did the average room rate. Tourist arrivals also dropped in 1996 from the preceding year.

Manila

A total of 60 hotels and 12,112 rooms were in operation in Manila in 1996 - an increase of 7 percent from 11,321 rooms in 1994. Strong economic growth supported improved performance in Manila's hotel market, with occupancies reaching 69.1 percent in 1996 compared with the 62.2 percent occupancy rate in the previous year. The number of rooms available also fell with hotels under renovation, including the Dusit Hotel Nikko, EDSA Plaza Hotel, the Heritage Hotel, the Manila Hotel and the Westin Philippine Plaza.

Between 1997 and 1998, 12 hotels and four extension projects totaling some 2,347 rooms - will come on stream, increasing the supply in Metro Manila to 14,089 rooms, about a 20 percent gain. These hotels, generally not managed by an international operator, are mainly mid-market.

New first class and luxury hotels planned for Manila include a Ritz-Carlton and a JW Marriott in Makati, as well as a hotel development by Mega World in Manila Bay reclamation area. None of these hotels, however, will open before the year 2000. Further supply of at least three Luxury hotels is expected in the new development of Fort Bonafacio with opening dates beyond 2001. Given literally no additional supply during the next two years, both Makati (next to the financial center and thus frequented by the business travelers) and the bay area (where most leisure travelers stay) should see further growth in occupancy and average rates, especially if tourism arrival growth continues at a 16 percent pace as was the case in 1996.

Hong Kong

As of December, 1996, the Hong Kong hotel market comprised 33,530 rooms and 88 properties. With growth in hotel demand outweighing supply, Hong Kong has enjoyed tremendous success as occupancy rates have climbed to 85 percent on average during the last five years and average room rates have risen to some of the highest in Asia. Supporting this economic success story are the commercial redevelopments of the Lee Garden, Victoria and Hilton hotels, which have been an economic benefit for other currently existing hotels. A mid-market hotel is able to demand at least US$125, first-class hotels US$190 and the luxury segment US$300 a night. Hotel profitability has thus increased substantially during the past five years as labour costs fell as a percentage of revenue.

As the price gap between the leisure and business segments has narrowed, Hong Kong is now facing a major challenge to further expand the leisure sector. Recent arrival figures, however, have been discouraging and the 100-day, posthandover public relations campaign by the Hong Kong Tourism Association had no immediate impact on business. With bargains on shopping becoming more and more difficult to find and no additional tourist attractions on the drawing boards, Hong Kong may see a long-term decline in leisure travelers unless new strategies are put in place by both the public and private sectors. High prices in Hong Kong are one reason for the drop in tourist arrivals.

The devaluation of major Southeast Asian currencies during recent months will also force Hong Kong to review its future pricing policy. Most Asian travelers have seen their local currency drop more than 30 percent against the U.S. dollar and the Hong Kong dollar. In addition, Hong Kong developers have 9,000 rooms on the drawing boards before the year 2,000, a 27 percent increase - pushing supply from 33,536 to 42,685 rooms. Given recent political and economic developments, however, it is unlikely that all projects will remain on time, while some may never materialise.

The majority of the new developments are planned along the new MTR railway to the Chek Lap Kok airport opening in mid - 1998. Given that this new supply is primarily in the mid-market sector, leisure travelers now staying at firstclass hotels may find themselves trading down in their accommodation once these new properties open. The growth in business travelers to Hong Kong should remain strong as the city will continue to benefit from being the financial and business center of Greater China.

International Hotel Groups in Asia

In almost every Asian country, there is a strong presence of independent or family-owned hotels with long traditions and are thus well established in the market. Yet international chains are dominating the major developments in Asia through their proven track record, management skills and access to international financing. The following highlights the development plans of select international and Asian hotel operators.

Accor

Accor Asia/Pacific - which manages hotels under the brand of Sofitel, Novotel, Mercure, Ibis and Formula I -

currently operates 75 hotels in Asia. Under an aggressive expansion plan, Accor will add 34 hotels with 6,053 rooms to its 75 property portfolio during the next two years alone. Expansion focuses primarily on Indonesia, the world's third largest country, Thailand and Vietnam.

Inter-Continental Hotels and Resorts

This international chain has more than 30 hotels and resorts in major Asian business centers and leisure destinations. Recent expansion has centered around joint venture agreements in Malaysia and China, which added nine hotels to the portfolio in 1996. The Forum brand remains an under-developed brand in Asia, although destined to grow.

Century International Hotels

The company currently has 21 hotels with more than 5,300 rooms in Asia. Lai Sun Hotels' recent 51 percent acquisition of Century International Hotels will provide the management company with further financial backing to expand throughout the region. Century International Hotels has been fully committed to developing mid-market hotels in this region as its only brand. The group plans to expand its midmarket portfolio to 60 hotels with 18,800 rooms by the year 2000.

Shangri - La Hotels and Resorts

A major player in Asia, Shangri-La Hotels & Resorts is rapidly expanding its portfolio of deluxe city hotels and resorts. Shangri-La presently operates 35 properties with a total of 17,000 rooms. Shangri-La Asia Ltd. recently acquired Slim, the privately held hotel management and marketing operation arm of the Kuok Group, which manages all Shangri-La and Traders hotels. Shangri-La has current plans to add 11 hotels with a total of 5,718 rooms in Asia, mainly in primary and secondary cities of China.

Westin Hotels and Resorts

Westin Hotels & Resorts currently manages 16 hotels with more than 7,000 rooms in Asia. Five hotel projects with some 2,354 rooms will come on stream in the next two years.

Challenges

Asia has experienced a hotel boom that is historically unprecedented. Is this trend likely to continue? Clearly, some markets are experiencing severe financial problems, the most serious being in Thailand and Malaysia. This will likely interrupt domestic developments for the time being until financial institutions have identified a new way forward. This comes at a time when both markets suffer from growth in tourism and a substantial oversupply in the firstclass and luxury segment of the hotel market. This time of uncertainty and volatility is bringing with it opportunities for investors as distress sales and acquisitions are likely to follow in select Asian markets during the next 9 to 18 months as some owners and operators may default on their payments.

This will create opportunities to buy hotel properties at minimal replacement cost primarily in Thailand, but possibly in Malaysia as well. This will occur as hotel owners are forced to adjust their assets to today's market value, and financial institutions seek buyers to purchase assets newly acquired by default. Lending for new construction will be very hard to come by, while new regulations will need to be put in place to reduce the lending risk for banks and other financial institutions going forward.

The intra-Asian business travel is on a rapid rise as the business interests of major Asian and international corporations drive further expansion in the region. A rapidly growing middle class in countries such as Indonesia and China also will assure the need for more affordable accommodation in the region, especially for individual leisure travelers. Owners and operators in Asia will increasingly face the following challenges:

Productivity

Shortage of skilled labour in almost all Asian markets remains a serious problem for the foreseeable future as new hotels come on line. This will inevitably drive labour costs higher as a percentage of revenue. Hotels will need to review and increase the productivity of all staff, from rank and file to executive, to stave off this rise in costs. Profit margins will inevitably slide if hotels do not reinvent their primary processes and eliminate services not sought by today's travelers. The high staff room ratios of the past may well decline during the next five years to levels much closer to what is common in Europe and the United States.

Training

Training is another major challenge, more so than ever, and must become an integral part of the human resource strategy. With turnover often exceeding 30 percent annually, training still focuses on getting newcomers assimilated to the company as quickly as possible. Limited funds are typically made available for training and developing existing staff to improve knowledge and productivity. Unless the industry embraces training and measures monetary pay- offs, service quality, productivity and turnover are unlikely to improve in the region.

Marketing

Increased marketing activities in main feeder markets and alliances with key suppliers of demand (such as wholesalers and airlines) will become critical in the future due to intense competition. In addition, electronic distribution systems, still in the infancy stage in Asia, will gain in significance. Often up to 70-80 percent of hotel bookings are currently made by phone or fax directly with the property. This must change. An interface with Global Distribution Systems (CDS) is one of many competitive advantages of international hotel management companies, yet their impact is reduced in Asia as travel agencies and wholesalers do not use the technology to the same extent as their counterparts in Europe or the United States. This is significant as the percentage of intra-Asian travel is rapidly increasing - with the ultimate effect of reducing dependency on overseas feeder markets during the next five to 10 years.

Investments in Central Reservations Systems (CRS) will allow hotel chains to control inventories and pricing through sophisticated yield management systems, as well as offer a one-stop shop for travel agencies to make bookings for the entire hotel portfolio. An interface with a recognised GDS is the next step only if a) the non-Asian business mix justifies the investment in added distribution and cost; and b) the Asian travel agencies use the available GDS technology to book hotel rooms in larger quantities.

Branding

Branding will become one of the most important issues

facing Asian-based owners and operators, many of whom have accumulated portfolios of assets without a proper framework for growth. Asset management and hotel management are two distinct businesses requiring different resources. Some Asian-based companies are trying to do both at the same time, often with disappointing results in developing a strong brand with a critical mass of properties.

The global trend of mergers and acquisitions will continue regionally with further rebranding and reorganisation of hotel property portfolios of Asian-based companies into two single asset and hotel management entities. Don't be surprised, however, if a seemingly "small Asian fish" swallows a "big Western fish" in the not too distant future as pockets are deep in this part of the world.

Diversification

With an oversupply of first-class and luxury hotels in most Asian cities today, the development of new mid-market hotels has the greatest potential, especially in population - rich countries such as China, Indonesia and India. Supply of internationally operated hotels does not currently meet the demand in these countries. International operators are eager to introduce their mid-market brands to the Asian market. For the past decade only Accor and Holiday Inns have made major strides in the region in the mid-market sector. Much competition is now expected from ITT Sheraton's "Compass," Marriott's "Courtyard," Shangri - La's "Traders" and Inter-Continental's "Forum" brand, which will push hard to get a market presence.

Secondary cities are also on the screens of international operators to guarantee management fee growth as primary Asian cities seem to enter the bottom of the cycle. These secondary cities are likely to gain in importance as a sound strategy to grow market share and a balanced network with all of the obvious economies of marketing and operational scale. Although the payoffs are usually longer-term in secondary markets, rapid growth in the economy and population should support future profitability. India and China are in desperate need of hotels in secondary cities, yet more often than not first-class and luxury hotels in Asia enter the market first followed by the mid-market properties years later.

Given the rise of an Asian middle class and the desire of Western tourists to look for culturally rich and less crowded vacation spots, Asian resorts are providing major international operators with additional growth opportunities. Four Seasons is expanding its resort portfolio in Bali and India. Sheraton and others have made similar strides to increase their resort portfolios. Although pristine destinations are harder to find, the future of the resort industry, especially in Malaysia, Indonesia and the Philippines, should be bright. Serviced apartments is another sector of significant potential growth. Despite high yields available, most international hotel operators have stayed clear. Given the scope for growth, however, their absence may not last for long.

Technology in the Hospitality Industry

In our contemporary world, hotel organisations are no longer constrained by physical location in serving customers. New media and systems technologies offer extraordinary efficiencies in delivering products and services with greater speed, lower cost and improved flexibility. Furthermore, technology offers unprecedented opportunities for innovation in an industry's changing menu of products and services. We are witnessing a period of major change as the fundamental value proposition of our industry is overturned. Customers -

not physical assets - drive wealth in all industries, and the hospitality industry is certainly no exception.

Technology deployed in enterprise-wide platforms makes it possible to get closer to customers. It provides tangible benefits as it offers opportunities to increase business value, reduce operational costs and create new opportunities for growth in the industry. Technology plays a key role, both in delivering products and service in virtual space, but also in enhancing the ability to listen and talk with customers in new ways. Sophisticated management information systems allow companies to identify with increasing precision the customer segments and markets that offer the greatest opportunities for growth, given the pace of change in a global economy.

A technology platform must incorporate two systems, however, to support the hospitality industry's potential for improving customer equity. Customer reservations systems track when and where customers are going, and what they will do when they get there. Customer information systems track who the customers are, what they purchase, and how they live and work. Hospitality companies already use reservation systems to get customers into the hotel. Information systems generate customer profiles based on tracking consumption patterns in the process defining a diverse range of wants and needs

This poses a number of challenges. Certainly, it will be important to integrate data generated at the property level with reservations systems and customer information in a total system solution that provides for data warehouses and networked communications. In such a system, customer information is captured from a variety of sources, and becomes the platform for the highly focused marketing and product development strategies of the future. The hospitality in the industry will thus require two types of infrastructure to do business - real estate and technology - to support a shirt from depending on "place" to a reliance on "space" to fully meet customer needs. This follows a four-stage evolution currently taking place in industries across the board.

The hospitality industry, for example, historically focused on developing major physical assets, with an almost exclusive orientation to financing and building individual properties. At this first stage, companies achieved relatively low customer equity, providing a narrow band of products and services, traditional to the hospitality industry, at various physical locations. As the industry matured, it differentiated itself to meet more diverse customer needs with properties matched to the various market niches. In this second stage, business hotels and all-suite properties are examples of such differentiation. A third stage involves serving customers in ways that do not require a physical address at all, including telephone marketing and catalogue sales. And in the fourth state - the age of electronic commerce - the "real estate" is actually owned by the consumers themselves in the form of a personal computer located on a desktop, eliminating the need for many types of businesses to own significant physical assets in order to create wealth.

At each of these stages, the potential for customer equity rises with increased access to customers, regardless of their physical location, while the costs associated with fixed-assets declines. The evolutionary track moves from exclusive reliance on major assets to combinations of physical assets and technology in reaching customers. Indeed, new media and systems technologies can be designed to give hotel organisations greatly enhanced access to larger numbers of customers - regardless of physical location. These technology platforms also spawn rapid innovation in products and services, combined with improved speed to market. The result enhanced business valuation and higher stock prices as a company's strategic, technological and financial architectures are aligned to generate customer equity.

Hospitality companies can dramatically improve the valuation of their companies by using new technology to bring them closer to their customers. This is particularly the case with major companies that have not fully served their large customer bases and have good potential to build customer equity. In many cases these organisations are our industry's major franchisors, whose goals are typically to sign up new franchisees and improve the yields from each property. In a nutshell, these companies are using franchising as a growth vehicle and their orientation is to maximising fee income.

For these organisations, an intermediate performance measure might be described as revenue-per-available-franchisee (REVPAF). The challenge here will be to develop ways to reach the primary customer (hotel guest) directly, rather than simply through the franchisee organisations - with the end game being improved REVPAC. The typical franchisor catches the primary customer in its reservation system, but typically doesn't "speak" to that customer again, either during the guest stay or after leaving the hotel property. Franchisors will benefit as they begin to develop the strategies and systems allowing them direct access to the primary customers, with a goal of increasing REVPAC.

In the years ahead, we will need to change the way we think about the hospitality industry. Indeed, we will need to transform ourselves with a new vision of serving customers, or the customers will do it for us. Are hotels an asset play - or a customer access play? The real values of the industry have always rested with the customers that stay in our hotels, but opportunities to serve them are vastly increased by technology. REVPAC is a performance measure that matches the capabilities of the Information Age, and underscores the strategic directions hotel organisations must consider in the years ahead to return shareholder value.

Globalisation on Hotel Industry

Globalisation is a natural outgrowth of trends that have evolved during the past 50 years. International hotel chains were invented after World War II; they grew in the 1960s, and expanded greatly in the following two decades. Industry and economic trends in this decade have further propelled the growth of internationally-oriented hotel companies for a variety of reasons. Severe overbuilding of hotel markets, particularly in the United States during the 1980s, halted new development almost entirely, while scarcity of growth and development opportunities in markets around the world has further supported the trend toward industry consolidation.

Many companies committed to growth have found that opportunities in their back yards have been limited because of overbuilding, and they have been forced to look beyond mature domestic markets to offshore opportunities. The pressures to expand beyond national boundaries have largely arisen from the need for growing hotel companies to reach 'critical mass'— the point at which a network of properties is sufficiently large to satisfy the travel needs of the hotel company's most valued customers. For different companies with varying products and locations, critical mass will vary in scope.

A hotel organisation, for example, may reach a point in which there is no other viable option than to expand across national boundaries if it wishes to grow, achieve critical mass and benefit from the economies of scale that accompany it. If this is the case, leadership will need to recognise the imperative of organising as a global company. As an example, consider an international hotel company that is well established in North America and Europe. In today's world market, company leadership may cast attention on the potential for moving into burgeoning Asia/Pacific markets to compete with established regional companies. Companics considering such strategic options can succeed against strong local and regional competitors only if they capitalise on the advantages derived from being a global company.

While the large international chains continue to expand on a global basis, there are in the United States a number of brand names that have yet to reach the critical mass required for marketing success. The question this presents to the industry can be stated simply. Will the demands of globalisation encourage further consolidation as smaller companies that have not achieved critical mass are acquired or put out of business? The need for hotel companies to achieve critical mass and the attendant economies of scale suggests that we will see a diminishing number of larger companies in the future as the imperatives of global expansion persist.

Economies of scale are real, not imagined, and marketing on a global basis creates a significant competitive edge. It is certain that brands and products will be increasingly marketed on a truly global basis. Growth and development functions will thus become even more critical for those organisations that have not yet achieved critical mass. For those companies pursuing a global strategy and accustomed to hotel management contracts, franchising relationships and non-recourse financing, significant adjustments will need to be made to the growth and development model.

In a number of markets around the world, the bifurcation of ownership from management and management from marketing is a concept yet to achieve real maturity. The process that promotes these concepts is a slow one and global-minded companies will need to respond accordingly. The differences in financing, owning, operating and marketing hotel properties will thus eventually narrow in a more global environment.

The challenge for companies growing into markets where local partnerships and alliances are required for success will be to convince their foreign counterparts of the benefits of structures that have been successful in their home countries. A company going offshore with a business concept, however, cannot assume that it will be wholly accepted. Differences will gradually break down, but for the time being it may be necessary to adjust to local realities.

Global Products

Hospitality customers increasingly seek predictable services that support their ability to move quickly and easily around the world. Indeed, the businesses and lifestyles of these multi-cultural travelers have themselves been shaped by globalisation. The concept of projecting single brands globally is thus alluring, as well as being fully within the grasp of many hospitality companies. Nevertheless, there continues to be uncertainty about the benefits of establishing a single-brand presence in a global marketplace, in contrast to responding to the unique conditions at the local level.

A number of international hotel companies have sought the economies of scale attendant to developing single brands and products, and providing them in a uniform fashion to as many markets around the globe as possible. A counter-vailing trend is that many people — both tourists and business travelers — seek the unique qualities and customs of an individual locale. In response, some international hotel companies have tried to reflect local culture in the way their hotels are designed and operated.

This is clearly an arena in which there is no one right answer, but rather a balance of complex factors required. For example, there is a general consensus that "global travelers," who travel frequently whether for business or recreation, usually prefer a uniform product, because they want the convenience and comfort of predictability, and they demand a high level of service. Those who travel less frequently, but have a fairly high level of sophistication may avoid such dominant global brand and product concepts.

A third group is looking for what they are accustomed to, and are attracted by brands they are familiar with; in essence, they prefer to stay in environments that reflect their home-based experience. Customer expectations are related to the level of the product, and hotel products at the lower end of the spectrum tend to be easier to standardise globally, in part because these properties are more clearly defined by physical attributes, which can be duplicated. At the upper end of the product quality spectrum, customers seek subtle differences in services and quality, which are not easily replicated.

Global Capital

As hospitality companies grow into the global economy, they will need to look to global capital markets for support. Investment capital, however, continues to be in short supply and this situation will continue for some time. Companies that wish to attract investors will need to demonstrate that they can offer better returns and performance than in the past. And, at least in the eyes of the world's financial markets, they will need to demonstrate their viability as companies in a global marketplace. For the first time real estate is now being traded as a commodity in securities markets, and we can therefore expect hospitality products in the future to be viewed in the same manner.

The securitisation of real estate in the United States represents a significant trend, and it behooves savvy futurists to track these trends as they develop elsewhere in the world. Indeed, the world's financial markets are at the cutting edge of globalisation, driven by the revolution in communications. With investment portfolios passed between the Americas, Europe and Asia/Pacific in a time continuum without interruption, 24-hour financial markets are here and are destined to impact significantly the way their customers use them.

Hospitality companies that seek capital from the public marketplace will need to function as global enterprises. If the public markets on a global basis are going to serve corporations and produce optimum results, those public companies that feed into any or all of the three major financial centers of the world need to view themselves and to be viewed as global enterprises in order to benefit fully from what these markets have to offer. Hospitality companies that want to trade in the financial markets will need a business concept that is relatively easy to communicate and comprehend. Those companies that provide homogeneity in products and market orientations will be the most attractive to global capital markets. Companies with simple and well-defined products such as Coca Cola have become recognised by customers and investors around the world.

Hospitality companies that want to trade in the financial markets will need a business concept that is relatively easy to communicate and comprehend. A truly global enterprise will have the ability to react quickly to market opportunities, no matter where they present themselves by applying business concepts that have been proven in the context of a global undertaking. Hotel companies expanding globally will also need to confront varying traditions, structures and attitudes to property investment and valuation in different countries. It is possible that there will be a more common set of standards in the future but we are still far from that level of standardisation.

3

Food Service Facilities

The food service industry continues to be more and more competitive, and the integration of marketing concepts into the creation of the atmosphere is desirable from the standpoint of increasing sales. One approach to this integration is to use attractive displays of food and beverages in the dining areas or lobby and lounge areas. Displays of wines, salads, desserts, or baked goods lend to the creation of a pleasing dining atmosphere as well as help increase the sales of these items.

The use of salad bars, dessert carts, carving carts, and refrigerated display cases are some of the methods used to accomplish this integration. Among other things, the atmosphere to be developed for a food facility should attract attention, be pleasing to the eyes, and provide an interesting change of pace. For example, an intimate, peaceful dining room provides welcome relief from noisy offices and industries. Likewise, a noisy cafeteria may actually be refreshing to students who are in quiet surroundings most of the day. The warmth and glow of a fireplace provides a welcome change in cold weather.

The development of the physical and psychological aspects of the atmosphere depends in great part upon the planners selected to design the facility. They must have a clear understanding with the owner of the particular needs and goals to be accomplished in developing the atmosphere. In addition to knowledge of the functional operation of the facility, the planners should be keenly aware of the type of clientele to be attracted. Only then can they come up with a suitable design that will be attractive as well as functional. It is then up to management to develop the nonphysical aspects of the atmosphere to complete the total concept.

COLOUR

This is one of the visual aspects of the atmosphere as perceived by individuals; it is also one of the best tools that planners have to create a variety of moods. Most people make a number of choices based on colour; they select their clothes, cars, houses, paints, and even foods by colour. Colour can be used to induce a feeling of happiness, to promote serenity, or to stimulate hunger. It can attract people to one type of dining room and drive them out of others. Certain colours are especially important to the development of dining areas.

Many experiments have shown that certain colours have a very strong emotional effect on most individuals. It is known that blue reduces excitability and therefore helps one to relax. Blue is also considered to be cooling and is "easy" on the eyes. Green is a colour that acts as a sedative. Yellow, on the other hand, is cheery, stimulating, and attention-drawing. On dull, sunless days, people exhibit mental and physical sluggishness which is partially attributed to the absence of yellow, red, and other stimulating colours. Red is associated with excitement and violence. Gray suggests coldness and is very depressing unless it is combined with livelier colours.

Colour sensations can sometimes produce physical reactions that are not just of the visual system but affect the entire body. For example, persons exposed to predominately red colours exhibit increased blood pressure, quickened muscular reactions, and greater emotions. Red also tends to produce restlessness and makes time seem to pass very slowly. In comparison, persons exposed to predominately blue and green colours have been found to exhibit slower muscle response and quicker mental and conversational response. Blues and greens also make time seem to go faster. Some of the common emotional responses caused by exposure to various colours. These may be used to develop the type of response desired in various areas of the food facility. The colours have to be predominant in an area and individuals must be exposed to them for a period of time.

Features

The strong effect colours may have on individuals, care should be taken in selecting them to achieve the desired result. One if the aspects of good colour planning deals with contrast. A single predominant colour, no matter how pleasing, cannot function alone. A restful green that is predominant would strain the part of the eye susceptible to it and eventually lead to eye and body fatigue. With a single predominant colour individuals would have to look harder to distinguish objects because of the lack of contrast. Extreme contrast between very light and dark colours is also undesirable since they too result in eyestrain. Achieving the right amount of contrast along with maintaining the desired emotional responses is necessary to the creation of a pleasing environment for dining.

Classifications of Colours

Red, yellow, and blue are the primary colours. They are referred to is primaries because other colours are derived from them. In their pure form the primary colours are too strong to use on large areas and therefore are used as accents. The secondary colours are green, orange, and violet and are mixtures of two of the primary colours. Green is obtained by mixing blue and fellow, orange by mixing red and yellow, and violet by mixing red and blue.

Mixtures of primary colours and secondary colours result in the intermediate colours. Examples of intermediates are red-orange, yellow-green, and blue-violet. Colours are also classified as warm or cool. Red, orange, and yellow are the warm colours; they seem to advance and convey a feeling of warmth. The cool colours are blue, green, and violet; these are retracting colours and are cooling and relaxing. A combination of one warm colour and one cool colour results in the complementary colours used in colour planning.

The problem of selecting colours that go well together or harmonise is solved by using one of five rules. These rules are related to harmonies and are identified as monochromatic, analogous, complementary, split complementary, and triad. Monochromatic harmony uses a single colour and is the simplest of colour schemes. The single colour can be expressed in the following ways.

— As the pure colour itself

— As a tint of the pure colour (a tint is the pure colour mixed with white) is a shade of the pure colour (a shade is the pure colour mixed with black)

— As a tone of the pure colour (a tone is the pure colour mixed with both black and white).

— Analogous harmony is obtained by using any three or four consecutive colours on the colour wheel. Examples of analogous harmony are red-orange, orange, and yellow-orange; or red, red-orange, orange, and Glow-orange.

— Complementary harmony results by using any two colours that are directly opposite each other on the colour wheel. Red and green, red orange and blue green, or yellow and violet are examples of complementary harmony.

— Split complementary or near complementary harmony involves three colours. Any one of the two complementary colours and two colours adjacent to the omitted complementary colour are used. On the colour wheel, the split complementaries are in the form of a Y. Examples of split complementary colours are yellow, blue-violet, and red-violet; green, red-orange, and red-violet; and red, blue-green, and yellow-green.

— Triad harmony also involves three colours. These are selected by king every fourth colour on the colour wheel. Two examples of triads are red, yellow, and blue; and yellow-orange, red-violet, and blue-green.

— After a particular harmony is selected, then a decision regarding the tints, shades, or tones of the colours is made. One or two of the colours selected will be used for the walls and other major surfaces. The other colours will be used as accents on smaller objects like drapes, table cloths, and dinnerware.

The important points in colour selection are as follows:

— Pure colours are usually too strong and brilliant when applied to large areas or surfaces.

— Colours should be selected under the kind of lighting that they will be used under. Colours selected under fluorescent lighting will appear different under incandescent lighting.

— Colours selected from a small sample will appear brighter when applied to large areas.

— Complementary, split complementary, and triad harmonies always result in a combination of warm and cool colours. The desired atmosphere will dictate which colour is to predominate.

— Black, white, brown, and gold usually go well with any of the colour harmonies.

— Texture is closely related to colour application and usage is best considered at the same time the colour choices are made.

Light and Colour

As light modifies colours in many ways, the type of light source and systems of lighting should be considered when selecting colours. Pink lights, for example, have been shown to pale lipstick colours. Green lights have a tendency to show up wrinkles and should not be used in an atmosphere where a feeling of well-being is to be created. Another problem is the use of amber lights which tend to wash out colours. A well-chosen colour scheme can be easily spoiled by poorly selected lights. Lights and colours for work areas are quite different from those desirable for dining areas and should be planned separately.

The uses of colour in foodservice facilities are so numerous that space will not allow a complete presentation of all of them. Therefore, a guide to the uses of colour is presented below. Note that many of the uses of colour are related to other factors that affect an individual's perception of atmosphere.

1) The use of warm reds, browns, yellows, golds, and oranges enhances the appearance of foods.
2) Where emphasis is to be placed on fast service and high turnover, warm colours should dominate the major areas.
3) Use colours in dining areas that are flattering to people. Colours that tend to make people look pale (green and grey) should be avoided.

4) Use light colours in small areas to create the impression of size.

5) Use warm colours in rooms that are windowless.

6) High ceilings can be made to appear lower by using dark colours.

7) Emphasising horizontal lines by dark colours will make a ceiling appear lower.

8) Low ceilings can be overcome by emphasising vertical lines with dark colours.

9) The end walls of long narrow rooms should be a warmer or deeper hue than the other walls to make them approach and make the room seem squarer.

10) Undesirable features of a room can be painted the same colour as their background so as not to emphasise them.

11) Each room or area should have a mixture of warm and cool colours.

12) Adjoining rooms or areas are best painted in harmonious colours.

13) Avoid using too many different colours in one room or area.

14) Use light colours to make objects appear larger if they are to be emphasised.

15) Use dark colours to make rooms appear smaller.

16) Use brilliant colours to bring attention to signs or other features.

17) Dark-coloured objects appear to be smaller than they really are.

18) Maintain proper contrast to permit differentiation of objects from their backgrounds.

(19) Avoid highly reflective colours that tend to tire the eyes.

The selection of colours is a very difficult task that requires skill, taste, and experience. Colour scheming does not end with the blending of wall colours with upholstery, fabrics, and carpets, but includes the considerations of menus, dinnerware, uniforms, and even the type of decorations. Just as the right colours can be used to make a food facility more attractive, the wrong colours can focus attention on features that should not be accented. Also, since colour is so influenced by fashion and trend, these factors must be considered in the colour scheme chosen.

LIGHTING

As with colour, proper planning of lights can achieve dramatic effects and aid in the creation of the desired atmosphere. Both sexes enjoy a type of lighting that makes them look their best. This factor is of great importance in the planning and design of lights for dining areas, bars, rest rooms, and other public spaces.

The best system of lighting for restaurants appears to be a combination of indirect, direct, and spot lights. These lights can be arranged to accomplish the desired flexibility required for the various meal periods. Areas should be well lit for breakfast and lunch, while less lighting is desired for evening meals.

The installation of rheostats will provide this flexibility. In considering the lighting system, the amount of daylight entering an area should be considered. Total glass area can be specified by the architect to adjust for this factor. The use of tinted glass may be considered for some situations. The ultimate type of lighting for dining areas has traditionally been considered to be candlelight. The reddish flame of candlelight is flattering to people and to most foods. The flickering of the flame adds to the creation of a desirable atmosphere.

Alternatives to candlelight are incandescent and fluorescent lights. The economy of operation of fluorescent lights favours their installation in large areas. Incandescent lights would be the best choice in dining areas because of their red colour enhancement. Properly selected fluorescent lights may also be used in dining areas if sufficient red tones are used in the colour scheme. The deluxe warm white fluorescent tubes are the closest in colour tint to incandescent bulbs and would be recommended. As with colour, lighting can do much toward creating atmosphere by correcting spacial deficiencies and accenting desirable areas.

To illustrate, a low ceiling can be made to appear higher if it is well-lit; high ceilings will appear lower if they are dimly lit. Care should be taken not to light the long walls brightly in a narrow room since it will appear to be even narrower. Dark walls will show up better with bright lights, and if the colour is to be accented, the illumination level has to be high. Bright lights are placed above normal eye levels to minimise glare. The same concept applies to candles since they too can create glare. Candles may be placed in frosted globes if they are at eye level or slightly below.

In dining areas, it is best to concentrate illumination on the seats and tables and perhaps on special design features. The ceilings and walls should not be so brightly lit that they detract attention from the room. Bright lights may be used to create a brisk atmosphere which, if service is fast, results in a high turnover of customers. Serving areas, should be well-lighted. Some operations may use full lighting for a high turnover at lunch and then dim the lights for evening meals in hopes of attaining higher check averages.

Coloured Lights

Careful selection of coloured lights will enhance the total

atmosphere. The first consideration is to coordinate the coloured lights with other coloured objects and colour schemes used in the room. This is important, since certain colours will take on strange off-colours when subjected to coloured lights. Red colours will appear very dark under blue or green lights and olive-green colours look brown under yellow lights. Coloured lights affect the appearance of the faces and clothes of people. Red lights have the advantage of flattering complexions and tend to enhance the colour of fabrics. Red lights also have a good effect on most foods.

Green and blue lights are undesirable for illuminating areas where people will be present. These lights tend to distort the red hues and are unflattering because of this. Green and blue lights may be used for inanimate objects that serve as accent pieces. The use of pink, ivory, or amber lights is suggested for areas where skin tone is important, as they are warm and impart a friendly and inviting feeling. It is better to use tints of colours rather than strong hues.

Lighting should not only provide atmosphere but should reach a satisfactory level of illumination from a practical standpoint. If the lighting level is too high, individuals will have a feeling of exposure; or if too dim, they may feel fearful. For these reasons, there should be enough light so persons can see, yet not so much that they feel uneasy.

One method of attaining such an arrangement is to lower the height of ceiling fixtures. This provides a sufficient amount of light and at the same time results in a comfortable soft effect. Foodservice lighting levels typically will range between 5 and 50 foot-candles (53.8-538 lux), with 30-50 foot-candles (323-538 lux) usually used for breakfast and lunch. A level of 5-30 foot-candles (53.8-323 lux), depending on the atmosphere desired, is used for evening meals.

The lighting level in all areas must be sufficient to make the other elements of the atmosphere visible. It is senseless to spend a great deal of time and money creating a striking colour scheme and then ruin it with poor lighting. Any area with less than 5 foot-candles (53.8 lux) of illumination may as well be colourless. In reality, the excitement of good lighting comes largely from its shadows and variations in brightness. Flat, shadowless lighting is dull and monotonous. The general lighting system for an area needs the accents of bright areas which come from direct light sources. These may take the form of wall brackets, chandeliers, downlights, or spot lights. Recessed ceiling downlights of low intensity are very satisfactory for lighting dining areas.

Sound

Aside from dinner music, sounds are to play a passive role and never attract attention. The design goal is to create a balance between quiet and noise. Many people are uncomfortable in a room which is very quiet. A noisy room creates tension and irritability. For dining rooms, a satisfactory acoustical environment has a reverberant sound level that is high enough to be heard, but not so high that individuals at nearby tables can distinguish what is being said. Correct planning for the acoustical environment contributes to the development of the desired atmosphere.

The sensitivities of individuals to various sounds require control of undesirable noise and maintenance of desirable sounds at an acceptable level. Sound may be considered to be a pressure wave and is compared to the ripples spreading out from a pebble dropped in water. If the sound is not restricted, it will spread out in all directions. The speed of sound in air is about 1100 feet per second (335 meters per second). Any sounds produced in open air will travel directly from the source to the listener. In a room, however, sound is reflected from the walls, floor, and ceiling and can build up a general sound level much greater than that which results from the same source in open space.

Sounds that are repeatedly reflected become noise or unwanted sounds. Noise at a high enough level causes irritation and fatigue. It can interfere with communication and concentration and become very distracting and disturbing. The intensity of sound is measured by the decibel. A sound intensity of one decibel is at the threshold of audibility for the normal human ear. A sound intensity of 20 decibels may be compared to a whisper. The normal speaking voice has an intensity of about 60 decibels. Any sound intensities over 100 decibels for any length of time are undesirable, and constant exposure can cause partial loss of hearing. When there is a source of sound in a room, the level of noise at any position is made up of two parts.

The first part is the direct sound travelling straight from the source to the position under consideration. The second part is the reverberant sound, which is the sound reaching the position after multiple reflection from the room surfaces. The intensity of direct sound falls off as the distance from the source increases. Direct sound is reduced by about 6 decibels each time the distance from the source is doubled. Reverberant sound levels will generally be at a uniform intensity throughout the room. Direct sounds are predominant at positions close to the source, while reverberant sounds will dominate positions remote from the source.

Noise Controlling

The problem of controlling noise levels is basically a matter of suppressing the sounds from the source or reducing the amount of reverberant sounds. Sound-absorbing materials are used to minimise both types of sounds. In some instances, the source of the sounds can be isolated by coverings or baffles. Kitchen areas are very difficult to soundproof because of the materials used in the construction of the room and the large amount of metallic equipment present.

Hard, dense materials, like quarry tile or clay tile used for kitchen floors and tiled wall surfaces, reflect a large portion of the sound striking them. Stainless steel surfaces actually act as sound surfaces much like a drum. In these areas, it is desirable to increase the amount of sound-absorbing materials as much as possible to overcome the severe noise problem. Service doors leading to the kitchen can be vestibuled to reduce the noise level before reaching the dining room. This is a compromise between the additional square footage needed for the vestibule and the desirability of reduced noise levels. Thus a facility designed for professionals may include a vestibule while a facility to be designed for other segments of the market may not consider one.

The following things that can be done to minimise noise from the kitchen include the following:

1. Selecting mechanical equipment such as fans and compressors for quiet operation.
2. Using installation techniques that minimise duct noises, the sound of water flow, and water hammer.
3. Using silent closing devices on doors and drawers.
4. Providing rubber bumpers for mobile equipment.
5. Soundproofing walls between kitchen and dining areas.
6. Placing a service station between the entrance to the kitchen and the dining room.
7. Creating a quiet work environment to reduce employee noise.

8. Using the spread load dishwashing concept where an adequate inventory of china, silverware, and glassware are maintained to handle the entire meal period. Dishwashing begins after the meal period to clean the dinnerware for the next meal period. This concept has several ramifications in terms of soiled and clean dish storage requirements, dishwasher size, impact on employee scheduling, and the total size of the dishwashing area.

In addition to acoustical treatment of walls and ceilings, carpeting where permitted will also help. Local sanitarians should be consulted before specifying carpet for production areas. The sound-proofing of metal surfaces by undercoating will reduce the noise created. One method of handling noise problems in dining areas is to vary the spacing of tables. The distance between diners at one table should be appreciably less than the distance to diners at adjoining tables. If a greater density of seating is desired, the use of screens or partial partitions will reduce the sound levels. Bar areas tend to be noisy and can be partially partitioned.

Music

Music is a desirable sound is one way of enhancing the audible environment. Music has a direct effect on the mood of individuals. Background music should be selected so it does not attract attention. It should be soft, inoffensive, and as characterless as possible. The correct use of background music can put customers in a good mood for dining.

CLIMATE

This is one of the important factors affecting the comfort of people. Most individuals are very sensitive to thermodynamic phenomena and variations from an ideal climate are easily noticed and quickly lead to discomfort. Customers will quickly respond to environmental conditions that are too hot, too cold, too drafty, too stuffy, or too damp. The ideal climate for dining consists of temperatures between 70 and 75°F (21.1 and 23.9°C) with a relative humidity of 50%.

Thermodynamic comfort is a function of activity and other factors such as age, sex, and the amount of clothing worn. Needless to say, the climate should be designed for the particular type of patron that the facility is to be planned for. Higher-priced operations will usually attract people who are accustomed to slightly higher temperatures. Women prefer higher temperatures than men, and children require less heat than both men and women. People who are in active occupations prefer lower temperatures. The amount of clothing worn during the different seasons reflects the needs of different temperatures.

People will be wearing lighter clothing in the summer; therefore, slightly warmer than normal temperatures would be appreciated. Clothing worn in the winter is heavier and temperatures should not be allowed to get too high. The effects of colours and lighting are evaluated before a particular temperature level is decided upon. Temperature can be used to some extent to affect a desired turnover of customers. Many fast-food operations may want lower temperatures to keep the customers on the move and thereby increase the turnover rate.

The opposite is true in more luxurious dining rooms where turnover is not stressed. Customers are inclined to be more relaxed in a higher temperature, and the warmth is conducive to a leisurely meal of several courses. The ideal design is to have a system where the temperature can be precisely adjusted for the particular situation. Climate control in most regions requires both heating and air conditioning. The systems should have sufficient capacity to maintain the desired temperature and relative humidity.

Pleasant Odors

Climate control also includes the control of odors. Odors are an important part of the atmosphere, because smell usually evokes much deeper memories in individuals than either vision or sound. People are often uncomfortable in odor-free surroundings, and pleasant odors can contribute to the desired atmosphere. The popularity of display cooking areas in the dining room is partially caused by the cooking aromas that are emitted. Odors have to be controlled or they will blend and can become quite offensive. This is very noticeable in dining areas where the air circulation system may bring in varied kitchen odors. Mixing the odors of fish and steak, for example, is not at all appealing to the person eating the steak.

Odors are very disturbing to individuals when dining because taste is largely a matter of smell. If the odors cannot be controlled and separated, or if they are undesirable, they should not be allowed to seep into the dining room. One method of accomplishing this is to maintain the air pressure in the dining room at a higher level than the air pressure in the kitchen. Exhaust systems designed to rid the interiors of smoke, fumes, and odors should be positioned to avoid affecting the immediate exterior environment. This is especially important for exterior walks and entrances into the public areas.

FURNISHINGS

Furnishings for the dining area are also correlated to the type of atmosphere to be planned. The first thing that an individual does upon entering a dining room is to look for a place to sit. Therefore, arrangement of tables, chairs, and auxiliary furnishings does much to affect the initial impression of customers. Many people do not like to sit at exposed tables because they feel observed. This problem is overcome by the use of booths or by planters that act as partitions.

Tables and Chairs

Tables, chairs, and banquettes should be large enough to seat diners comfortably without crowding. Distances between tables are sized to enable waiters or waitresses to move through the area while serving and allow diners to eat and converse without being distracted. Selection of chairs is critical since the greatest body contact is made with them. Chairs must have suitable shape, angle of seat and back, size, relationship to table, and tactile qualities to be comfortable.

Table space of at least 26 in. (660 mm) should be allowed for chairs without arms to provide elbow room. Armchairs require a minimum table space of 28 in. (711 mm) for comfort. The preferred height of chair seats is 17 to 18 in. (432 to 457 mm), for adults. A minimum of 12 in. (305 mm) of space is needed between the top of the chair and the bottom of the table. The shape of the table should be considered in relation to the dining mood to be created. Round tables, for example, tend to promote communications among the diners and may result in a lower turnover but higher check averages. Square or rectangular tables tend to increase turnover and are more efficient in the use of dining space.

Counter seating can be used to accommodate single customers and also increase turnover rates. Combinations of tables, booths, banquettes, and counters are frequently planned to appeal to a variety of market segments. Cashier areas should be placed for ease of access and in consideration of flow patterns. Bars, buffets, wine displays, or other merchandising setups are placed for maximum visibility and exposure to the customers.

Fabrics

The selection of drapes, carpeting, and fabrics is guided by the need for variations in textures, colours, and shapes. These materials may be chosen to blend with or contrast with the architectural features of the building. Drapes and floor coverings are selected to give an overall appearance of unity and balance. Various fabrics are selected to add warmth and cosiness to a room and to relieve any monotony in the shape of the room. Fabrics contribute not only by their visual impact, but by the fact that they are more pleasant to touch than hard surfaces. Designers may use grass wallpapers, ceramic tile, cork, linen, silk, brick, and other materials that are textured and appealing for wall coverings. Carpeting adds a feeling of intimacy and comfort because it is a point of contact.

Pictures and Prints

Pictures and prints used to decorate wall areas add considerably to the atmosphere. An advantage in using these items is that they can be easily changed. The pictures selected should not clash with the decorative scheme. The shape and size are correlated to the walls on which they will be placed. Colours within the pictures or on frames should blend with the overall scheme of the room to give a coordinated appearance. Table settings can enhance the appeal of the dining atmosphere. Customers notice the tableware they are using and will thus form an impression of the restaurant. Each item placed on the table is selected to add to the feeling and mood to be created in the room. This pertains to dishes, glasses, silver, napkins, and tablecloths.

Food Facilities or Exterior Design

The term exterior, as used in food facilities design, is taken to include signs, landscaping, parking areas, building structure, doors, and windows. The objective of exterior design is to attract customers. To perform this function effectively, the exterior must convey the correct impression of the type of food facility into which the customer is being invited. Exterior design is to be coordinated with interior design to provide the total atmosphere.

Problem of Visibility

One problem to be dealt with in exterior design is the matter of attracting initial attention. This is a problem of visibility as seen through the eyes of pedestrians and people in slow- or fast-moving cars. An attractive sign, large enough for the situation, is generally accepted as the best method of attracting attention. The placement of the sign must ensure that drivers are aware of the facility before it appears in view. In some locations, signs may have to be placed at considerable distances from the building. The most effective signs are those that are short and to the point.

Attraction is also gained by the exterior treatment of the building. This includes the size, shape, colours, and materials used in construction. The first impression of an interior of a facility is gained from the exterior. This impression- is derived not solely by the exterior design but from glimpses of the interior that are provided by windows. Windows are so located as to frame the parts of the interior that they expose. Colour usage on the exterior can follow the same general guidelines presented for interior use. An additional consideration is to let any natural landscaping provide much of the colour. In this case, the building elements can be finished as plainly as possible so as not to compete.

Floodlighting is frequently used with success when the architectural features of the exterior are appealing or dramatic. Care must be used in sizing and placing windows in floodlighted areas to prevent glare into the building. Some designers may prefer to rely on the elegance of simplicity and use little, if any, decorative detailing. On the other hand, facilities with perhaps a national theme may require carefully selected exterior details to complete the concept of total atmosphere.

Planning of Parking Areas

Parking lots and areas is important in creating the right impression with the customers. The ease of entering and leaving the parking lot as well as the individual parking space is critical to good design. Consideration should also be given to the placement of walkways from the parking lot to the building.

The locations of exterior trash and garbage containers have to be selected carefully. It may be desirable to sacrifice a parking space or two to give special treatment to these undesirable areas. The customers' first impression of a foodservice facility as they leave their cars should not be the sights and smells of trash and garbage. Management should stress the cleanliness of exterior areas at all times.

The entrance door to the facility can form the climax of the exterior attractiveness. It should be selected in accord with the overall design of the building exterior. Doors may be all glass, half glass, wood, or metal, plain or with panels. Separate entrances to the bar are provided if the bar will be used by nondiners. Entrance doors are located for easy access from streets or parking areas. Whether to provide an entrance area or not is largely a matter of choice. An entrance area can have several desirable functions: it can convey a sense of spaciousness and enhance the atmosphere. Entrance areas also provide a meeting place for people and can be used is waiting space during rush hours.

Landscaping provides the setting for -he facility. Another use of landscaping is to hide undesirable service areas or views from dining areas that are not pleasant. The landscape architect may use contours, plant textures, heights, rocks, pathway surfaces, or garden furniture to achieve the desired exterior appearance. In laying out the landscape, important views are selected and foregrounds and backgrounds are developed for them. The landscaping must harmonise with the exterior features of the building so that a good impression is created from all angles of view.

Employees

The importance of retaining good employees and keeping them in a pleasant mood cannot be underestimated as a vital part of the atmosphere. A cold welcome, poor service, or indifferent attitude can ruin all the friendliness which the colour, lighting, decor, and furnishings have created. These physical components of the atmosphere are ineffective unless they are complemented by the human components.

Food Service Industry

The food service industry generally encompasses those places, institutions, and companies responsible for any meal eaten away from home. This industry includes restaurants, school and hospital cafeterias, catering operations, and many other formats. Major foodservice providers include Compass Group, Sodexho, Aramark, and the Crown Group.

The companies that supply foodservice operators are called foodservice distributors. Some companies manufacture products in both consumer and foodservice versions. The consumer version usually comes in individual-sized packages with elaborate label design for retail sale. The foodservice version is packaged in a much larger industrial size and often lacks the colourful label designs of the consumer version.

HOTEL

The hotel food and beverage department provides food-related guest services throughout a hotel, conference, or resort property. Outlets for food and beverage services can include the following:

— Full-service restaurant.

— Coffee shop.

— Catering facilities.

— Room service.

— Recreational areas.

— Lobby area bars.

— Food market or delicatessen.

Food items for these combined foodservice areas are provided from a central kitchen, with the exception of large hotel facilities where satellite kitchens provide auxiliary production and service areas. An executive chef supervises production for all areas, consulting with the manager of each foodservice area. Of the seven food service areas, catering affords the possibility for the greatest profit, in addition to providing much-needed cash flow during periods when room sales are slow. Hotel catering services are usually classified as:

— Business.

— Convention/conference.

— Social.

The volume of catering service available to a hotel is based on the size and number of facilities that can be used for private functions as well as the availability of production and service staff and related equipment. The primary catering market for a hotel is based on three factors:

— Location.

— Hotel facilities.

— Customer profile.

The location of a hotel determines the demand for in-house catering. In house catering is defined as guest-related foodservice functions associated with business meetings, conferences, conventions, and social concerns. A hotel with a remote location focuses its catering efforts on the business booked into the hotel. Resort locations often provide additional opportunities for catering services at sports facilities and landscape venues throughout the property. A hotel with a suburban or downtown location can expect to develop a large volume of outside catering business, both business-related and social in addition to conferences and conventions.

The amount of combined catering business that can be handled at any one time in a hotel is based primarily on the number and size of the facilities available. The major function rooms are usually referred to as the ballroom areas. These are complemented by a series of meeting rooms, some adjacent to the main ballroom area and some located in other areas of the hotel. The customer profile for hotel catering services is made up of both business and social clientele. Customers who use the hotel as a location for a two or three-day meeting consider meal functions as part of the total meeting package. This arrangement not only enables customers to work within a budget that covers the entire project, but also fits with an approach to planning catering functions that considers the success of the overall meeting rather than each individual function.

The catering manager is generally given the responsibility of creating a menu plan for the entire programme along with theme functions and special events. The target market for hotel catering functions is a customer who reflects the social, business, and economic profile of the community. Hotel catering services attract a wide base of customers with a broad range of requests. Customers who plan business functions on a regular basis are familiar with the catering staff and services of the hotel. Their needs are often quickly identified and provided for. Customers who plan social functions on a one-time basis, however, need more personal guidance throughout much of the planning stage. Pricing is a primary concern of this customer group.

Hotel food and beverage departments are often requested to handle the arrangements for functions to be held away from the hotel property. If a company wants to retain as much revenue as possible from business, convention, and social customers, an off-premise catering policy should be developed. Using the off-premise catering organisational guide, hotel catering departments can easily develop an off-premise catering programme. Often, a hotel will have the facilities in place to offer a limited menu of take-out items. Items have been selected from the hotel dining room menu to offer to the general public on a take-away basis.

Hotels have the advantage over many private catering companies of being able to use their own equipment. In addition, kitchen and storage facilities are available to handle large volumes of both food and beverage as well as equipment. If the volume of on-property business requires the use of hotel equipment, rentals can cover the additional needs, with costs being charged back to the customer.

RESTAURANTS

A restaurant is an establishment that serves prepared food and beverages to be consumed on the premises. The term covers a multiplicity of venues and a diversity of styles of cuisine. Restaurants are sometimes a feature of a larger complex, typically a hotel, where the dining amenities are provided for the convenience of the residents and, of course, for the hotel to maximise their potential revenue. Such restaurants are often also open to non-residents.

The term restaurant (from the French restaurer, to restore) first appeared in the 16th century, meaning "a food which restores", and referred specifically to a rich, highly flavoured soup. The modern sense of the word was born around 1765 when a Parisian soup-seller named Boulanger opened his establishment. The first restaurant in the form that became standard (customers sitting down with individual portions at individual tables, selecting food from menus, during fixed opening hours) was the Grand Taverne de Londres, founded in 1782 by a man named Beauvilliers.

Whilst inns and taverns were known from antiquity, these were establishments aimed at travellers, and in general locals would rarely eat there. The restaurant became established in France after the French Revolution broke up catering guilds and forced the aristocracy to flee, leaving a retinue of servants with the skills to cook excellent food; whilst at the same time numerous provincials arrived in Paris with no family to cook for them. Restaurants were the means by which these two could be brought together—and the French tradition of dining out was born. In this period the star chef Antonin Carême, often credited with founding classic French cuisine, flourished, becoming known as the "Cook of Kings and the King of Cooks."

Restaurants spread rapidly to the United States, with the first (Jullien's Restarator) opening in Boston in 1794, and they spread rapidly thereafter. Most however continued on the standard approach of providing a shared meal on the table to which customers would then help themselves, something which encouraged them to eat rather quickly. The modern formal style of dining, where customers are given a plate with the food already arranged on it, is known as Service à la russe, as it is said to have been introduced to France by the Russian Prince Kurakin in the 1810s, from where it spread rapidly to England and beyond.

Cafeteria

A cafeteria is a type of food service location in which there is no table service, whether a restaurant or within an institution such as a large office building or school; a school dining location is also referred to as a canteen. Instead, there are food serving counters/stalls, either in a line or allowing arbitrary walking paths, and customers take food they require as they walk along, placing them on a tray, and pay at the check-out (buffet system).

For some food items there may be the system that while at the counter one orders it and it is served by personnel behind the counter. Sometimes, for some food items and drinks, one collects an empty cup, glass, etc., pays at the check-out, then fills that after the check-out. This system may be combined with being allowed to take a free second serving.

Due to the consumption pattern of people, this system is rarely or never used for alcoholic beverages. As cafeterias require few employees, they are often found within a larger institution, catering to the clientele of that institution. For example, schools, colleges and their halls of residence, department stores, museums, and office buildings often have cafeterias. At one time, cafeteria-style restaurants dominated the dining-out culture of the Southern United States, and there were several prominent chains of them: Bickford's, Morrison's, Apple House, K&W, and Blue Boar among them. These institutions, with the exception of K&W, went into a decline in the 1960s with the rise of fast food and were largely finished off in the 1980s by the rise of "casual dining".

However, newer chains, notably Luby's and Piccadilly Cafeteria, have arisen to fill some of the gap left by the decline of the older chains. A cafeteria in a US military installation is known as either a chow hall, a mess hall, or, more correctly, a dining facility, whereas in common British armed forces parlance, it is known as a cookhouse or mess. Some monasteries and boarding schools refer to their cafeteria as a refectory. Students often refer to cafeterias as lunchrooms, though breakfast as well as lunch is often eaten there. Cafeterias serving university dormitories are sometimes called dining halls. A food court is a type of cafeteria found in many shopping malls and airports.

College Cafeteria

A college cafeteria is one that is designed to serve college students at the university. These cafeterias can be a part of a residence hall or in a separate building. Many of these colleges employ their own students to work in the cafeteria. The amount of meals served to students varies from school to school, but is normally around 20 meals per week. Like normal cafeterias, a person will have a tray to select the food that they want, but instead of paying money, they pay beforehand by purchasing a meal plan. The method of payment for college cafeterias is commonly in the form of a meal plan, whereby the patron pays a certain amount at the start of the semester and the details of the plan are stored on a computer system.

Student ID cards are then used to access the meal plan. A meal plan is not necessary to eat at a college cafeteria however. Meal plans can vary widely in their details to best fit the needs of the students. Typically, the college tracks the student's usage of their plan by counting either the number of pre-defined meal servings, points, dollars, or number of buffet dinners. The plan may give the student a certain number of any of the above per week or semester and they may or may not roll over to the next week or semester. Many schools offer several different options for using their meal plans.

The main cafeteria is usually where most of the meal plan is used but smaller cafeterias, cafés, restaurants, bars, or even fast food chains located on campus may accept meal plans. College cafeterias are prone to having poor food due to the lack of competition. A college cafeteria system often has a virtual monopoly on the students due to an isolated location or a requirement that residence contracts include a full meal plan.

Catering Services

Catering is the business of providing food service at a remote site. Catering is covered by two different groups. Independent caterers and companies with a catering business on the side.

Event Catering

An event caterer serves food with wait staff at dining tables or sets up a self-serve buffet. The food may be prepared on site or shipped in but often some combination depending on the menu and facilities at the site. The event caterer staff is responsible not only for preparing the food but also setting up the dining area and waiting tables. This service is typically provided at banquets, conventions, and weddings. Any event where all the attenders are provided with food and drinks or sometimes only hors d'oeuvres is often called a catered event.

A catering company or specialist is expected to know not just food preperation, but how to make it attractive. A wedding requires working with the entire theme or colour scheme of the wedding. Much catering is sold on a per-person basis, where adding additional people is a flat price per person. Keeping the cost of the food and supplies below this is required to make a profit on the catering.

Mobile Catering

Mobile catering is the business of selling prepared food from some sort of vehicle. It is a feature of urban culture in many countries.

Industrial Catering

Industrial catering includes providing food for airline passengers, schools, prisons and other institutional settings. It can include contract management of client foodservice facilities.

Airline Catering

Airlines often have divisions or hire third parties to provide food for passengers. Food on airlines has dropped in frequency of flights it's offered on. Today a drink and snack item are common on shorter flights. Airline food is often seen as bad by the people who eat it.

Private Clubs

Private clubs offer a self-contained facility that operates both full-service dining rooms and private function space along with a variety of food and beverage outlets. Private clubs are generally dependent on their membership for both dining room and catering business. Functioning as nonprofit organisations, clubs are, in many areas, prohibited by law from accepting or soliciting business from nonmembers. If such is the case private clubs may, however, cater functions that are sponsored by members and attended by nonmembers, allowing them to service both social and business activities.

Factors that influence the success of restaurant and hotel catering services, such as location, facilities, and customer profile, also affect private clubs. Off-premise catering services can also be offered to private club members.

Private clubs may also contract out their foodservice operation to a contract foodservice operator. Clubs are broken down into two general classifications: private clubs and country clubs. Private clubs are generally situated in the downtown areas of larger towns and cities. The club facility is used primarily as a location for meetings, private dining, social and business functions.

Country clubs require a suburban location and usually promote a combination of golf, tennis, and/ or boating as their primary recreational facilities. Private dining and catering facilities are located in the clubhouse. Acceptability of location is based primarily on general location and accessibility to major transportation routes. Downtown city locations can create problems regarding parking and security for people travelling into the city.

— *Facilities*: Club facilities can greatly influence the volume of catering business. Clubs offering spectacular settings, access to garden areas for outdoor functions, or well designed interiors will easily attract social business.

— *Off-premise catering*: A club's ability to accept off-premise catering function business is controlled by the same laws and regulations as the solicitation of nonmember business. Beyond these restrictions, the same considerations for restaurants and hotels concerning transportation, staffing, production, and service apply.

Basic Requirements

The basic requirements considered are equipment and space. For each function or task, the planner will determine the type of equipment to be used, and this in turn leads to the development of space requirements. The capacity of the equipment is not usually determined at this time because a careful analysis of the menu and scheduling are required. In the development of equipment and space requirements, the planner has to decide how each of the tasks for a particular function is to be performed in terms of the materials and processes involved.

To illustrate, consider the task of making a stew as one of the components of the cooking function. Some of the variations of the materials that may be used in making the stew are:

1. Entirely from fresh raw ingredients; both meat and vegetables
2. Partially fresh vegetables and partially canned (i.e., fresh potatoes and other canned)
3. Partially fresh vegetables and partially frozen vegetables
4. All canned vegetables and fresh meat
5. All frozen vegetables and fresh meat
6. Fully processed canned stew
7. Fully processed frozen stew

It can be seen that each of these variations in the ingredients will require different tasks and different processes for production. This in turn leads to different equipment types. The planner will evaluate the menu items to be produced and make the decisions regarding the type of production equipment to use. This same concept is used for all the other functions and tasks required to operate the facility. Considerations of space requirements are also evaluated in a similar manner. The mere identification of the functions and tasks alerts the planner to the fact that some kind of space will be needed.

The planner does not necessarily need to determine the final square footage of space now, but does consider whether a particular task requires floor space, work space, and/or storage space. The designer is essentially developing the basic concepts for the operation of the facility. This is done prior to the planning of the actual physical areas. In other words, the planning of the operational methods is the key to the functional planning for the facility. A short discussion of some of these functional areas will illustrate and clarify the concept.

Receiving Function

The receiving function is very similar for most: foodservice operations. The receiving of incoming foods, beverages, and supplies is planned according to the types and volumes of different materials handled. The frequency of deliveries and the type of delivery service are considered for each type of material to be received. For large facilities, materials-handling systems may be utilised to simplify the movement of materials into and out of the receiving area. Many suppliers offer their products in palletised form, which simplifies the movement. The use of carts, trucks, and conveyors will solve most materials-handling problems. Planning of the materials-handling system for the recciving area is only a part of the total system for the entire facility, and the planner should consider all the various components of the handling system before making a final decision.

Some may decide to use a single type of handling equipment for everything from the initial receiving to final service. Other planners may conceive a system which uses several types of equipment, each selected for its characteristics for handling certain types of materials. For example, mobile carts and trucks may be selected for handling food items, while conveyors may be chosen to handle dishes and other nonfood items. The availability of a wide variety of materials-handling equipment enables the designer to develop many different systems. Some temporary storage in the way of floor space and table space is required to check deliveries for quantity and quality. This space is designed on the basis of the larger amounts of frequently delivered materials.

Additional space is planned for scales, storage of skids and hand trucks, and for other necessary equipment for the receiving function. Consideration of waste disposal is also a factor in planning for the receiving function, since some partial trimming and cleaning of materials may be needed before they are placed in storage. Disposal of boxes, cartons, and other packaging materials removed during the receiving function is also involved. Architectural features, including the size and location of unloading docks and doors, may be developed at this time.

Storage Function

Planning for the storage function in food facilities includes dry storage, refrigerated storage, freezer storage, beverage storage, and storage for nonfood supplies.

Dry storage: The dry storage function, like other storage functions, is necessary for the on-the-site storage of frequently used materials. Storage requirements will depend upon the types of materials, frequency of delivery and the volume of each delivery. These variables are evaluated before functional planning of the storage area begins. Dry storage areas for food items are planned to maintain temperatures between 50° and 70°F (10° and 21.1° C).

The desired relative humidity is approximately 50%. For this reason, heat-generating equipment, such as motors and compressors, should not be planned for this area. Pipes carrying steam or hot water are insulated to minimise heat gain of the storage area. Protection against moisture from sweating cold water or refrigerant lines is also important. Planning for protection of the foodstuffs from insects and vermin is required for sanitary reasons. Some space for storage of frequently used dry items can be provided in various work areas of the facility. This concept will reduce the amount of movement required to obtain the materials.

Refrigerated storage: Refrigerated storage areas maintaining temperatures of 32°-37° F (0.0°-2.8° C) are required for fresh meats, vegetables and fruits, dairy products, beverages, and carry-over foods. Many planners are specifying smaller but more numerous reach-in refrigerators strategically located throughout the facility instead of one large walk-in storage. The use of reach-in units minimises employee movements in obtaining items. A combination of walk-in and reach-in refrigerators seems to be a good design for many types of foodservice facilities.

The reach-ins are usually located adjacent to preparation and production equipment or may be built-in under tables and counters. The design of walk-in refrigerated areas is similar to the dry storage areas except for the refrigeration system required to maintain the desired temperature. The size and type of foodservice operation and the frequency and volume of deliveries will determine whether a walk-in refrigerated space is needed. It is thought that a walk-in refrigerator is feasible for operations serving over 300-400 meals per day.

Reach-in refrigerators are generally designed to store for a shorter period of time and are ideal for smaller operations. Pass-through refrigeration units may be specified where their use will simplify the storage and movement of foods. The increased use of frozen foods necessitates planning refrigerated space for thawing purposes. Requirements will depend on the volume and type of frozen foods to be used in the operation. Thawing space is generally designed to handle one day's production.

Freezer storage: Temperatures of -10° to -15°F (- 23.3° to - 26.1° C) are needed to safely store frozen foods. Designers are aware of the increased use of frozen foods that are partially or fully preprocessed, and plan accordingly. Some operations have gone almost exclusively to frozen foods. Freezers may be walk-in or reach-in, and requirements are dictated by several factors including the availability of seasonal items. The possibility of buying seasonal items in volume lots should be evaluated before the design of freezer storage is finalised.

Storage of nonfood items: The design of storage areas for nonfood items like dishes, glasses, flatware, utensils, paper goods, linen, cleaning supplies, and furniture can take many different forms. They may be stored in rooms, on shelves, in cabinets, or on specially designed racks. In smaller operations, some items may be incorporated in the dry food storage area, but separate areas are best for larger operations. All chemicals, soaps, sanitising compounds, and other cleaning supplies should be stored separately because of their danger to foods. Separate areas are also desirable for cleaning equipment such as brooms, mops, pails, scrubbers, and polishers. In-process storage of items may be accomplished by special equipment such as self-levelling dispensers. The self-levelling dispensers are a very satisfactory method of providing storage for dishes.

Preparation Functions

The preparation functions for a foodservice facility are

meat/fish/ poultry preparation, vegetable preparation, salad preparation, and sandwich preparation. Speciality restaurants may have different or additional functions depending on their menu items. An example is Le fish and shellfish preparation function for seafood operations. The various preparation functions are sometimes combined and performed in one area. Smaller facilities frequently combine the salad and sandwich preparation areas. Combined vegetable and salad preparation areas are also common.

Cooking Function

The heart of all foodservice facilities is the main cooking function, and special care in planning for it is required. In addition to cooking ill meat and vegetable items, the cooking area serves as the hub between the production and service functions. In many table-service operations, for example, the pick-up of food for serving is directly adjacent to the main cooking area. The design of cooking areas varies from very limited facilities, as in fast-food and limited-menu operations, to the very extensive facilities of luxury table-service operations or in large institutional food-services. In all cases, the design of cooking area is closely correlated with the various menu items to be processed.

Baking Function

Except in a relatively few cases, foodservice operations will not be involved in the production of a full line of baked goods. Even many large institutional operations in universities and hospitals confine heir baking function to cakes, cookies, and pastries, other items being obtained from commercial bakeries. Even the operations that do a good portion of their own baking will use basic mixes that simplify he tasks of the baking function. Full bakeries are occasionally planned for commissaries or central kitchens that supply several outlets. These may be planned to handle the conventional tasks of formulation, scaling, mixing, handling, and make-up.

The advent of high-quality pre-prepared unbaked goods that require only thawing and baking has also had an impact on the design of baking areas. Many of the pre-prepared items can be processed in the main cooking area, eliminating the need for a separate baking area completely. An economic analysis of the cost of full baking on the premises versus the use of pre-prepared baked goods may also influence the design of the baking system.

Serving Function

The different ways of performing the serving function result in a variety of serving facilities that may be planned. Basic table-service operations require pick-up areas immediately adjacent to the cooking battery. Separate pick-up areas are used for salads, beverages, and desserts. Some items, including rolls, bread, butter, and water, are stored at waiter or waitress stations located in dining areas. Serving-line facilities are planned for cafeterias, employee feeding, and school or university feeding operations. Several- configurations of serving lines can be used, depending on the total number of people to be served and the time allowed for serving.

Straight-line configurations, are the most basic and are characterised by easy access and well-defined traffic flow. The major problem with the straight-line configuration is its limited serving capacity per line. Variations of the straight-line include the U-shaped counter and the herringbone design. These configurations give more linear space and increase serving-line capacity. The sopping centre or scramble serving line system is characterised by an open-square configuration of counters at the perimeters that allow traffic to flow freely in the centre.

Total serving capacity of the shopping centre or scramble system is much greater than that of the basic straightline configurations. Other types of serving functions that may be planned are tray make-up conveyors for hospitals, cart assembly areas for banquets, and room servicc facilities for hotels. Each of these has special requirements and should be planned for efficient handling of the food to be served.

4

Marketing of Tourism and Hospitality

Tourism is primarily a service based industry, the principal products provided by recreation/tourism (R/T) businesses are recreational experiences and hospitality. These are intangible products and more difficult to market than tangible products such as automobiles. The intangible nature of services makes quality control difficult but crucial. It also makes it more difficult for potential customers to evaluate and compare service offerings.

In addition, instead of moving the product to the customer, the customer must travel to the product (area/community). Travel is a significant portion of the time and money spent in association with recreational and tourism experiences and is a major factor in people's decisions on whether or not to visit your business or community. As an industry, tourism has many components comprising the overall "travel experience."

Along with transportation, it includes such things as accommodations, food and beverage services, shops, entertainment, aesthetics and special events. It is rare for one business to provide the variety of activities or facilities tourists need or desire. This adds to the difficulty of maintaining and controlling the quality of the experience. To overcome this hurdle, tourism related businesses, agencies, and organizations need to work together to package and promote tourism opportunities in their areas and align their efforts to assure consistency in product quality.

Developing a Marketing Plan

One of the most important steps a business or community can take to improve the effectiveness and efficiency of their marketing efforts is to develop a written marketing plan. This plan will guide their marketing decisions and assist them in allocating marketing resources such as money and personnel time. The plan should include:

- the overall business objectives-what you want to accomplish;
- an assessment of the market environment-what factors may affect your marketing efforts;
- a business/community profile-what resources are available,
- market identification (segmentation)--the specific groups or clientele most interested in your product;
- the marketing objectives for each segment;
- the marketing strategies (or mixes) for different markets you target-the best combination of the 4 Ps (product, price, place, promotion) for each segment;
- an implementation plan-how to "make it work;"
- the marketing budget-how much you have to spend; and
- a method for evaluation and change.

Business Objectives

Businesses, agencies, and communities should develop overall objectives and regularly monitor their progress. The objectives should provide guidance for all decisions including finances, personnel and marketing. They should be quantitative and measurable statements of what the business or community wants to accomplish over a specified period of time. Business objectives are often stated in terms of sales, profits, market shares and/or occupancy rates.

Communities frequently establish objectives relating to such things as increasing the number of tourists, developing or changing their image, facility and activity development, cooperation among tourism related businesses and increasing length of stay and local expenditures. It is important that the objectives be reasonable given the market conditions and the firm's or organization's resources. Establish a few reasonable objectives instead of a long, unrealistic "wish list." This is especially true for new businesses or communities which do not have much experience in tourism development and/or marketing.

Market Environment Analysis

The next step in developing a marketing plan is to assess the impact of environmental factors (such as economic, social and political) on present and future markets. Changes in these factors can create marketing opportunities as well as problems.

Demographic and lifestyle trends

Changing demographics and lifestyles are having a major impact on R/T participation. An assessment of these trends is important to understand how they will likely affect your business or community. Some of the important trends that bear watching:

— population growth and movement;
— rural community growth compared to metropolitan areas;

— number of adult women employed outside the home;
— the number of households is growing, especially non family and single parent households, but family size is decreasing;
— the impact of two wage earner households on real family income;
— the number of retired persons with the financial ability to travel;
— better health to an older age; and
— continued aging of the population (we are becoming a middle aged society).

Economic conditions

Overall economic conditions can have significant impacts on recreation and tourism markets. A marketing strategy that is effective during periods of low unemployment rates may have to be significantly adjusted if unemployment increases. Businesses and communities should monitor and assess the likely impact of factors such as unemployment rates, real family income, rate of inflation, credit availability, terms and interest rates. Consideration should also be given to the prices of complementary products, such as lodging, gasoline and recreation equipment.

Laws and government actions

As a complex industry, tourism is significantly affected both positively and negatively by laws and by actions of governmental agencies. For instance, rulings on such things as liability issues or decisions regarding building and health codes may change or possibly prevent the construction of a proposed facility. If a public facility changes the prices of its services, this could affect the service offerings of associated private businesses. These actions may have both positive and negative effects on the marketing efforts of the business and community. To avoid wasting valuable resources it is important that R/T businesses, agencies, and communities continually monitor and evaluate governmental actions.

Technology

Technological developments are increasing rapidly. New recreation products, such as all-terrain vehicles and wind surfers, provide new ways for people to satisfy their recreational preferences. New production technologies and materials offer recreation and tourism businesses ways to reduce costs and improve the quality of their products/services. Advances in telecommunications have and will continue to create new promotional opportunities. Technological innovations, in relation to jobs and the home, have resulted in increased leisure time for many people.

Competition

Businesses and communities must identify and analyze existing and potential competitors. The objective of the analysis is to determine the strengths and weaknesses of the competition's marketing strategies. The analysis should include the competition's:

— product/service features and quality;

— location relative to different geographic markets;

— promotional themes and messages;

— prices; and

— type of customer they are attracting.

Community Profiles

Too many communities attempt to market themselves as tourist destinations without accurate information about their resources (facilities, services, staff), image, and how well their customers are satisfied. Without this information, it is difficult to make other decisions in the planning process. Included should be such things as recreational and entertainment facilities, cultural and historic sites, overnight accommodations, restaurants, shopping opportunities, special events and activities, staff size, and transportation. Each item of the "inventory" should also be assessed in terms of quality and availability.

Market Segmentation

Recreation and tourism businesses and communities often make the mistake of attempting to be all things to all people. It is difficult, and risky, to develop marketing strategies for the mass market. Strategies designed for the "average" customer often result in unappealing products, prices, and promotional messages. For example, it would be difficult to develop a campground that would be equally attractive to recreational vehicle campers and backpackers or promote a property to serve both snowmobilers and nature oriented cross country skiers. Marketing is strongly based on market segmentation and target marketing. Market segmentation is the process of:

- taking existing and/or potential customers/visitors (market) and categorizing them into groups with similar preferences referred to as "market segments;"
- selecting the most promising segments as "target markets;" and
- designing "marketing mixes," or strategies (combination of the 4 Ps), which satisfy the special needs, desires and behavior of the target markets.

There is no unique or best way to segment markets, but ways in which customers can be grouped are:

- location of residence---instate, out-of-state, local;
- demographics---age, income, family status, education;

— equipment ownership/use---RV's, sailboats, canoes, tents, snowmobiles;

— important product attributes---price, quality, quantity; and

— lifestyle attributes---activities, interests, opinions.

To be useful, the segment identification process should result in segments that suggest marketing efforts that will be effective in attracting them and at least one segment large enough to justify specialized marketing efforts. After segments have been identified, the business or community must select the "target markets," those segments which offer them the greatest opportunity. When determining target markets, consideration should be given to:

— existing and future sales potential of each segment;

— the amount and strength of competition for each segment;

— the ability to offer a marketing mix which will be successful in attracting each segment;

— the cost of servicing each segment; and

— each segment's contribution to accomplishing overall business/community objectives.

It is often wiser to target smaller segments that are presently not being served, or served inadequately, than to go after larger segments for which there is a great deal of competition. Marketing objectives which contribute to the accomplishment of the overall business objectives should be established for each target market. Objectives serve a number of functions including:

— guidance for developing marketing mixes for different target markets;

— information for allocating the marketing budget between target markets;

— a basis for objectively evaluating the effectiveness of the marketing mixes (setting standards); and
— a framework for integrating the different marketing mixes into the overall marketing plan.

The target market objectives should:

— be expressed in quantitative terms;
— be measurable;
— specify the target market; and
— indicate the time period in which the objective is to be accomplished.

For example, increase the number of overnight stays by people from the Chicago market over the next two years by five percent. Remember, rank objectives by priority and carefully evaluate them to ensure that they are reasonable given the strength of the competition and resources available for marketing.

Definition of Marketing

Marketing is defined most simply as "providing the right products [or services] at the right price in the right place and promoting them in a way that will appeal to the target market". More specifically:

> "marketing is a managerial process involving the setting of organizational goals and objectives, analysis, planning, and implementation. It is a set of activities that results in the formulation of plans and programs. Through these activities an organization seeks to bring about a voluntary exchange of values by providing benefits to its clients and potential clients and, through this, benefits to the organization and its constituent parts or members".

Marketing can be visualized at three levels. Firstly, any "exchange" of products or services in order to satisfy needs and wants is considered marketing. Secondly, marketing is a "system," which includes the providers of goods and services, those purchasing the goods and services, and those responsible for delivering goods and services from the producers to the consumers. The marketing system also encompasses the flows of money, communications, and information between the industry and the market, and the surrounding environment in which these flows occur. Thirdly, a marketing "management philosophy" is one of five management philosophies, including the "production concept," the "product concept," the "selling concept," the "marketing concept," and the "societal marketing concept", that may be adopted by organizations involved in exchanges with consumers.

Organizations that focus on providing their products and services in the most efficient manner possible are said to have a "production" orientation, whereas organizations that concentrate their efforts on producing the best product possible have adopted a "product" orientation. The "selling" philosophy involves "large-scale selling and promotion effort[s]" in order to stimulate purchases. A "marketing philosophy" involves "determining the needs and wants of target markets and delivering the desired satisfactions more effectively and efficiently than competitors do". Some companies go further by adopting a "societal marketing concept" in order to "deliver the desired satisfactions more effectively and efficiently than competitors in a way that maintains or improves the consumer's and society's well-being".

According to this philosophy, marketers should make every effort possible to find out what it is that consumers really want and need, and then endeavour to provide these products and services in an ethical and socially-responsible way. One example of the societal marketing concept for tourism can be seen in the case of bike tours of Africa. The tourist experiences the outdoors, improves his/her well-being by obtaining exercise, learns about the history, culture, ecology, and economics first-hand, all the while avoiding the pollution and environmental damage that would be produced by renting a vehicle.

The marketing system comprises many complex, interrelated elements and processes. Despite the fact that the individual, specialized elements in a marketing process vary, and the order in which the steps should be followed is flexible, there is a general consensus on the process to be followed regardless of the product or service being marketed. Strategic marketing planning is the first step in the marketing process, and involves developing the business portfolio, creating the mission statement, determining goals and objectives, and designing functional strategies for each department of the business (e.g., human resources, accounting, purchasing). A business portfolio is "the collection of businesses and products that comprise the company".

The mission statement is a statement of a company's overall reasons for doing business, and provides guidance for all the various departments, products, and services which make up the company. Goals and objectives are set in order to help the company and its various departments fulfill the mission statement, and to provide direction for every aspect of the business. Functional strategies are plans which help each business unit to achieve its goals and objectives. Another major step in the marketing process is the selection of the target market, defined as the group of consumers sharing similar characteristics or needs that the company has chosen to satisfy. This in turn is made up of four steps: "demand measurement and forecasting;" "market segmentation;" "market targeting;" and "market positioning".

Demand measurement involves determining whether or not there exists a market for the product or service at the present time, and forecasting is used to estimate the demand for the product or service in the future. As it is nearly impossible to satisfy every consumer with a particular product or service, market segmentation is performed to identify "distinct groups of buyers with different needs, characteristics, or behaviours who might require separate products or marketing mixes".

The selection of the particular markets to be satisfied by the company's product or service is called market targeting, and is followed by marketing positioning, which involves determining the distinctive position (e.g., most luxurious, most economical) the product or service will occupy in the market relative to competing products or services. The development of "competitive marketing strategies" requires the examination and evaluation of competitors so as to discern "areas of potential advantage and disadvantage". This is followed by the development of the "marketing mix," which is "the set of controllable tactical marketing tools — product, price, place, and promotion — that the firm blends to produce the response it wants in the target market".

The marketing mix is of great importance as "[i]t determines how the marketing budget is allocated, forms the foundation of the marketing plan's strategy, and provides the marketing manager with the techniques to optimise his [sic] budgetary expenditure". "Product" refers to the product or service that the company has chosen to offer to its target markets, and the "price" is the amount that consumers will have to pay to obtain the product or service. "Place" refers to the physical location in which consumers may access the product or service, and encompasses the distribution of the product or service. Lastly, "promotion" involves the activities that the company undertakes in order to make consumers aware of its products and services.

Businesses also must undertake the management of their marketing efforts, which includes analysis, planning, implementation and control. Marketing analysis involves "complete analysis of the company's situation . . . to determine which opportunities it can best pursue". Through the process of marketing planning, a company develops a marketing plan, which "will help the company attain its overall strategic objectives" and includes an "executive summary, current marketing situation, threats and opportunities, objectives and issues, marketing strategies, action programs, budgets, and controls". The third step in marketing management is implementation, which involves "turn[ing] marketing strategies and plans into marketing actions to accomplish strategic marketing objectives". Lastly, marketing control is used to evaluate the performance of the plans and strategies against preset goals.

In this way, marketers may analyse the performance of their plans, and then take "corrective actions" in order to improve future performance. The preceding description of the marketing process highlights the fact that marketing is a complex, time-consuming, and expensive undertaking, made even more so because it occurs in an environment that is constantly changing, and involves competitors that are trying to gain competitive advantage. Businesses (and tourist destinations) must realize the importance of their marketing efforts, and continually monitor and modify their marketing strategies and plans in order to survive in this competitive environment.

Tourism Marketing Materials

The most visible tourism marketing materials are those involved in the process of promotion, as its purpose is to create and increase awareness of a business' products or services and involves communicating with prospective clients. Promotion encompasses the areas of personal selling, direct marketing, sales promotion, public relations, and advertising and of these, advertising is usually the most obvious as it is conducted on a larger scale than the other four. Personal selling consists of one-on-one interactions between a company's salespersons and their prospective clients, and is one form of direct marketing, which involves communicating with potential customers, usually by direct mail and telephone, and measuring the response.

Public relations involves "building a good reputation and image", and "handling or heading off unfavourable rumours, stories, and events". Sales promotion includes "short-term incentives to encourage purchase or sales of a product or service", such as rebates, coupons, or contests. Advertising can occur through a number of different media, including print materials (such as brochures, magazines and newspapers), direct mail (flyers, announcements), television commercials, videos, radio advertisements, window displays, and through the newest communication channel: the Internet. These advertisements usually consist of pictures, graphics, drawings, videos, maps, animation, and text, in varying amounts depending on the advertising channel employed.

Consumers access marketing materials by either seeking them out, coming across them while pursuing other activities, or receiving them directly from the company undertaking the advertising effort. Once discovered, they can choose either to ignore the information, to express interest, to request further information, or to put the information to use. In addition, marketing may be either direct or indirect. Direct marketing is that which attempts to make a sale immediately, whereas indirect marketing is aimed at making a sale eventually. Images of space and place play a prominent role in promotional materials, as their goal is the creation of a desirable image of the destination region, with the hope of causing consumers to seek further information and eventually select the destination as the site for future tourism experiences.

Images are created through textual description, pictures, drawings, graphics, maps, music, audio, video, and animation. Even the overall "look and feel" of the promotional materials, the choice of promotional methods, and the communication channel used, may influence the image of a destination. However, there are other factors which may influence images of place. Indirect influences (both positive and negative) on place images include movies, television shows, web sites, books, magazines, clothing, sporting events, music, posters, myths, rumours, stories, legends, and word-of-mouth from family and friends.

Process of Perception

The process of perception has been defined as "both the response of the senses to external stimuli and purposeful activity in which certain phenomena are clearly registered while others recede in the shade or are blocked out". During interaction with the environment, the senses of sight, hearing, smell, taste, touch, and the sixth sense of "feel", constantly and selectively sense and collect information about that environment, in the process known as environmental perception. A concise explanation of the environmental perception process is provided by Goodey:

> "In operating within any environment, man [sic] is involved in the 'image system.' He [sic] perceives, selectively, certain information by means of his [sic] various senses and adds this information to his [sic] store of mental images. Images from other environments, as well as the image of the environment under consideration, will be 'consulted' before behaviour is decided upon. Behaviour itself will be varied by motivation and the play of social, political and economic factors, but when it does take place the environment itself will be affected and the individual's information on that environment will be supplemented. During and after activity within the

> environment, perception by the individual will continually change."

Berlyne notes that "perception is gradual and takes time . . . involves difficulty and effort . . . has emotional accompaniments . . . [and] can be rewarding and pleasurable." For the purpose of this research, this type of perception is considered 'on-site' perception. It may be argued that there are three different stages of perception: pre-visit perception, on-site perception, and post-visit perception. Pre-visit perception is that which occurs before direct, on-site perception has occurred, and is a result of information collected (both consciously and unconsciously) from sources other than the environment itself.

On-site perception, is perception that occurs during interaction with the environment, but is influenced by pre-visit perception. Post-visit perception occurs after interaction with the environment, and is influenced by various information sources. Post-visit perceptions may continue to change, as memory tends to be selective and may fail over time. An image is defined as a "mental conception, perception or idea" of something, and is the product of the perception process.

As Porteous explains, "the personal image one has of the phenomenal environment is said to be one's perception of the environment." However, "the perceived environment or image is more than the sum of direct perceptual experiences", as additional, indirect, information about environments may come from ". . . simulative exploration, cinematic and photographic displays, sketches, drawings [and] replicas".

All three stages of perception, and therefore also the image an individual has of the environment, are influenced by numerous factors, including physical and mental ability, gender, age, familiarity with and affection towards the surroundings, socioeconomic status, religion, ambitions, education, time, weather, fashion, and the political situation. Images are influenced further by the media, television, radio, the Internet, movies, books, magazines, advertisements, stories, myths, legends, and rumours, and discussions with friends and family. As individuals interact with the environment, the information they receive may be used for: classification and description; appraisals involving emotions, meanings and values; or "predictions and inference which give to the image a depth, continuity, pattern or meaning beyond that justified by experience of a particular scene alone".

Once information about the environment has been collected, from both direct and indirect sources, and during all three stages of perception, the process of environmental cognition organizes, stores and recalls the information when necessary. Thus, personal perceptions, evaluations, preferences, attitudes, aesthetic judgments, appraisals and images of the environment are formed as a function of direct and indirect experiences, before, during, and after interaction with the environment. These explanations reveal the intricate link between perception and the formation of images of space and place

JUDGMENTS OF SPACE AND PLACE

In terms of tourism destination selection, space and place always play a role because tourism is "the experience and consumption of place", but this role varies in significance. Often it is the specific place, such as a specific city (e.g., Venice) which attracts tourists. However, in certain situations, the place is the deterring factor. These may be considered a "real place" typology. Alternatively, sometimes the specific place doesn't matter as much as the specific attribute(s) that the place possesses, such as the climate (e.g., sun, sand, surf); recreational resources; status (e.g., most luxurious); special events (e.g., festival or type of sporting event); location relative to home; or even special pricing. These types of destinations are somewhat "interchangeable" because the desire for travelling could be satisfied by visiting any place that satisfies these criteria.

These are similar to Tuan's "environments of persistent appeal" which include the tropical forest, seashore, valley, and island. In this situation, place plays a less prominent role. These are sometimes referred to as "generic place" typologies. Judgments of environments are based on numerous criteria, both tangible and intangible. Tangible criteria involve such factors as air and water quality, noise pollution, recreation facilities, transportation systems, amount of green space, safety, crowding, remoteness, climate, natural resources, infrastructure, and tourist or recreation amenities. Intangible criteria upon which individuals form judgments of space and place include abstract concepts such as aesthetics, landscape quality, "style" or status, and the meanings or significance attached to place, such as biological, ecological, cultural, moral, economic, political, symbolic, and emotional.

Perceived Environment Quality Indices (PEQI) have been developed in order to assess environmental quality using measurements such as air and water quality, noise pollution, crowding, and even aesthetics. Traditionally, tangible criteria have been given more "weight" when judging space and place, as they are scientifically quantifiable, and therefore considered objective. Measurement of intangible elements is performed "indirectly, in terms of human experiences", and is therefore considered "subjective." But does this necessarily mean that they are less important, or perform a lesser role in the formation of environmental judgments? Craik & Zube point out that:

> "all indices of the quality of environmental components, however concrete and tangible the components may be, are based upon human

> perception and judgment. The identification of a component as a determinant of environmental quality, and the determination of appropriate standards of quality for that component, rest upon human (subjective) judgments."

Generally, PEQIs have been used for decision-making by organizations rather than individuals. Personal judgments of space and place may be based on some of the same criteria as PEQIs, such as safety, climate, recreational amenities and aesthetics, but these judgments vary "with experience and perspective . . . novelty and familiarity . . . distance and memory," and are influenced by the intensity of feelings towards the environment, especially in crisis situations. Furthermore, environments that are valued today, may not be valued tomorrow, as "value is a dynamic concept". PEQIs changes as a typology of place goes in or out of fashion. The media, societal trends, fashion and prestige change, as do variables such as safety.

Recommendations and opinions from both formal (e.g., the media, travel agents, and tourism magazines) and informal (e.g., friends and relatives, myths and legends) sources play a significant role in the formation of personal judgments of space and place, particularly in the selection of a holiday destination.

Judgments and images of space and place depend on what individuals have done, are doing, or plan to do, in that space and place, their individual perceptions of that space and place (influenced by factors such as age, gender, beliefs, etc.), their experiences in and of that space or place, and the surrounding circumstances in which the judgments are formed (i.e., political situation, climate, culture). Therefore, it is obvious that images of space and place will affect decision-making, especially in the process of "holiday selection."

Destination Selection

Individuals are constantly interacting with, and collecting information about, their immediate environment as well as distant places. When the decision is made to plan a holiday, individuals will consult their personal images and information in order to begin the process of "holiday selection". The first step is "problem recognition," and encompasses the factors motivating the individual to take a holiday. At that point, a "preferential image" is formed, based on the type of holiday the individual wishes to take and which he or she believes will best satisfy the reason for traveling. Obviously, this is subject to various constraints and outside influences, such as time, money, and peer pressure.

As an individual's information about the "total set" of holiday possibilities is limited, the individual undertakes an "information search". Information is gathered from both formal and informal sources, and may be promoted or unpromoted. Unpromoted, informal information usually is judged by potential tourists to be more credible, as these sources do not have a "vested interest" in promoting a certain destination. In addition, perceived destination image is influenced by the communications channel through which the information is received and the environment in which the information is received. Now that the individual has information on a number of different sites, forming the "awareness set", these are compared against the "evaluative image" that the potential tourist has created.

The information gathered is used to form attitudes, preferences, and aesthetic judgments, and these in turn are used to form "naive or factual images" of each of the destinations in the "consideration set". These images are continually compared against each other, the "evaluative image" and the reason for traveling, until the number of destinations under consideration is narrowed down to the "choice set". Other significant influences upon the consideration set include numerous trade-offs between, for example, time at the destination versus en-route travel time, destination versus cost, and cost versus length of holiday.

From the final choice set, the destination which is expected to "exceed the aspiration level by the greatest amount" is chosen, unless the decision to travel is aborted. Goodall articulates the essential role of destination images in the holiday selection process:

> ". . . unless a given destination figures amongst a would-be tourist's current set of mental images it has no chance of being selected as the holiday base. [W]here it does figure in the tourist's image set a very positive image of that destination must be projected in the tourist's mind for it to be selected in preference to an alternative. [W]here the tourist is successfully enticed to a destination it is equally important that the satisfaction derived from the holiday at least matches the expectations created by the image - otherwise the tourist will not wish to return and will not recommend that destination to friends (indeed, the dissatisfied tourist may be instrumental in implanting a negative image in the minds of friends)."

Destination marketers must be aware of their image as perceived by potential tourists. If this image is not positive, place marketers must attempt either to alter or to recreate their image. But this should be done in an ethical manner. With large amounts of money at stake, place marketers sometimes "stretch the truth" in order to persuade and attract tourists. Deceptive or unrealistic images can lead to tourist disappointment and dissatisfaction, loss of repeat business, bad "word-of-mouth" advertising, and a poor reputation.

As Kotler et al. state: "[n]o amount of advertising and public relations can fool the public for long if the reality fails to match the image." Therefore, destination marketers must strive to create and project desirable and realistic images of their destination.

Place Marketing

As stated earlier, "contacts and communication are vital elements" of tourism. Within the tourism marketing process, communication refers to transferring an image of the tourism destination through various promotional channels to potential tourists. The purpose of this is "to create, maintain, or change attitudes or behaviour toward particular places", and:

> "to persuade the potential tourist to make a holiday purchase where none was made before: to induce a change in holiday behaviour by getting the tourist to purchase a different destination or type of holiday; or to reinforce the tourist's existing behaviour by maintaining the purchase of a given holiday 'brand'".

Destination marketers must first conduct research in order to determine how consumers view the destination. As different markets have different needs, wants and, therefore, different images of the destination, the consultation must be performed within the chosen "target markets," the groups of consumers sharing similar characteristics that the destination has decided to attract and "serve", in order "to avoid the problem of unstable or inconsistent images". If the image is unsatisfactory, destination marketers will have to determine why the projected image is inadequate.

Does the image need to be coordinated, enhanced, altered, or completely recreated? Was the marketing emphasizing the wrong things? What is the nature of the desired image? How will the new image be created and promoted? How will the current political, economic, and technological environment affect the creation and promotion of the projected image? Kotler et al. outline the various strategies that may be adopted by tourism marketers in order to improve a destination's image.

First, the actual, physical attributes of the destination may be improved, a process termed "real repositioning"; or tourism marketers may undertake "psychological repositioning" to influences people's beliefs about the destination. "Competitive depositioning" and the highlighting of "neglected attributes" of other destinations may be employed, in order to influence beliefs about competing destinations.

Finally, they may change the "importance weights" by "persuad[ing] buyers to attach more importance to the attributes in which the place excels," or attempt to "shift the buyer's ideals". Selection of the appropriate positioning method is dependent upon the natural, competitive, social, cultural, political, technological, and economic environments in which the destination exists.

If planned carefully, an image promotion campaign may be successful in influencing people's beliefs and perceived images of a destination. In order to be effective, projected place images must be simple, distinctive, appealing, believable, and valid. As tourism services are "interdependent" (i.e., they are made up of several services) the coordination of the images of these services is necessary for the creation of a simple and distinctive image. This prevents tourist "confusion" and aids in distinguishing the destination from competitors. The image must be appealing and believable in order to attract tourists, and then must be valid in order to avoid tourist dissatisfaction and disappointment.

To achieve a simple, distinctive, and appealing image, tourism marketers may employ "slogans, themes and positions," "symbols and branding," or "events and deeds". Aesthetics play an essential role in the creation of a destination's identity, and its image as perceived by target markets. This argument is forwarded by Schmitt & Simonson:

> "Aesthetics is not esoteric. The vitality of aesthetics in customers' lives provides opportunities for organizations to appeal to customers through a variety of sensory experiences and thereby benefit both the customers and the organizations through customer satisfaction and loyalty. These opportunities are not limited . . . Any organization whatsoever, in any industry, for any customer base, for profit or not for profit, governmental or private, consumer, industrial or service can benefit from using aesthetics."

Projected images, including the aesthetic qualities of these images, may be considered important "pull factors" for tourism destinations. That is, they may attract or "pull" tourists toward a certain destination. Place marketers must understand the image formation process, and the role of aesthetics in this process. After tourism marketers have decided on the nature and design of the image they wish to project, they must decide how, and through which channels, this image will be projected or communicated to potential tourists. An important concept regarding marketing communications, known as the "AIDA model," (Awareness, Interest, Desire, Action) is identified in the literature.

Before a tourist selects a destination, they must be aware of the destination and have the interest and desire to visit the destination. Interest and desire may be created through the design and delivery of a positive place image to potential tourists. At this point the tourist may choose to perform the required actions to visit the destination, but this will only happen after a desirable image has been formed in the mind of the potential tourist and that image has out-bid all other potential destination sites in the choice set. No matter how good the marketing strategy, how low the price, how available the product, and how visible the advertising, if a consumer's image of the destination is not sufficient to make the choice set, nothing will convince them to choose the site as a tourism destination. This awareness, interest, desire, and action may be created through promotion of the destination region, but marketing and promotional efforts will differ depending upon which phase of the AIDA model the tourism marketer is trying to address.

Promotion encompasses personal selling, sales promotion, public relations and advertising. Each of these elements can influence perceived images of a tourism destination, however, advertising is the most visible factor as it is undertaken on a larger scale than the others. Both informative and persuasive advertising may be used to increase awareness of, and demand for, products and services, including tourism. Informative advertising is generally used to increase awareness of new products, features, or destinations, whereas persuasive advertising is an attempt to convince consumers that the destination will best satisfy their "need" for traveling.

Promotional materials and information about tourism destinations may reach consumers through a number of "communication channels", including television and radio, print ads in magazines and newspapers, brochures and flyers, and most recently, through the Internet. Although tourists may obtain a "virtual" tourism experience through videos and web sites, in reality the tourism product is 'intangible.' Therefore:

> "[t]o reduce uncertainty [and increase tangibility], buyers look for 'signals' of service quality. They draw conclusions about quality from the place, people, price, equipment, and communication material that they can see".

It is essential for tourism marketers to realize that not only does the quality, design, and timing of these materials have an influence on tourists' images, but the communication channel itself can play a role. The Internet is the newest and most powerful communications and research tool available to tourism marketers. Use of the Internet may make tourism information available to a larger audience, as the Internet is quickly spreading worldwide. Moreover, a well-designed, informative web site that provides information and value to potential tourists may help to create a positive and professional image of the destination.

Image Creation

People travel for many reasons, such as: to experience change or "to 'get away from it all;'" to "see different places, things and people", or in MacCannell's words, to "consume culture" to research ancestry; to "recover. . .wholeness and structure"; to learn or appreciate something; for "self-actualization or self-realization"; to be different; for rest and relaxation; for prestige or status; to "escape personal problems"; to experience "reduced constraints on behaviour"; to play out a "fantasy"; or to get closer to relatives.

Tourists have also been described as "myth-chasers". In order to better understand tourists' needs and motivations, researchers have developed various tourist typologies. As Jafari explains "tourist typologies reflect the diversity of individual motivations, styles, interests and values, and the subsequent differences often correlate with specific disciplinary research interests."

Gray defined two typologies based on the type of travel undertaken. These included "sunlust" and "wanderlust," the first being travel undertaken for "rest and relaxation," the second being "motivated by the desire to learn." Cohen identifies two groups of tourists - institutionalized and non-institutionalized. Institutionalized tourists are those which desire comfort and safety and rely heavily upon the tourism industry, whereas non-institutionalized tourists are those which prefer to follow their own path and have little contact with the tourism industry.

In 1979, Cohen amended his typology, and defined two groups of tourists - those who "search for pleasure" and those who undertake a "modern pilgrimage." Pleasure-seeking tourists include the recreational tourist, who simply desires "entertainment and relaxation" and the diversionary tourist, who wishes to "escape the routine of everyday life." Modern pilgrimage tourists encompass three different typologies: the experiential tourist who "seeks an authentic experience... but does not totally identify with the foreign culture;" the experimental tourist who wishes to "seek an alternative lifestyle but does not become totally immersed in a foreign culture;" and the existential tourist who becomes totally "immersed in the foreign culture."

A typology based upon tourists' personalities was developed by Plog. The three personalities, including psychocentrics, mid-centrics, and allocentrics, are located on a continuum similar to bell-curve. Psychocentrics are "anxious, somewhat inhibited, non-adventuresome, inner-focussed and classified by their lower income levels." This typology is located at one end of the continuum. At the other end of the continuum are allocentrics, characterized as "adventurous, self-confident, curious, outgoing... and hav[ing] higher income levels." Mid-centrics, those who travel "for relaxation and pleasure, or the need for a change" make up the middle of the continuum, and are the largest in number.

Yet another typology was created by Smith, who proposes that there are seven types of tourists: charter tourists, mass tourists, incipient mass tourists, unusual tourists, off-beat tourists, elite tourists, and explorers. These typologies gradually progress from tourists who "arrive by the planeload in large numbers and are just there to enjoy their holiday", to the few tourists who explore new areas and "fully accept local culture" (explorers). Regardless of the reason for travelling, the choice of a destination is dependent upon the potential tourist's perception of the ability of that destination to satisfy the reason, or "need" for travelling. The key word here is perception, which has been defined as "both the response of the senses to external stimuli and purposeful activity in which certain phenomena are clearly registered while others recede in the shade or are blocked out".

Porteous explains that "the personal image one has of the phenomenal environment is said to be one's perception of the environment." From this it may be seen that image and perception are intricately linked, as an image is based upon and formed by one's perceptions. An image is an "idea" or "conception" of something and is the "basis of the evaluation or selection process". Furthermore, perceptions, and thus images, are also dependent upon a number of influencing factors, such as age, sex, physical and mental ability, weather, time, political factors, money, fashion, social ambitions, personality, culture, and lifestyle.

Other external influences include movies, books, and legends, and therefore images are not simply the result of promotions put forward by various companies or destinations. Such issues are discussed at length in Goodey, Tuan, Porteous, and Gifford, and in the tourism marketing literature by Goodall & Ashworth and Kotler et al.. The creation of desirable and realistic images is of utmost importance in the effective marketing of space and place. This is corroborated by Murphy's statement that "tourism is built upon imagery".

The purpose of image creation within marketing is either to create, to confirm and enhance, to alter, or to completely recreate or change the existing image, thereby motivating the consumer to choose the product or service being marketed. The Internet can be of great assistance in this process, but the effectiveness of various elements, specifically maps, in the image creation process when marketing tourism destinations on the Internet is still unknown.

Maps and Tourism

Maps and tourism are inseparable. From early adventurers who used rudimentary maps and charts to explore "new" worlds, to the modern-day tourist who uses a travel map to navigate within a chosen destination, maps play a significant role in how we discover, learn, and communicate information about the world around us. By definition, tourism involves travel to a place where the tourist normally does not work or live. Therefore, the traveller has limited spatial knowledge of the visited environment and maps perform an essential function in the acquisition of spatial information by tourists. Their importance is emphasized by Jakle:

> "Maps are indispensable to strangers orienting themselves to new places . . . Sightseeing rarely starts without . . . a map. Maps direct seeing, visualization serving to validate expectations predicated on map use."

A map is "a representation of things in space", and thus facilitates spatial visualization, perception, learning, and image creation. As a means of communicating spatial information, maps appear unsurpassed:

> "One has to regard cartography as visual communication of a special kind which, with regard to its two-dimensional and systematic information, is superior to all other means of communication as far as certain messages are concerned".

> "Maps break down our inhibitions, stimulate our glands, stir our imagination, loosen our tongues. The

> map speaks across the barriers of language; it is sometimes claimed as the language of geography".

Maps perform a valuable function throughout the entire tourism process. They are a source of inspiration and daydreaming about future travel destinations. Maps may be used by tourists in the decision-making stage in order to visualize and imagine potential destinations. They may be used in the trip-planning phase, to decide how to travel to, from, and within the selected destination, where to stay, which attractions to visit, and even which neighborhoods or regions to avoid. They are used during travel, to assist with navigation and orientation. And maps may be used after traveling, to remember places visited, or to help with post-trip visualization and reminiscence.

Since the "goal of map making is to communicate information and ideas about places", maps are fundamental vehicles for communicating spatial information and creating images of space and place. Just as a "picture is worth a thousand words," a well-designed map can speak volumes about a travel destination. Maps are an important part of most tourism experiences, and it makes intuitive sense that maps should be part of any marketing campaign promoting a travel destination. Although maps have traditionally played a significant role in tourism marketing, and although the Web provides significant opportunities for the communication of spatial information and image creation, this area of tourism marketing is not being used to its full potential.

From a preliminary examination of the content and design of tourism web sites and maps, it appears that some tourism marketers overlook the importance of maps in the tourism marketing process. In other cases it seems that tourism marketers realize the importance of maps, but fail to use them effectively. Frequently, maps are underutilised, poor in quality or design, hard to find with the web site, unsuitable, illegible, or so complicated that they take a long time to load or crash the computer.

5

Tourism Planning and Operations

Tourism planning has evolved from two related but distinct sets of planning philosophies and methods. On the one hand, tourism is one of many activities in an area that must be considered as part of physical, environmental, social, and economic planning. Therefore, it is common to find tourism addressed, at least partially, in a regional land use, transportation, recreation, economic development, or comprehensive plan. The degree to which tourism is addressed in such plans depends upon the relative importance of tourism to the community or region and how sensitive the planning authority is to tourism activities.

Tourism may also be viewed as a business in which a community or region chooses to engage. Individual tourism businesses conduct a variety of planning activities including feasibility, marketing, product development, promotion, forecasting, and strategic planning. If tourism is a significant component of an area's economy or development plans, regional or community-wide marketing plans are needed to coordinate the development and marketing activities of different tourism interests in the community.

A comprehensive approach integrates a strategic marketing plan with more traditional public planning activities. This ensures a balance between serving the needs and wants of the tourists versus the needs and wants of local residents.

A formal tourism plan provides a vehicle for the various interests within a community to coordinate their activities and work toward common goals. It also is a means of coordinating tourism with other community activities. Like any planning, tourism planning is goal-oriented, striving to achieve certain objectives by matching available resources and programs with the needs and wants of people. Comprehensive planning requires a systematic approach, usually involving a series of steps. The process is best viewed as an iterative and on-going one, with each step subject to modification and refinement at any stage of the planning process. There are six steps in the planning process:

- Define goals and objectives.
- Identify the tourism system.
  - Resources
  - Organizations
  - Markets
- Generate alternatives.
- Evaluate alternatives.
- Select and implement.
- Monitor and evaluate.

Fundamental Design Principles

Most fundamental design principle is creating the visitor domain with a sense of place that is unique and authentic, and that contains a diversity of potential experience. Reid and Smith encourage development of gateways in designing tourist spaces. The gateway is a physical symbol of entrance to the tourist domain. The gateway also marks the transition from ordinary into extraordinary places and experience. Clustering and concentrating attractions and services is the technique of creating the visitor domain.

Use of these principles leads ultimately to a critical mass of tourist products which establishes a place as a tourist destination in the tourist market. With a critical mass, tourists become aware of the place and will purposely begin to choose to go to that place. The application of the market research technique of product/ market match is the means to achieve a supply of the right tourism products, particularly attractions and services, for the targeted quality tourists of a tourism destination plan.

Targeted tourists are statistically defined; the products suitable to their tastes are what should be developed at the destination. Statistically defined tourist segments usually come from defined geographic areas, fall into specified age and gender groups, have specified education and income levels and have specific preferences for what they like to do, see and eat. Well signed transportation linkages are necessary to ease the movement of people in the tourist domain. Where large crowds of people are concentrated during the tourist season, such as now at the Grand Canyon with four to five million visitors per year, mass transit interventions are rapidly replacing automobile use.

Protecting the environment-natural, cultural and social-is now an accepted mainstay of successful tourism planning. This can be achieved by attracting quality tourists and by managing tourist flows and access while they are in the visitor domain. The Grand Canyon intervention of mass transit is a direct result of the Park Service's goal to protect the environment and preserve the visitor experience. This year Park Service introduced use of a quiet helicopter and will require commercial areal sightseeing operators to use noise-reduced equipment starting next year.

There already are restricted air space regulations. Grand Canyon will be a quieter place soon. The seasons-high, low and shoulder-can be the bane of a tourism planner's life and a test of her skills. In most cases, tourism flows are seasonal but with heavy investment in service and attraction facilities, there is generally a desire by the operators of these facilities to generate year round tourists and thus cash flow. The flip side of this principle is that the seasons with low tourist volumes give local residents periods of reduced stress and rest.

Partnership is another principle to incorporate into successful tourism planning. Because of the pluralistic nature of tourism, there needs to be destination partnerships created or formed which can more effectively take advantage of the product offerings of each member of the partnership. It is the idea of "synergy" where the total is more than the sum of the parts. Another principle to consider in tourism planning is product life cycle. Tourism products, like many others, grow in popularity and after a while fall off in popularity. The key is to be prepared when popularity begins to wane and have plans prepared to breathe new life into the attraction or service.

A final principle for successful tourism planning is the planner should insure there is ample opportunity for economic benefits to be captured. Tourists are generally willing to spend money, but as in the Hopi situation, there may be little planned opportunity for them to spend it. For example, most tourists to Hopi are day visitors; they spend money for accommodation in the border towns of Flagstaff, Winslow and Holbrook. There are only a few places to buy food and gas. Planners are experts, but it takes community vision and community involvement to create a successful tourism plan that reflects the willingness of local residents to go the cost necessary to support tourism in their living space.

Murphy provides a comprehensive model for community-based tourism planning. Implementation and action plans are a must in tourism planning because these are the vehicles that create coordination among people and organizations in a destination area. Without coordination-who is going to do what when with what resources-specified in written or chart form people will forget to do what needs to be done. Monitoring and evaluation are important to measure the success of the plan and to modify it if it is not working out. Successful monitoring depends on establishing a baseline of data from which to measure change. It is unnecessary to measure everything about a plan; select several key indicators and work with those over time.

Scales in Tourism Planning

The range of scale in tourism planning is from site specific physical plans to intermediary community and regional destination plans to national policy plans. No matter at what scale of tourism a planner is working, it is important to incorporate and account for all the components of structure, element, principle and process that have been described. In this way balanced, sustainable tourism development has a chance of being achieved. Promotion is not Tourism Planning & Development - This misconception has been mentioned several times before, but it is worth reiterating that promotion is only part of successful tourism structure and is only one of four vital components of tourism supply.

Tourism is not an Industry - Tourism is made up of several different indus-tries-aviation, accommodation, food and beverage, attractions-and modes of business enterprise range from a few transnational companies to numerous local small businesses. Government, the public sector, is another major player in tourism development. Governments provide numerous "public good" attractions and conduct or subsidize promotional campaigns of their regions. The nonprofit, volunteer sector also operates attractions of various kinds; most common are county historical museums.

Tourism is not a Smokeless Industry - Tourism can and unfortunately does bring pollution, overcrowding, congestion, destruction of natural and cultural resources, contamination of water supplies, decay of landscapes and vistas with oversized and insensitive physical development and cross cultural clashes in customs and values. Tourism planning must be sensitive to these issues and attempt to anticipate and mitigate the more dire impacts before they develop. Tourism is the Salvation of Rural & Small Town Economies - Not necessarily! Rural and small towns must have reasonable access to tourist markets and be a special enough place to appeal in order to become successful tourist destinations.

Clever rural and small towns see their large urban neighbors, a half hour to an hour driving time away, as their tourist market and they develop attractions and products which interest these people. For some places, all the boosterism in the world will not overcome an intrinsic lack of natural and cultural resources on which to build a tourism attractions strategy. In other places, there is no distinct sense of place or the authentic and unique have been replaced by homogenized commercial development. In yet other places, local residents do not want tourism development; without local support successful development will be difficult at best.

Community-Based Tourism Planning

The Community-Based Tourism Planning (CBTP) model proposes that tourism planning should build from an awareness of community values and organisational needs to guide more locally-appropriate tourism development that fits with other community needs, initiatives, and opportunities. This brings otherwise established strategic planning and community development principles to tourism planning practices so that stakeholders (residents, operators, government) can together guide a more sustainable and consistent tourism industry for communities, not at the expense of communities and local ecosystems.

There is a growing and more genuine appreciation of the need for increased community involvement in tourism planning to help preserve and maintain unique, special, or valued local features and tourism attractions. Such planning can better prepare a community to "adapt to the unexpected, create the desirable, and avoid the undesirable[and] promotes the opportunity for improving the total community rather than improving one part of the community at the expense of other parts". Every tourism decision must be made on a community-wide consensus basis.

In corporations and institutions, values and visions are commonly clarified at the outset of strategic planning processes and form the basis of short- and long-term decisions and actions. A similar approach can be used as the basis for tourism planning. "Community demands for active participation in the setting of the tourism agenda and its priorities for tourism development and management cannot be ignored". Though more time-consuming than a top-down approach to planning and development, when a community guides their own development, "the results are often longer lasting and more effective over the long-term".

Making and pursuing conscientious and co-operative choices for community development requires patience and perseverance from all stakeholders. Independent operator initiatives, government promotion, and market responses to tourist demands commonly drive tourism development.

Tourism planning, development, and marketing typically focus on tourist trends and desires, thereby insufficiently identifying, upholding, or pursuing the aspirations of affected communities or local residents in a "destination area".

All travel is linked with communities no matter how urban or remote the purpose may be. This inescapable fact can be a blessing or a curse depending upon how well a community accepts its tourism role and maintains a balance between traveller and resident development and management. Rather than "accepting their role", CBTP promotes that the community should define their own- and the tourism industry's-role.

To accomplish this, a community needs to create opportunities for stepping back from tourism marketing and product development pressures. Then, stakeholders can evaluate their tourism experiences and local values while setting a direction for their own tourism development in partnership with other significant stakeholders.

This community-based approach is fundamentally linked with a "belief in human potential for favorable growth" which relies on community members having a positive view and understanding of their own potential. CBTP relies on an initial and periodic community assessment process that harnesses the experience, expertise, desires, and support of local residents together with tourism operators and other stakeholders (government, organisations, and industry). Such assessment can generate an inventory of perceptions about tourismrelated changes (experiences, concerns, hopes, fears, and dreams). This "social or perceptual inventory" can complement other tourism resource inventories (infrastructure, services, attractions, biophysical features, and cultural features) for making more informed and accountable decisions while building organisation and infrastructure capacity.

Careful thought and discussion about "what matters to us", "what we can offer", and "how we want tourism to affect our home/community/area" can help to chart a clear course with guiding principles for local tourism planning and development. This process is invaluable when rural, remote, and first nations communities are involved where there are often close communities, shared lands, common resources, and sensitive cultural heritage. Similarly, in more populated destinations, insightful guidance and collaboration can emerge from an assessment process within the many layers or sectors of the community, i.e., "the many communities" affected. Community-based tourism planning is about:

— introducing more "strategic" and "future" thinking or visioning to tourism development;

— relying on residents and community leaders as their own "experts" about community needs and desirable tourism influences; and

— providing opportunities to clarify community strengths, challenges, obstacles, and opportunities for social, economic, and ecological well-being.

CBTP encourages and facilitates reflection about how a "destination" is also a "home" (for residents, flora, and fauna). Tourists are more likely to appreciate and return if they feel a "good fit" between aspects of "destination" and "home" rather than experiencing tourism as a source of tension or negative impacts.

This CBTP process model emphasises the need for catalysts from events or individuals to initiate an assessment process, and to keep the process going through tasks that stimulate co-operation, trust, tourism awareness, and links with the broader community development context. The actual "little steps" will vary by community and depend on previous experiences from working or planning together.

The success or failure of reducing negative tourism impacts on communities and ecosystems clearly depends on how relationships are valued-relationships between people, and between people and their ecosystems. The Kyuquot Sound area on the Northwest coast of Vancouver Island is one of the island's last remote coastal tourism destinations, and has one of the most isolated communities of its size. By most accounts, tourism activity is slowly increasing here, but has not yet seriously influenced local planning and development in the community and surrounding wilderness and protected areas.

During Kyuquot's two month peak tourism season in 1997, the four sportfishing lodges, three B&Bs, and one sea kayaking and marine tour company were operating at about 60% of their combined capacity of about 90 clients/day. There is currently no monitoring of recreational tourist numbers, however, a rough estimate is that commercial tourism accounts for approximately one sixth of visitors to the area. Though not promoted as such, the many provincial protected areas adjacent to Kyuquot Sound are undoubtedly tourism draws.

Tourism is creeping northward on Vancouver Island and the people of Kyuquot are only beginning to more carefully consider its implications and opportunities. In the peak of the summer, there are an estimated 300 seasonal and full-time residents. About two thirds of this population are from the Ka:' yu: 'k' t 'h' (Kyuquot) and Che:k'tles7et'h' (Checleset) First Nation. This is the northernmost band of the Nuuchah-nulth Tribal Council (NTC) which spans most of Vancouver Island's west coast.

Kyuquot's past is generally described as that of a small and remote commercial fishing village that has survived several boom and bust cycles in the whaling and fishing industries during the last 80 years. As in many coastal regions of BC, most local residents are struggling with an almost collapsed local economy that has relied on fishing and forestry.

Assessment

The community assessment provided many tangible and less-tangible outputs from, and for, the many stakeholders. In summary, some tangible tourism planning outputs included:

— A background inventory of tourism planning efforts and dynamics.

— A summary of related influences on the future of tourism.

— A summary of direct, indirect, and potential stakeholders and their roles.

— A set of potential guiding elements for tourism planning.

— A summary of significant hurdles for tourism planning.

— A possible tourism steering group model.

— Initial task suggestions as planning catalysts.

Each of these outputs provides a valuable reference for ongoing tourism-related discussions, organisation, and planning, or for later evaluating the path and successes of tourism planning and development efforts. Some less-tangible community assessment outputs included:

— Encouraging stakeholder awareness about tourism implications and possibilities.

— Identifying shared community and stakeholder interests not otherwise being discussed.

— Demonstrating the collective community wisdom and potential of combining stakeholder input, experience, and expertise.

— Stimulating constructive and cooperative discussions.
— Clarifying relationships and needs.
— Prompting links with other local issues, decisions, and initiatives.

Each of these less-tangible outputs adds to the momentum necessary for stakeholders to begin having a more community-based influence on how tourism affects their lives and the area. Several stakeholders felt that tourismrelated decisions and initiatives could become opportunities for the community to begin addressing chronic economic, social, and cultural challenges. Some of these same stakeholders worried that continued haphazard tourism growth could add to economic, social, and cultural conflicts, including lingering tensions between the Native and non-Native local residents. Regardless, awareness is increasing about how tourism is beginning to influence other aspects of community and area well-being.

The most significant assessment outputs were the potential "Guiding Elements" for Kyuquot's tourism planning which came from themes identified through stakeholder comments. With some further discussion, refinement, and community ratification, these can serve as the foundation principles for tourism-related decisions in Kyuquot. These are a starting point for providing more clear and consistent community messages to tourists, tourism operators, government agencies, politicians, and others who influence how tourism affects the community and area. This helps to demonstrate the comprehensive collective wisdom that can be tapped through a community assessment rather than suggesting or imposing a prescribed list of tourism principles. These stakeholdergenerated Guiding Elements offer more depth and local meaning than what could otherwise be suggested to the community with concepts of eco-or sustainable tourism.

One resident astutely commented that it is much easier to simply make a 2° shift in tourism development directions now, than having to eventually make a 90o shift to change and repair undesired impacts from tourism. This pinpoints the purpose and advantage of identifying guiding elements early in tourism planning. Another resident reflected that, "You have to feel good about your home before you can invite others to it." This is at the heart of community-based tourism planning. Not surprisingly, there are important ways in which all tourism stakeholders can work to support Kyuquot as a healthy home and place to visit.

Several native and non-native residents increasingly avoid or resent tourists who appear to take the community, fishing, and favourite local places for granted. A few residents described their observation that some tourists see the village like an incidental "backdrop for their experience," and not as a living community with real people. Others have had tourists stare at them as though studying "a real Native" like a "monkey in a cage". These types of encounters and experiences can quickly shatter local confidence, respect, and hospitality in residentvisitor relationships.

One Native resident insightfully added that, if local residents increasingly withdraw from contacts with tourists, this will unfortunately only add to the potential for conflicts and stereotyping in both directions, and may subsequently increase tensions within the community. Many described essential links between the "visitor experience" and the "local community experience" whereby each affects the other.

Kyuquot's remoteness, quaint village, local services, sportfishing, secluded beaches, and protected areas are linked to the collective "stakeholder experience" of residents and tourists alike. One tourism operator described hopes that tourists can become more knowledgeable, educated, and inspired from the area and from local people-that tourism can catalyse more meaningful understandings and respect for coastal ecology, remote and rural communities, and Native people. There was almost a universal stakeholder concern about-and desire to move away from-the status quo of continuing with haphazard, marketdriven, and externally imposed tourism development.

Co-operative, inclusive, and community-based tourism planning can be approached as casually or intensively as suits the local context. For Kyuquot, many of the tourism planning "task suggestions" focused on education and training, initiating community co-operation, discussing tourism implications, clarifying community expectations and messages, and stimulating local pride and stewardship.

Given the stakeholder awareness of both desired and negative tourism impacts, there is ample reason to believe that these same stakeholders can prioritise ways of working together to address tourism concerns, and to refine and follow some guiding elements for their own tourism future. "Sustainability", many of the resultant "Guiding Elements" describe an interest in balancing tourism development to "meet the needs of the present without compromising the ability of future generations to meet their own needs". The importance of resident satisfaction for visitor satisfaction. The need to "balance the commercial imperatives of tourism with the cultural integrity of the community".

In tourism planning, issues of sustainability are often linked with other resource and protected area management efforts, especially where protected areas attract visitors. In Kyuquot, many residents have felt alienated from local protected area management. Policies and activities that have emphasised land or marine areas as everyone's resource, playground, or treasure (the "public good" and "provincial interests") typically overlook the greatest potential stewardship asset the local residents. All residents aren't necessarily "connected with the land" or setting stellar examples of treating their home area with care; but if not included in the planning and management, they feel even less of an obligation or need to be stewards.

The community assessment identified the need for tourism and protected area management strategies formed through partnerships between local residents and government agencies. Otherwise, the "tragedy of the commons" remains a tragedy of approaching it as the commons. If tourism and protected area policies are drafted with nobody's home in mind, then nobody in that home is likely to respect, welcome or embrace those policies. Similarly, Kyuquot residents will be reluctant to respect tourists who don't acknowledge that they are visitors or guests to somebody's home area.

It remains to be seen whether the community assessment will stimulate further community-based tourism planning in the Kyuquot area. Nothing more may happen without significant increases in tourism-related pressures and conflicts or without further initiatives from key stakeholders. Nevertheless, stakeholder feedback has been positive about the community assessment contributions to clarifying tourism-related issues and relationships.

The CBTP Process Model makes the following three assumptions:

— That local capacity building and organisational development can be most effectively guided using the knowledge and insights of stakeholders.

— That most stakeholders can look beyond their immediate circumstance.

— That with community values identified, most stakeholders will move together toward acknowledged desires that respect local area and community well-being.

These assumptions relate to community development and strategic planning principles. Only time and examples of CBTP initiatives elsewhere will provide more insights about the value of this Process Model and validity of its assumptions. A CBTP approach doesn't ignore or preclude more market-conscious tourism planning and development, but first establishes a common framework for shaping a locally appropriate tourism industry.

In the CBTP Process Model, the three major feedback loops allow for tourism development to be guided and massaged by community, area, and marketconscious inputs. Subsequent assessments could be done after every tourism season, once a year, or at two- or three-year intervals the frequency would depend on the intensity of tourism pressures, other shifts in the local planning context, and stakeholder satisfaction.

The specific community approach taken will vary by population size, cultural context, local need, tourism intensity, seasonality, and previous tourism planning efforts. Nevertheless, the CBTP concepts and framework can remain the same. Along the planning path, it is the recipe of individuals-their talents, skills, experience, limitations, commitment, time, patience, and perseverance-which ultimately determines the success of any community-based process.

Tour Operator as Travel Agent

These people are solely into marketing the concept of travel. They plan and `sell' trips to individuals and groups. They book tickets - for air, rail, sea or road travel, arrange hotel reservations or guest houses, hire taxis etc. Besides domestic, all travel agents undertake international bookings and special business tours or conferences. Tour operators are mostly into travel management. They organise and put together package trips and holidays. These could be for incoming tourists from abroad or outbound tours or even domestic travellers. They can offer special packages, which could include such diverse attractions as deep-sea diving, snorkelling, Himalayan trekking or even camel safaris in the Thar Desert.

Working in this field means dealing with people directly on a daily basis. Helping people plan their itinerary, providing ticketing services to company executives, co-ordinating with the airlines, railways or transport company staff, arranging passports and visas, booking hotels - all these require not only a great deal of mobility but also regular contact with representatives of the various services. One must be up-to-date on rules and regulations governing foreign travel, documents required, hindrances if any; so as to correctly advise the clients.

All the staff, be it in marketing, counter sales or guide services must be knowledgeable about the places their clients intend to visit - the best way to reach your destination, places to visit, facilities available etc. Major areas of work in a travel agency include counter work, marketing and management. Counter work involves helping clients with their itineraries, chalking out travel routes, procuring tickets, arranging for passports and visas, making hotel reservations, organising cargo transport and the like.

Counter clerks must be able to have easy access to timetable information and be extremely accurate with the information provided to clients. A small slip on their part could result in embarrassing or even disastrous consequences. Marketing area includes advertising and an aggressive promotion of the agency to potential customers. Procuring steady business for the company is their major job. The management staff deals with the administration of the agency. The managers co- ordinate and streamline the work of the clerks and select brochures of the various tours and packages available with them, among other things.

Roles of a Tour Operator

— *Planning*: The planning of the tours is done by the tour directors or once-in-a-while by experienced counter clerks. Planning involves chalking out the tour programme, working out the cost, confirmation of accommodation and other facilities like food and entertainment, and consulting tourist officials.

— *Sales and Reservations*: The staff has to ensure that travel brochures are on display at agencies. They also take bookings from travel agents or individuals.

— *Representatives/guides*: These are freelancers mostly whose job involves accompanying tourists to their destination and looking after their needs while travelling. A smattering knowledge of different languages can be useful as well as a general awareness and history of the place visited. This job can be easily done by students or even office workers and others who are interested in travelling. Tour operators or local tourism departments often employ professional guides who have a thorough knowledge of the history and cultural significance of a place. Many tour operators, nowadays specialise in areas such as adventure tourism, beach tourism, mountain holidays etc.

— *Entry*: A basic diploma in travel and tourism management can be advantageous to a person seeking to work in this field. Advertisements appear from time to time for jobs available in travel agencies and tour operating companies or for a position in a government department or corporation. In general, the minimum requirement for entry into this industry are: (i) 10+2 and fluency in the spoken language up to tourist guide level. (ii) for higher positions, a graduate degree in any discipline with a specialisation in history and architecture or geography and archaeology can be a great asset as is the knowledge of one or more foreign languages. If one is applying for a government post, he/she has to clear a written test, a personal interview and a medical examination. On-the-job training is provided to all new entrants.

— *Training*: With the demand for trained people increasing by the day, it is wise to gain some insights into the field through professional training. There are a number of institutions in the country which offer training courses on different aspects of the industry. There are equally good correspondence courses too.

— *Career prospects*: A career in travel and tourism can be exciting and full of fun. Not only is it flexible, but certain jobs in the field can provide excellent travelling opportunities. Job prospects include working in: travel agencies as tour operators, in airlines (domestic and foreign) transport and cargo companies, travel consultancy services and in the government run tourism departments. With enough experience and capital, one can even start one's own travel consultancy.

The tourism industry is thus a high-growth industry which can only expand with time, what with more and more people finding the means and the inclination to discover new places and seek new adventures. At the rate the industry is growing, it is certain to be the industry of the 21st century, providing ample job opportunities to all kinds of people at all levels.

Challenges of Tour Operators

The tourism industry has been expressing much concern

over the five million Indian outbound tourists that are amounting to a revenue outflow of about Rs 25000 crore annually. In an endeavour to divert some of this revenue toward domestic tourism, the industry is all geared up to develop this segment further to give it a much needed thrust. Tour operators have awakened to the fact that domestic tourism is the foundation of strong tourist inflow. With an intent to focus on inter-regional tourism promotion and to boost the potent domestic tourism segment, Indian travel agents and tour operators have for the first time joined hands to aggressively tap this lucrative sector. Until a few years back, India's domestic tourism was limited to only pilgrim tours.

However, today the movement of the domestic market has increased tremendously. This is evident from the fact that even time-share, which till recently was one of the most infamous segments of the industry is now gaining popularity as an easy vacation option. To attract customers, travel agents are now exploring new territories and are sprucing up their itineraries and products. According to the latest travel surveys, there has been a phenomenal rise of ten per cent annual growth in the domestic tourism segment.

The explosion of domestic tourism is an inevitable by-product of economic development in the country. As there is an increase of disposable income, the demand for travel has grown exponentially, diverting most of the traffic toward the outbound segment., putting domestic tourism on the back burner. Where as Indian tourism has been equated with foreign visitors alone or the inbound tourism segment which has been sluggish over the last few years. It is time that India starts equating domestic tourists at par with the foreign tourists to boost its domestic tourism.

Experts believe that Indian tourism has no foundation and lacks projection and awareness. In addition, whenever

India has tried to pep up the scenario, several uncalled for events like 9/11, attacks on the parliament and other natural calamities have become major deterrents in the movement of travellers internationally. Weighing the socio-political scenario globally and its adverse impacts on the international movement of both the business and leisure traffic it is only natural that all tour operators have turned focus on domestic tourism, which is both a profitable and feasible proposition in the given scenario.

Tour operators are now diverting outbound tourists by enticing them with attractive domestic packages. The industry is now working with various airlines and state tourism departments to work out incentives for the domestic travellers. To promote domestic tourism, the biggest hurdle has been the inadequate infrastructure. Now the Ministry of Tourism is becoming aggressive as far as infrastructure development is concerned, development of the tourism circuits is has received a big impetus by the same. While infrastructure development is a continuous process, many agents believe that it is not a burning issue.

Tourism experts observe that infrastructure development will take place automatically once there is aggressive movement of tourists. To strengthen the country's tourism, the geographical diversity can be fruitfully marketed nationally and internationally. This exercise has a lot of significance even regionally. For people in the South, Snow holidays and Himalayas are new attractions and similarly, the beaches and temples of the South can be promoted to the people of North. These products are to be co-ordinated to compete with the attractive packages available for the outbound tourists. Moreover, domestic tourist movement is not limited by seasons, but each season has its own unique selling proposition (USP).

Initiatives like re-introduction of Leave Travel Concession (LTC) are much required to boost domestic tourism. The government's decision to restore the LTC facility to its employees with the hope that the consequential additional outgoing from the exchequer on this account, will at least benefit the tourism industry, has been a welcome decision. Two years ago, the ban on LTC came as a serious blow to the domestic travel agents (since ticket bookings for the employees for the leisure travel generated a good business), depriving them from booking travel tickets for government employees willing to go for leisure tours.

LTC has been termed as a good tool to offer a fillip to the leisure travel. The withdrawal of LTC for last two years was counted as an obstacle to the growth of the domestic tourism and was criticised by prominent tour operators. The government employees with the allowance as a disposable income would now be prominent travellers.

In order to create adequate awareness, tourism practitioners point out that media can create the desired hype amongst the populace. Besides, state tourism offices should carry out extensive marketing campaigns jointly with the help of media, tour operators and travel agents, finance companies, hotels and airlines by offering attractive holiday packages to lure the consumers.

Due to the lack of publicity, public is unaware of the destinations within the State and outside which are worth seeing and comes under one's budget to spend holidays. States should organise inter-state Travel Marts/Exhibitions to expose the tourism potential in their areas. Development of integrated tourist circuits as envisaged in the National Tourism Policy need to be aggressively promoted by the travel trade. This will enable the tourist to visit more than one destination at a given time while planning holidays. Indian Railways can play a major role in this regard by developing special holiday packages for domestic tourists.

Community-based Ecotourism

The community-based ecotourism is a form of ecotourism where the local community has substantial control over, and involvement in, its development and management, and a major proportion of the benefits remain within the community. How the community is defined will depend on the social and institutional structures in the area concerned, but the definition implies some kind of collective responsibility and approval by representative bodies.

In many places, particularly those inhabited by indigenous peoples, there are collective rights over lands and resources. Community-based ecotourism should therefore foster sustainable use and collective responsibility. However, it must also embrace individual initiatives within the community. Some further general characteristics of ecotourism have been identified by UNEP and the World Tourism Organisation as:

— involving appreciation not only of nature, but also of indigenous cultures prevailing in natural areas, as part of the visitor experience;

— containing education and interpretation as part of the tourist offer;

— generally, but not exclusively, organised for small groups by small, specialised and locally owned businesses;

— minimising negative impacts on the natural and socio-cultural environment;

— supporting the protection of natural areas by generating economic benefits for the managers of natural areas;

— providing alternative income and employment for local communities; and

— increasing local and visitor awareness of conservation.

The processes involved in ecotourism include all aspects of planning, developing, marketing and managing resources and facilities for this form of tourism. Visitor provision includes access to natural areas and cultural heritage, guiding and interpretative services, accommodation, catering, sales of produce and handicrafts, and transport. Appropriate recreational and special interest activities, such as trail walking, photography and participatory conservation programmes, may also be part of ecotourism.

In some locations, hunting and fishing may be included as appropriate activities, provided that they are carefully researched and controlled within a management plan that supports conservation. This kind of sustainable use relies on local knowledge, provides significant local income, and encourages communities to place a high value on wildlife, resulting in net conservation benefits.

WWF's Tourism Position Statement states that WWF and the tourism industry should share a common goal: the long-term preservation of the natural environment. It presents a vision that tourism development and practice should:

— be part of a wider sustainable development strategy;

— be compatible with effective conservation of natural ecosystems; and

— involve local people and cultures, ensuring that they have an equitable share in its benefits.

Ecotourism is receiving considerable attention from international and national conservation, development and tourism organisations, such as UNEP and the World Tourism Organisation. At the same time, there has been growing international concern that ecotourism should be genuinely community-based. There are many reported incidents where forms of 'ecotourism', which are not sufficiently community focused, are having a negative impact on the environment, and where indigenous communities are not receiving sufficient benefit.

Moreover, many small scale community-based ecotourism initiatives have been set up which have failed owing to a lack of market assessment, organisation, quality and promotion. Ecotourism is no panacea. It is important not to exaggerate the opportunities and benefits it can bring. Careful planning and improved knowledge is needed. Ecotourism and responsible tourism should be part of wider sustainable development strategies, whether at a community or an international level.

In most ecotourism projects, a fundamental objective is improved conservation of landscapes and biodiversity. Community-based ecotourism should be seen and evaluated as just one tool in achieving this. Its role may be to:

— provide a more sustainable form of livelihood for local communities;
— encourage communities themselves to be more directly involved in conservation; and
— generate more goodwill towards, and local benefit from, conservation measures such as protected areas.

There needs to be clear initial understanding of the relationship between local communities and the use of natural resources in the area concerned. The following are important issues to consider.

1. What actions are currently being taken, and by whom, which are supporting or damaging the environment? A challenge for community-based ecotourism is often one of being seen to benefit sufficient numbers of people in the community to make a difference.

2. What type and level of incentive might be needed to change attitudes and actions in order to achieve worthwhile conservation benefits? Could ecotourism deliver this? How does it compare with other development options which may have worse environmental impacts?
3. What additional problems for conservation might be brought by ecotourism, to set against possible gains? This might include not only development and visitor pressure but also an over-emphasis on certain species compared with biodiversity as a whole.
4. Could alternative sustainable livelihood options achieve the same or better results with less effort or disruption?

The capacity of ecotourism to support a positive attitude towards conservation is not only achieved in proportion to direct economic benefits delivered. With many ecotourism initiatives it has been found that simply raising awareness that there is some realisable value in wildlife and attractive landscapes has been sufficient to make a considerable difference, both within communities and also politically at a regional or national level. It is important to avoid spending time pursuing ecotourism and raising expectations in circumstances which are highly likely to lead to failure. An initial feasibility assessment should be made before instigating a communitybased strategy. Some preconditions relate to the situation at a national level, others to conditions in the local area. The main aspects to check are as follows. Reasonable conditions for undertakingtourism business are:

— an economic and political framework which does not prevent effective trading and security of investment;
— national legislation which does not obstruct tourism income being earned by and retained within local communities;

— a sufficient level of ownership rights within the local community;
— high levels of safety and security for visitors (both in terms of image of the country/region and in reality);
— relatively low health risks and access to basic medical services and a clean water supply; and
— practicable means of physical access and telecommunication to the area.

Some basic preconditions for community-based ecotourism are:

— landscapes or flora/fauna which have inherent attractiveness or degree of interest to appeal either to specialists or more general visitors;
— ecosystems that are at least able to absorb a managed level of visitation without damage;
— a local community that is aware of the potential opportunities, risks and changes involved, and is interested in receiving visitors;
— existing or potential structures for effective community decision-making;
— no obvious threats to indigenous culture and traditions; and
— an initial market assessment suggesting a potential demand and an effective means of accessing it, and that the area is not over supplied with ecotourism offers.

Some preconditions may be more relevant than others, depending on the local circumstances, and these may change over time. For example, in Namibia cross-border conflict in Caprivi has seriously affected market demand in that region but action is being taken to enable promising ecotourism initiatives there to resume when the situation stabilises. If the preconditions are met, this does not necessarily mean that ecotourism will be successful, only that it is worth proceeding to the next stage of consultation and assessment.Checking these preconditions will require informed judgement. The concept of preconditions and fast pre-feasibility checks is increasingly applied among donor agencies in the tourism field.

Integrated Community Approach to Ecotourism

The small scale of most community-based ecotourism initiatives means that their impact, both on nature conservation and on income and employment for the community as a whole, is limited. They can be more influential and successful if they are integrated within other sustainable development initiatives at a regional and local level.Ecotourism can be integrated with other sectors of the rural economy, creating mutually supportive linkages and reducing financial leakage away from the area. It can also be coordinated with agriculture, in terms of the use of time and resources and in providing markets for local produce.

In principle, multiple sector activity within local communities should be encouraged. Ecotourism markets are small, seasonal and sensitive to external influences such as political changes or economic instability in the host or generating country. On the other hand, ecotourism can shield against threats to other sectors. As well as horizontal integration within the community, the success of local ecotourism initiatives may depend on vertical integration with national level initiatives to support and promote responsible tourism.

In addition to making linkages with what may already exist, efforts should be made to influence national policies in favour of ecotourism, including coordination between tourism and environmental ministries and policies. National level support is needed in terms of linking conservation and tourism activities and responsibilities, appropriate legislation and assistance towards small enterprises and community initiatives, and national and international promotion.

Community Involvement

Involving the community is a critically important and complex subject for successful community-based ecotourism. Opportunities and solutions will vary considerably in different areas and between communities. An important principle is to seek to work with existing social and community structures, though these can create challenges as well as opportunities. It can also help to identify potential leaders and people with drive. The main objective should be to achieve broad and equitable benefits throughout the community. Issues of gender may also be important and ecotourism can provide good opportunities for women.

Community-based ecotourism requires an understanding, and where possible a strengthening, of the legal rights and responsibilities of the community over land, resources and development. This should apply in particular to the tenure of community-held lands and to rights over tourism, conservation and other uses on these lands, enabling the community to influence activity and earn income from tourism. It should also apply to participation in land use planning and development control over private property.

It is important to remember that ecotourism is a business. As well as community-led initiatives, private enterprise and investment should be encouraged where appropriate, within a structure which enables the community to benefit, and have decision-making power over the level and nature of tourism in its area. There are various ways in which the community can relate to private enterprise. The degree of community involvement and benefit can develop over time. For example, there are some ecotourism initiatives in the Amazon where lodges, that have been built with private investment, offer a concession to the community, an agreement to hand the business over to them after a specified period, and provision for an employment and training programme for local people.

Community-based Ecotourism Strategy

All community-based ecotourism initiatives should be centred on a clear strategy agreed and understood by the local community and all other stakeholders with an interest in tourism and conservation. The strategy should enable a comprehensive picture to be formed of needs and opportunities in an area, so that a range of complementary actions can be taken. One of the main benefits from working on a strategy is to provide the community with the tools and knowledge necessary for decision making. The strategy should be community-led and community-focused. However, it is essential that people with experience and knowledge of tourism and conservation are involved in its preparation.

People involved should include representatives of the local community, knowledgeable tourism operators, local entrepreneurs, relevant NGOs, conservation agencies including protected area managers, and local authorities. Links should be made as appropriate to the regional and national government level. Inputs to the strategy should include:

— careful consultation within the community covering attitudes and awareness of tourism, possible opportunities and pitfalls, existing experience, concerns and level of interest;

— a comprehensive market assessment; and

— an assessment of the natural and cultural heritage, including opportunities presented for ecotourism and sensitivities and constraints.

It is also helpful to set out a clear statement of strengths, weaknesses, opportunities and threats.The output of the strategy process should be an agreed vision for ecotourism over a specified period, together with an identification of aims, objectives and strategic priorities, an action plan, and a way of monitoring results. The action plan should identify practical initiatives, including a timescale and an indication of responsibility and resources required. It is very important, in order to avoid frustration, not to be too ambitious in terms of targets and timing.

The actions identified may include specific development or marketing projects. In some locations at least as much, or more, attention may need to be paid to action to manage tourism, including policies on development control and the handling of existing visitors. In many places, the relationship between the local community and a protected area may be an important element of the strategy, including agreed action on the level of any park admission fees and their subsequent use for conservation or within the community, which is an important issue for ecotourism. A fundamental characteristic of community-based ecotourism is that the quality of the natural resources and cultural heritage of an area should not be damaged and, if possible, should be enhanced by tourism.

Adverse impact on the natural environment should be minimised and the culture of indigenous communities should not be compromised. Ecotourism should encourage people to value their own cultural heritage. However, culture is not static and communities may wish to see change. A practical approach is to identify the limits of acceptable change that could be brought by tourism and then to consider what level of tourism activity would generate this change. It is very important that communities decide on the level of tourism they wish to see.

Consultation during the process of drawing up an ecotourism strategy should reveal the kinds of changes that might be viewed positively or negatively by local people. They can then be helped to consider what this might mean in terms of the numbers and types of visitor to look for, when they should come and their length of stay. For example, in one community in the Amazon it was felt that more than eight visitors per month would be disruptive. Two important principles are: products developed should be based on the community's traditional knowledge, values and skills; and the community should decide which aspects of their cultural traditions they wish to share with visitors.

A similar approach can be adopted with respect to determining limits of acceptable change and of acceptable use as far as the natural environment is concerned. Here scientific knowledge may be required to enable a judgement to be made, taking account of the conditions of different sites at various times of the year. Often it is found that the quantity of visitors at any one time is a more critical factor than the overall level of visitation. Useful tools in the management of visitors include the following.

1. Agreements with tour operators over the number and size of groups to bring.
2. Codes of conducts for visitors.
3. Application of systematic environmental, social and cultural impact assessment on all proposed development. This should also be concerned with

details of what is offered to visitors, such as the choice of products sold to them or the use of inappropriate sources of fuel.

4. Zoning both within and outside protected areas. This should cover both the siting of facilities and the degree of access allowed. In some locations, village communities have identified specific zones for ecotourism, both with respect to facility provision and wildlife conservation measures. A common approach is to locate tourist lodges some distance away from community villages. The planning process should ensure that monitoring measures are in place so that it is possible to tell when limits of acceptable change have been reached. Furthermore, strategies for making the necessary adjustments to overcome any problems identified will need to be established. There are many examples in the Mediterranean where environmental degradation has occurred but also places where sound planning control and community involvement have prevented over-exploitation.

Promotion of Community-based Ecotourism

The main reason why many community-based ecotourism projects have failed is that they have not attracted a sufficient number of visitors. Often, assumptions made about the marketability of a particular location or experience have been unrealistic and not based on research. As a result, promotional activity has been misdirected.

A problem has been the lack of tourism knowledge not only among local communities themselves but also among advisors and supporting agencies. A thorough market assessment should be undertaken for the destination as a whole and for the individual ecotourism project. This should consider the following.

1. The patterns, profiles and interests of existing visitors to the area, based on visitor surveys. In principle, it is far easier to get more out of existing visitors than to attract new ones.
2. The location of the area with respect to established tourist circuits in the country. Proximity to these and opportunities for deflection make a considerable difference.
3. The level, nature and performance of existing ecotourism products which are competitors but also potential collaborators.
4. The activities of inbound tour operators and ground handling agents in the country and coverage by international tour operators.
5. Existing information and promotional mechanisms in the area.

The unique or particular qualities that an area might offer in comparison to other existing products should be identified. From knowledge of the market, an initial profile of target visitors should be drawn up. Attention needs to be paid to the different opportunities and requirements of experienced ecotourists, more general mid-market visitors who enjoy seeing nature and local culture, backpackers, and educational markets. In some areas, the domestic visitor market may offer more potential than international travellers. The level and nature of marketing should also take into account the environmental and cultural integrity of the area and implications for visitor numbers.

A marketing plan should be prepared for all projects, which relates market research to a promotional programme. A vital ingredient for many projects is to form a close working relationship with one or more specialist tour operators. These should be selected carefully to ensure they are well established and are delivering reliable business. Contact, directly or through handling agents, should be made in the early stages, before the development of the offer has occurred, so that the operator can advise on what can be sold and adjustments, if necessary, can be made. Setting up a fully saleable programme can take time. An initial step may be to test market the programme with one or two groups. This also has the advantage of acquainting the community with the experience of handling guests.

6

Development of Health Tourism

Up until 30 years ago, the most commonly referred to definition of health was that it explicitly implied "the absence of illness." In 1970 however, the World Health Organisation (WHO) formulated a definition of health that has influenced the medical model of health care and challenged our perceptions of what it means to be healthy. The WHO defined health as "a state of complete physical, mental, and social well being, not merely the absence of disease of infirmity".

More recently, contemporary definitions for health have been enhanced by the concept of "wellness" and the values and principles that have evolved from it. "Wellness," in this instance, can be described as "a process in which an individual makes choices and engages in activities in a way that leads to healthpromoting lifestyles, which in turn positively impact the multiple dimensions of the individual's well being."

Some experts engaged with defining "wellness" have proposed that there are four essential ingredients associated with it. They are:

(1) A lifelong approach emphasising permanent lifestyle changes;

(2) Taking responsibility for one's own actions;

(3) Adding to the quality of one's life, not simply extending the length of life, and

(4) Making choices that improves an individual's position on the lifestyle continuum.

In this sense, the idea of wellness has paved the way for a more holistic approach to health. Other researchers, for example those affiliated with the German Well Association, reached the conclusion that the numerous definitions of wellness share common features. Key among them is the importance of life style, self-responsibility for health, and the exploitation of a person's potential for a better quality of health. More than the absence of illness, contemporary definitions of health fundamentally include elements of "wellness." By many accounts, "wellness" can be seen as "a state of health featuring the harmony of body, mind and spirit with physical fitness, healthy nutrition and diet, relaxation, meditation, mental activity/learning, environmental sensitivity and social contacts."

Although there appears to be no single definition for today's health and wellness tourism, a simple and succinct description comes from Mary Tabacchi, a registered dietician who teaches at Cornell University's School of Hotel Administration. Tabacchi is also the researcher behind the first ever Spa-related consumer research. According to Tabacchi, health tourism is any kind of travel to make yourself or a member of your family healthier.

Wellness tourism is sometimes regarded as a sub-category of health tourism. However, it is often difficult to separate the two types of products and services being offered to visitors in the contemporary health and wellness tourism industry. For example, some experts define "health tourism" as "the sum of all the relationships and phenomena resulting from a change in location and residence by people in order to promote, stabilise and, as appropriate, restore physical, mental and social well being using traditional public or private health services. This is quite different than the same experts' definition of "wellness tourism" which is proposed to be "the sum of all the relationships and phenomena resulting from a journey and residence by people whose main motive is to preserve or promote their health.

Health and wellness tourism activities are, and will be, pursued, in the main by "healthy" people and that their primary goals will be to prevent illness and preserve, promote or enhance their overall health and well being. Therefore, a HWT will likely involve a view of wellness that involves the travel motivations and activities of healthy people and their desire to prevent problems so they stay well, both physically and mentally. In their research and marketing literature, the Canadian Tourism Commission (CTC) supports the idea that health tourism and wellness tourism are two different products.

On the one hand are found clients with various medical conditions who are motivated to travel so that they can experience therapies that will help to make them well or to improve their health. On the other hand are clients who are generally healthy to start with and who are motivated to travel so that they can experience therapies and activities that will promote, enhance, and otherwise maintain a sense of well being. The CTC explain that, "it may sound like hair-splitting, but they really are very different needs and are addressed in different ways."

Health and Wellness Industry

Today's health and wellness consumer seeks to look and feel better; to lose weight; to slow the effects of aging; to relieve pain or discomfort; to manage stress; or to partake in the use of natural supplements like vitamins and minerals to improve their health. In response to this, today's health and wellness programs respond to the growing consumer demands for fitness level improvement;

for healthy lifestyle education; for nutrition counseling; for healing; for preventative medicine; for solving personal problems like stress or depression; and for holistic, naturopathic, alternative or eastern medicinal practices/ therapies.

Combining the consumer's quest for health and wellness with travel, leisure, and fun (products of the travel industry) is, "simply stated, spa, health and wellness tourism."If follows that since people take part in recreational, cultural, and entertainment and educational activities while on vacation, that "tourism is a perfect vehicle for promoting wellness." The earliest forms of health tourism that are directly related to contemporary health and wellness include visits to mineral and hot springs.These activities date back to the Neolithic and Bronze ages in Europe and that "legend says Bath, England was founded by Bladud, father of King Lear, in 863 BC." The use of mineral and hot springs during the Middle Ages are characterised by a firmly established belief in the curative powers of thermal springs.

Ponce de Leon brought the concept to the New World in the 16th Century when he traveled to Florida in search of the fountain of youth. By the 1700s and 1800s, "taking the waters" at spa towns such as Baden-Baden was popular with the upper crust on both sides of the Atlantic. In the late 19th Century, the emerging urban middle class sought the healthful benefits of fresh sea or mountain air as an antidote to the overcrowding and pollution wrought by industrialisation. Ross states that, "a new era of health tourism began in the US in 1939 with the opening of a $17.50-a-week bring-your-tent spa, and healthy-living retreat, which became the renowned Rancho La Puerta Fitness Resort.

By 1958 the healthy living idea had moved north to the San Diego area with the creation of the Golden Door, a luxurious destination spa well known for its lavish individual service and successful mind-body programs." In the same vein, Tucson's Canyon Ranch was opened in 1979 and still provides pampering, fitness and medically supervised wellness programs. The early 20th Century saw the emergence of "health farms" or "fat farms" where the emphasis was on "fitness and good diet." The notion of spas for the mass tourism market, however, didn't take off until the late 1980s. Moreover, it was not until 1991 that the International Spa Association was formed. Since that time, the number of spas has grown exponentially.

In the late 19th and early 20th centuries, the warm dry climate of the Southwest attracted those with respiratory problems.Today, promoting the healthful and health-care benefits of a destination is gaining popularity because tourism marketers need ways to differentiate their products and their destinations. An Internet search finds dozens of countries touting their health tourism activities, including some that many tourists would not normally associate with health promoting conditions. Among them are, for instance, Ethiopia, Pakistan, Yemen, Bulgaria, Siberia and El Salvador. Canada and the Yukon, with their resplendent natural and wilderness settings are environments that increasingly symbolise all the elements that are conducive to good health and well being.

Heading into new century, health and wellness industry remains the top priority for food manufacturers and consumers alike. The overall number of health messages and the nuances in the messages themselves resulting from increased scientific understanding require a more sophisticated level of comprehension today than ever before. Marketers have the challenge of determining what impact this should have on product formulation, claims, and label content, and how to communicate with consumers. While some messages, their rationale, and call to action are straightforward, such as that associated with reduced consumption of trans fats and nutritional labeling of them, others are much more complicated or ambiguous, such as identifying and labeling specific, individual omega-3 fatty acids.

Consumers are becoming both less receptive to dietary advice and confused when recommendations made one day are later refuted. To some extent, consumer skepticism of the latest information is on the rise for this reason. Key challenges for future will be to avoid creating consumer confusion as a result of the growing quantity and specificity of scientific information available, to enhance credibility by leveraging sound science, and to create compellingly positioned products so that consumers can purchase with confidence.

Factors Affeting Health and Wellness Industry

The most dominant factor impacting upon the growth of the HWT industry is the ever-increasing number of aging "Baby Boomers": there is an estimated 78 million Baby Boomers in the United States alone. Boomers' interest and desire for travel opportunities that also meet their health needs is becoming a market force that greatly influences the development of this tourism niche market. In fact, Boomers already represent 60 percent of the spa market.

A second factor is North America's, and indeed the worlds', fascination with fitness and alternative therapies and their use for promoting and enhancing health and healing. Some statistics help tell the story: 42 percent of Americans spent $21 billion on nontraditional medical therapies and products in 1997. Between 1998 and 2001, nearly 25 million U.S. travellers began using a fitness center or gym to combat obesity while traveling. The story is just as compelling in Canada: the Berger Population Health Monitor reported that 61% of Canadians use vitamins and 38% use plant based natural health products.

Another study done by the Tzu Chi Institute found that reimbursements by insurance companies for alternative medical treatments rose from less than 50 million dollars in 1989 to more than 250 million dollars in 2000.A third element that contributes to the increase in health tourism is the fact that today's consumers are well traveled. As a result they seek something new and different in a holiday experience. They often want something educational or experiential,and many aspects of health and wellness tourism also fulfills those requirements.

Just how "healthy" is health and wellness tourism? The first Canadian Tourism Resource Guide released in 2003/04 included a directory of new products and services with a special section on spa vacations. They describe this niche market as "generating US $2 billion worth of business in North America" and as providing "some of Canada's top travel options."

India's Tourism Sector

India is gradually gathering popularity as a health tourist destination. A study by McKinsey and Confederation of Indian Industry (CII) says that at its current pace of growth, healthcare tourism alone can rake over US$ 1.7 billion additional revenues by 2012. Medical tourism is now a US$ 299 million industry, as about 100,000 patients come each year. The country needs to exploit the cost advantage it can offer to a health tourist, the study said. The biggest driver for healthcare tourism is the disparity in costs.

— A heart surgery in the US costs US$ 30,000 as compared to US$ 6,000 in India.

— A bone marrow transplant in the US costs US$ 250,000 and US$ 26,000 in India.

With yoga, meditation, ayurveda, allopathy, and other systems of medicine, India offers a unique basket of services to an individual that is difficult to match by other countries," the CII study said. Clinical outcomes in India are at par with the world's best centres since India has internationally qualified and experienced specialists. It is boom time for India's Tourism and Hospitality sector. Driven by a surge in business traveller arrivals and a soaring interest in India as a tourist destination, the year 2005 has been the best year till date, with foreign visitor arrivals reaching a record 3.92 million, resulting in international tourism receipts of US$ 5.7 billion.

According to global hotel and hospitality consulting firm, HVS International, the strong performance in tourist arrivals in 2005 can be attributed to a strong sense of business and investment confidence in India inspired by:

— India's strong GDP performance
— Strengthening of ties with the developed world, and
— Opening of sectors of the economy to private sector/ foreign investment.
— The efforts made by the Ministry of Tourism & Culture in the last few years have had a salutary effect on India's tourism industry.
— Foreign tourist arrivals are expected to witness a growth of 78 per cent in 2006 over 2001 (last 5 years)
— Growth in foreign exchange earnings is expected to be of the order of 122 per cent during this period.
— As per estimates (Ministry of Tourism), on an average, about 3.1 million additional jobs per year have been created directly and indirectly in the tourism sector in the last four years.

India is fast emerging as one of the most enticing destinations for the global leisure traveller. The Readers Travel Awards 2006, conducted by Condé Nast Traveller has recently placed India at number four among the world's must-see countries, up from number nine in 2003. The Incredible India campaign has also been a huge success. As an engine for economic growth, the tourism and hospitality sector cuts across the rural-urban divide, and bridges economic boundaries.

According to The World Travel & Tourism Council's 2006 Travel and Tourism Economic Research, the travel and tourism sector in India is expected to generate a total demand of US$ 53,544.5 million of economic activity in 2006, accounting for nearly 5.3 per cent of GDP and 5.4 per cent of total employment. According to the report, the sector is expected to grow at a rate of 8.4 per cent in 2006 and by 8 per cent per annum, in real terms, between 2007 and 2016. As travellers surge into India, the demand for rooms, across segments, has skyrocketed. Hotels in the luxury and business traveller segment are recording nearly 100 per cent occupancy, spiralling tariffs, and a strain on capacity and manpower.

Anticipating this demand, around 10,856 hotel rooms in Delhi, 9,318 rooms in Mumbai, 7,794 rooms in Bangalore and 7,408 rooms in Hyderabad are expected to be added by 2011, according to estimates by HVS International. The objective of the existing Tourism Policy of the Government of India is to position tourism as a major engine of economic growth and to harness its direct and multiplier effects for employment and poverty eradication in an environmentally sustainable manner.

The present government's major policy initiatives include:

— Liberalisation in aviation sector

— Pricing policy for aviation turbine fuel which influences internal air fares

— Rationalisation in tax rates in the hospitality sector

— Tourist friendly visa regime
— Immigration services
— Procedural changes in making available land for construction of hotels
— Allowing setting up of Guest Houses

The Indian Ministry of Tourism has identified 31 villages across the country to be developed as tourism hubs. The states in which these villages have been identified include Himachal Pradesh, Gujarat, Maharashtra, Bihar, Karnataka, Madhya Pradesh, Andhra Pradesh, Kerala, Tamil Nadu, Orissa, Assam, Sikkim, Rajasthan and West Bengal. The government's Open Skies policy, permission for domestic airlines to commence international flights, start-up of various low-cost carriers, and fleet expansion by domestic players has created a huge incentive for domestic travellers to explore far-off destinations within and outside India.

The booming aviation business is bringing an ever-increasing number of passengers to India, and pulling Indians out of their homes and into hotels. The numbers, according to the Ministry of Tourism, speak for themselves:

— The number of domestic and international passengers has increased fifteen-fold to 73.34 million in 2005/06 since 1970.
— Domestic air passenger traffic grew by 16.8 per cent in 2005/06 compared to 2004/05.
— International passenger traffic observed a growth of 16.9 per cent in the same period.
— Private airlines accounted for 77.0 per cent of the total domestic traffic.

Travel and Tourism Sector

The travel and tourism sector creates more jobs per million

rupees of investment than any other sector of the economy and is capable of providing employment to a wide spectrum of job seekers from the unskilled to the specialised, even in the remote parts of the country. The Tenth Plan approach towards tourism signifies a distinct shift from the approach adopted in earlier Plans. Apart from acknowledging the wellaccepted advantages of developing tourism for the promotion of national integration, international understanding and earning foreign exchange, the Tenth Plan recognises the vast employment generating potential of tourism and the role it can play in furthering the socio-economic objectives of the Plan.

In order to create a supportive environment for the promotion of tourism, the New Tourism Policy, 2002, that is to be implemented during the Tenth Plan, will generate awareness about the benefits of tourism for the host population. It will mobilise state governments to use tourism as a means for achieving their socio-economic objectives, encourage the private sector to enhance investment in tourism and provide legislative and regulatory support for sustainable tourism and to protect the interests of the industry and the consumer. The policy envisages involving the rural sector in the promotion of rural, heritage, adventure and eco-tourism and will promote the development of competitive high quality products and destinations.

Most importantly, it will remove the barriers to growth and resolve contradictions in policy to achieve inter-sectoral convergence of activities that help the growth of tourism. The initiatives taken by the state so far have not yielded the desired result and India's tourism performance has failed to match its potential even as countries not blessed with its natural and cultural endowments have taken the lead in reaping the benefits of tourism development for their people. The reasons for this poor performance need to be speedily addressed to enable tourism to make an appropriate contribution to national development.

The public sector made a significant contribution to the growth of tourism in the initial stages of planned development by providing a reasonable infrastructure base. During the Ninth Plan it was recognised that a reappraisal of the role of the State in tourism development and the extent of its participation was needed as it is neither necessary nor feasible for the State to make large investments in areas that are best left to the initiative of the private sector. The state can contribute through infrastructure development, the planning of broad development strategies, the provision of fiscal and monetary incentives to catalyse private sector investment and devise an effective regulatory and supervisory mechanism to protect the interests of the industry and the consumer.

The acceptance of this view also led to the commencement of the process of disinvestment in 18 hotels of the India Tourism Development Corporation (ITDC) hotels. The ITDC will have to redefine its role in the Tenth Plan. The State can also play an effective role in ensuring that tourism development does not harm the environment. The interaction between tourism and environmental pollution requires sensitive handling. There is complementarity, not conflict, between the high quality environmental requirements of tourism and the imperatives of maintaining the ecological balance.

Global Market Trends

Although global recession and the September 11, 2001, events are estimated to have resulted in a temporary decline in travel and tourism demand in 2001-02, international and domestic tourism is expected to boom over the next two decades. The World Travel and Tourism Council (WTTC) estimates a 4.5 per cent per annum increase in the total amount of travel and tourism economic activity between 2002 and 2012. This is largely attributed to a rise in global wealth, liberalisation of international airspace, cheaper flights and the use of the Internet as a travel tool.

The earnings from tourism have made it one of the world's largest industries and the fastest growing sectors of global trade accounting for 10.7 per cent of global gross domestic product (GDP), 12.8 per cent of global exports, 8.2 per cent of global employment (or one in every 12.2 jobs), and 9.4 per cent of global capital investment. Tourism in the least developed countries is growing faster than the world average, holding the promise of prosperity for many. International tourist arrivals worldwide reached 698 million in 2000, generating $ 595 billion revenues.

International tourism flows are expected to reach 1.5 billion by 2020 and revenue estimated to cross $ 2000 billion. Today, only 3.5 per cent of the world population travels internationally but the number of Asian, particularly Chinese, tourists is predicted to grow enormously as the region becomes more integrated with the global economy.

The scale of world domestic tourism, on the other hand, exceeds world international tourism by a ratio of 10:1. In India, for every interna-tional tourist, there are 80 domestic tourists. Domestic tourism can form the basis of a viable and sustainable tourism industry in India. Consumer trends in tourism are gradually changing and require an appropriate response in terms of both policy formulation and investment.

Current market trends indicate that:

— Long haul travel will grow faster than intra-regional travel. A growth of 24 per cent is expected by 2020.

— People with less time for leisure are likely to take more frequent but shorter trips nearer home, opening up opportunities for 'neighbouring country' tourism.

— The experienced traveller wants authentic, off-the-beaten-track vacations in remote and less well-known places as against luxurious five-star vacations, leading to an interest in rural and ethnic tourism.

— The increase in the number of people with lots of money but little leisure time has resulted in a growing emphasis on rest and relaxation, and 'wellness' and 'health' holidays.

— The elderly population in key tourismgenerating markets has shown a preference for cultural tourism against sun-and-sand vacations.

— There is notable and increasing interest in spiritualism.

— The demand for eco-tourism and naturebased holidays is expected to double and even triple in the next 20 years. Sports and adventure holidays continue to be popular with the young.

The interest in cultural tourism, spiritualism, 'wellness' holidays, eco-tourism and rural tourism would tend to favour India, provided the country can avail of the opportunities offered to maximise its natural advantages in these areas.

The development of new tourism products and destinations during the Tenth Plan must be based on market research and demand, keeping the source markets and the age groups of the tourists in mind. At the same time, the Government must develop new source markets nearer home and make India a safer destination for women tourists and family holidays.

India's Place in World Tourism

The World Tourism Organisation forecast indicates an increasing tourism preference towards East Asia, the Pacific, West Asia and South Asia, although Europe and America still remain the world's foremost tourism destinations commanding 77 per cent of the global market. East Asia/Pacific achieved the highest rate of growth of 14.5 per cent in tourism and travel in 2000 followed by West Asia and South Asia. With this gradual shift in focus, the outlook for the growth of tourism in the region is promising. In Asia, China has emerged as a leading tourist destination and is poised to become the world's top tourist destination by 2020.

The WTTC has identified India as one of the world's foremost tourist growth centres in the coming decade. After Turkey, India is expected to achieve the fastest rate of growth of the total amount of economic activity likely to be generated by travel and tourism, at 9.7 per cent over the next 10 years. Also, the largest employment creation after China is expected to take place in India over the same period. The growth in 'visitor exports' or spending by international tourists, is likely to be the fastest in India at 14.3 per cent per annum over the next decade. On the whole, the WTTC forecast for India is promising, subject to key policy issues that affect the growth of the sector being addressed.

If India is to realise its enormous potential in tourism it must provide exclusive world-class tourism products and destinations to compete successfully for a larger share of the Asian tourism market. Today, outbound tourism from India far exceeds visitor traffic to the country partly because there is a lack of world-class destinations within the country and partly because the domestic tourism policy has been largely directed towards those in the lower end of the spending spectrum.

The high spender from India prefers to visit neighbouring countries as he gets better value for money. The scope and reach of domestic tourism will have to be broadened in the Tenth Plan through the development of competitive destinations that match international standards in terms of price and quality and also satisfy the international traveller. India's international arrival figures have not been able to keep pace with neighbouring countries and have been exceeded by Thailand, Malaysia, Indonesia, Dubai and the Maldives.

Since 1995, India's share of the world market has remained virtually stagnant at 0.38 per cent, while domestic tourism has grown at a phenomenal rate and India now accounts for 4.6 per cent share of domestic tourism worldwide. In terms of tourism receipts, India has shown relative buoyancy because of the interest shown by visitors in traditional handicraft items and particularly in diamonds. The Tenth Plan visualises a mutually supportive role for tourism and handicrafts by encouraging haats and shilpgrams and recognising shopping as an integral part of the tourism experience to promote the 'Made in India' brand.

India's Tourist Profile

India receives the largest number of overseas tourists from the United Kingdom, which is its largest source market, followed by the United States, Sri Lanka, France, Germany, Canada, Japan, Australia and Singapore. Of the tourists coming to India, 27.5 per cent are in the age group of 35-44 years, 23.4 per cent in the age group of 25-35 years and 20.8 per cent in the age group of 45-54 years. Women constitute only 30.5 per cent of India's total international arrivals. Repeat visitors account for 44.9 per cent of the overseas visitors.

A substantial number of these may be non-resident Indians, as hotel reservations do not correspond to the number of international arrivals in the country. The average length of stay of foreign tourists in the country in 1998 was 31.2 days. Domestic tourism, on the other hand, is largely pilgrimage-oriented and requires improvement in travel facilities and pilgrim destinations.

Tenth Plan Objective

Tourism in India has tended to be regarded as an elitist activity conducted primarily for the purpose of earning foreign exchange. Its vast potential as an engine of growth and employment generater has remained largely untapped. Although, with 25 million jobs, India ranks second in terms of number of persons employed in travel and tourism, yet the contribution of the sector as a percentage share of all employment is amongst the lowest in the world.

The Tenth Plan objective is to integrate tourism with the socio-economic objectives of the Plan by creating 3.6 million jobs a year through the promotion of domestic and international tourism and to enhance India's share of international arrivals from 0.38 per cent to at least 0.62 per cent by 2007.

Department of Tourism

Being the nodal agency for the development of tourism in the country, the department of tourism needs to make greater efforts to co-ordinate and integrate the policies of central ministries that have an impact on the development of tourism and to mobilise state governments and the private sector to develop unique and competitive tourism products and destinations. Crucial decisions affecting tourism are taken by other ministries viz. the Ministries of Finance, Home, Civil Aviation, Surface Transport, Environment and Forests, Urban Development, Rural Development, Ocean Develop-ment etc.

The Department of Tourism has tended to concentrate largely on its role as the promoter of international tourism and generator of foreign exchange earnings while paying relatively less attention to inter-sectoral policy co-ordination and the all-important development of tourism infrastructure and product quality. In the Tenth Plan, the Department will redefine and expand its role and work towards intersectoral convergence and policy integration to remove the barriers to the growth of tourism.

Barriers to growth

There are several factors that are responsible for the inadequate growth of the tourism sector in India. These are: barriers related to approach, barriers that discourage private investment, factors that affect competitiveness and factors that affect the long-term sustainability of tourism. The effective and early removal of these barriers during the Tenth Plan is an essential determinant for the success of the New Tourism Policy. The need for a national consensus on the role and level of tourism deve-lopment in the country has been voiced repeatedly but a concerted effort to achieve a consensus has not been made.

Tourism should not be limited by state or regional boundaries if distortions in policies are to be avoided. It is important that a consensus among all states is evolved through the National Development Council (NDC) and the barriers to the growth of tourism removed. Tourism has been denied the priority it deserves over successive Plan periods because its potential as an engine of economic growth has not been appreciated. This is visible in the low allocation of resources. Allocation to tourism has averaged 0.16 per cent of the total Plan outlay from the Third Plan to the Ninth Plan. In the Tenth Plan, it is likely to receive an allocation of 0.72 per cent.

According to the WTTC, India is one of the lowest spenders on tourism - 153rd out of 160 countries - while its neighbouring competitors and China invest far more: Malaysia (5.1 per cent), Nepal (5 per cent), Indonesia (8.4 per cent), Maldives (15.7 per cent), China (3.8 per cent). The growing domestic and international demand, which is set to boom, reinforces the need for higher investment. Failure to measure up to additional investment demand for domestic tourism is likely to lead to the over-exploitation of existing facilities, discouraging foreign visitors while leading to an increase in the outflow of high-spending domestic tourists from the country.

Most State Governments give scant importance to tourism even though they virtually control the tourism product located within their boundaries. They are responsible, inter alia, for local infrastructure, transport systems, sanitation and hygiene, leisure and recreation, law and order, the upkeep of local monuments and the general well-being of the tourist. Their support and participation is essential for tourism to succeed and spread its benefits among the host population. Their lack of interest has resulted in an unprofessional ad hoc approach that acts as a deterrent to the growth of tourism. The approach of the state governments needs to be focused, highly professional and result-oriented if India is to avail of the opportunity that the currently favourable market trends have to offer.

Apart from the State Governments, the private sector plays a vital role in the growth and development of tourism. Although the Central Government and certain state governments have, from time to time, announced incentives to involve the private sector in tourism development, the results achieved have fallen short of expectations. To provide a conducive environment for private sector investment, it is important to realise that the travel and tourism sector is adversely affected by the lack of synergy in inter-sectoral policies.

The growth of the sector requires well-integrated and co-ordinated policies and stability in approach. Contradictions and arbitrary changes in policy send confused signals to the investor. Unless infirmities in policy are expeditiously removed well before the end of the Tenth Plan period, the New Tourism Policy is unlikely to succeed. Being a long haul destination, India is more conveniently accessible by air and cannot be easily reached by rail or road.

A restrictive air transport policy has a very deleterious effect on tourist traffic. There are insufficient connections to most tourism destinations. The situation could be eased if the large number of regional airports could open up as international airports. The existing international and national airports also require improvement.

The price of aviation turbine fuel needs to be lowered to make air transport competitive and affordable. Today, it is cheaper to travel by air to neighbouring countries from India than to travel to certain parts of India itself. A more liberal aviation bilaterals regime and a new aviation policy to benefit the economy of the country as a whole rather than the national carriers alone would greatly aid the development of tourism. Central and state governments need to evolve a taxation regime, which is revenue generating without being burdensome.

Accommodation and transport taxes tend to be very heavy in certain states while the excise policy in others is extremely harsh. The land policy in some states makes the setting up of a hotel a formidable exercise and as many as 48 clearances are required for the construction and running of a hotel. Such policies deter private sector investment. The importance of protecting private investment in tourism must also be appreciated and activities such as mining, unauthorised construction, encroachments and haphazard development around tourist resorts must be prevented through appropriate legislation and public support.

As tourism is a highly competitive industry; the traveller has a wide range of choices and looks for good value for money. The lack of quality infrastructure, uncompetitive rates, indifferent or poor product quality, difficulty in getting access to information on travel and tourist destinations, untrained service providers, and above all, the lack of hygiene, have an enormously negative effect on the competitiveness of the tourism product. A world class destination requires professional planning to prevent haphazard, uncontrolled growth, spatial and land use planning, strict architectural controls, sewerage infrastructure and water treatment plants. It requires improvement of entry points and appropriate facilitation services.

The lack of a visaon-arrival regime on account of security considerations places India at a disadvantage vis-a-vis its competitors. It is necessary that India strikes a balance between security considerations and the need for tourism development and reviews its visa policy to permit tourists from its major source markets to obtain visas on arrival. Equally important is the behaviour of the host population. Training programmes are required not only for hotel managers but also for tourist guides, taxi-drivers, staff at eating places, porters etc., as the manner in which they conduct themselves affects the tourist's experience of the country. Important do's and dont's in terms of a code of ethics need to be inculcated among the service providers.

During the Tenth Plan, the Department of Tourism will organise capacitybuilding programmes for service providers through mobile training units. A major impediment to the growth of tourism in India has been the lack of awareness about the benefits that it can bestow upon the host population. Unless the host population, both in the rural and urban areas, is supportive of tourism, it cannot become a vibrant economic force. The rural sector, in particular, has been largely ignored in tourism development and has consequently been deprived of the benefits of employment and income generation accruing from tourism.

The Tenth Plan will seek to rectify this, particularly in view of the world-wide interest in rural tourism. While an awareness campaign that elicits local support for travel and tourism is essential for the long-term growth of the sector, it is also important to create awareness about the environmental impact of tourism by generating respect for the carrying capacities of tourist destinations. This is imperative as excessive exposure of ecologically fragile areas to human interference can lead to irreparable environmental degradation. As the demand for ecotourism is expected to grow enormously in the next decade, it is important to have regulations in place to prevent such damage.

The local population must be convinced of the need to support such regulations in the interest of long-term sustainability. India's hill resorts have already suffered seriously from a lack of concern for their carrying capacities and the unchecked influx of tourists during the summer months. If India's forest sanctuaries and pristine beaches are not to suffer the same fate, attention will have to be paid during the Tenth Plan to obtaining regulatory and public support for sustainability concerns.

Tenth Plan Strategy

The Tenth Plan strategy is to work towards a national consensus on the role of tourism in national development and to focus on the removal of barriers that hamper its growth. To make public sector investment more effective, it is necessary to work towards the inter-sectoral convergence of policies and programmes that could benefit tourism.

The New Tourism Policy envisages a framework, which is Government-led, private sector driven and oriented towards community welfare, with the Government creating the legislative framework and basic infrastructure for tourism development, the private sector providing the quality product and the community providing active support. The overall vision of the development of tourism embodied in the new policy will be achieved through five key strategic objectives. These are:

(i) Positioning tourism as a national priority.

(ii) Enhancing India's competitiveness as a tourist destination.

(iii) Improving and expanding product development.

(iv) Creation of world class infrastructure.

(v) Effective marketing plans and programmes.

Positioning tourism as a national priority

A concerted effort will be made, through the NDC, to arrive at a consensus on the role of tourism in the development agenda of the nation. Inclusion of tourism in the Concurrent List of the Constitution will provide constitutional recognition to the tourism sector and enable the central government to legislate for tourism development.

A proposal to this effect has been circulated by the Department of Tourism to the state governments for comments and has also been discussed at a Chief Ministers' conference and a majority of the states have agreed to the proposal. Other initiatives include the setting up of Tourism Advisory Council with key stakeholders functioning as a think tank and the constitution of a Group of Ministers on Tourism to improve policy integration and co-ordination.

The adoption of a tourism satellite accounting system is underway to gauge more precisely the contribution of tourism to the national economy. A national awareness campaign in order to create a popular movement in favour of tourism is being planned through a professionally managed communication strategy. Most importantly, the efficiency of public investment in tourism supporting activities will be improved through effective inter-sectoral coordination and prioritisation.

Enhancing India's competitiveness as a tourist sestination

As air capacity available to India is woefully short during the peak travel months, ranging from October to March, especially for the main tourism originating regions such as North America, Western Europe and South Asia, it is necessary to open India's skies to increase capacity and help enhance tourism. Additional seat capacity from the major tourism generating destinations would significantly benefit the national economy and provide a major impetus to tourism.

Improvement in the standard of facilities and services at the international and national airports will need to be speeded up by employing professional manage-ment agencies and by privatising and leasing out airports. To enhance India's competitiveness as a tourist destination, it is proposed to simplify the visa procedures and consider strategies for the speedy issue of visas including electronic visas and visas on arrival.

An attempt will be made, through a consensus, to reduce the heavy and multiple taxes that reduce the competitiveness of the Indian tourism product. Special tourism police will be deployed at major tourist destinations during the Tenth Plan to provide security to travellers and promote India as a safe destination.

Improving and expanding product development

Product development strategy during the Tenth Plan will be related to the special interests of tourist target markets.

— Cultural and heritage tourism will be expanded. India has a vast array of protected monuments with 22 world heritage sites, 16 of which are monuments. The integrated development of areas around these monuments provides an opportunity for the development of cultural tourism in India.

— For the development of beach and coastal tourism, a number of sites on the west coast of India will be identified for the development as beach resorts by the private sector. The sites will be offered on long term lease at preferential terms. These sites will primarily be on the beaches of Goa, Kerala, and North Karnataka because of easier access by air.

— During the Tenth Plan Kochi in Kerala and the Andaman and Nicobar Islands will be developed as international cruise destinations because of their proximity to international cruise routes and their exotic appeal.

— India's unmatched variety of cuisine is becoming increasingly popular in the world and will be developed as a special attraction. It is proposed to create a highly skilled workforce of culinary professionals through an innovative incentive scheme not only for India but also to promote Indian cuisine internationally.

— Village tourism will be promoted as the primary tourism product of India to spread tourism and its socio-economic benefits to rural areas.

— India's great wildlife variety has not been developed as a tourist attraction. Wildlife sanctuaries and national parks will become an integral part of the Indian tourism product. Priority will be given to the preparation of site and visitor management plans for key parks. The quality of tourist facilities available at the parks will be enhanced after a prioritisation of parks. Tentatively these will be: Corbett National Park, Kanha National Park, Bandhav Garh National Park, Kaziranga, Madhumali, Bharatpur, Periyar, Ranthambore, Little Rann of Kutch, Chilka, and the Sunderbans.

— India has the greatest adventure tourism assets in the world in the Himalayas and its rivers. Mountain-based adventure activities will be developed and promoted. Regulations and certification for adventure tourism operators will be introduced so that the minimum standards of safety and conservation are met.

— India receives only a minuscule proportion of the global meetings, conventions and exhibition market. It is important that India develops a world class international convention city not just for the sake of tourism development but also for international and domestic trade and commerce.

— India's most unique tourism product during the Tenth Plan will be holistic healing and rejuvenation packages. In focussing on this, it will capture the essence of Indian culture for international and Indian visitors alike.

— India's fairs and festivals, some of which are already well established such as the Pushkar mela, the Desert Festival at Jaisalmer, the Kumbh Mela etc. will be promoted as unique products of India. The Festivals of India programme will be re-introduced in the top 12 future markets for India - initially with an annual event in the United Kingdom and the United States, to be followed by triennial events in the other markets.

— Shopping will be recognised as an integral part of tourism. The development of dedicated shopping centres for traditional crafts designed along the lines of village haats such as Dilli Haat and Shilpgram will be encouraged and information on where to procure specific crafts made available through shopping guides.

— Delhi will be positioned as the cultural capital of India supported by an ongoing and vibrant calendar of cultural events. The development of such a niche-based special interest productmix will position India as a unique and competitive destination.

Creation of world class infrastructure

The need for physical infrastructure for tourism ranges from ports of entry to modes of transport to destinations (airways, roadways, railways or waterways), to urban infrastructure such as access roads, power, water supply, sewerage and telecommunication. This underscores the need for inter-sectoral convergence of infrastructural schemes and programmes that could support tourist destinations. The road network is vital for tourism as almost 70 per cent of passengers in India travel by road. Many tourist circuits are entirely dependent on roads.

The current government plan for the road system in the country covering both inter-state highways and improvements to rural roads directly supports tourism development. There is urgent need to construct and improve highways linking the 22 world heritage sites and places of tourist significance. The Ministry of Road Transport and National Highways will collaborate with the Ministry of Tourism in this effort. The Indian railway system can also become an enormous asset to the development of the tourism and hospitality industry in the country.

The railways hold a special fascination for foreign tourists who wish to travel the country. For the vast majority of domestic tourists also, the railways is the most affordable means of travel linking the length and breadth of the country. Introduction of special tourist trains with pre-set itineraries and private sector participation will be encouraged. The Indian Railways plan to establish 100 hotels at railway stations to serve specific tourist centres. The private sector will be given incentives to operate these hotels on long-term leases. These hotels will provide clean and inexpensive accommodation for budget tourists.

The Indian Railways also owns a number of heritage structures, which, if effectively maintained and marketed, could serve, both as railway stations and places of tourist interest. India has five hill railways, which compare with the best hill railway systems in the world. The enormous tourist potential of these products will be tapped during the Tenth Plan. As steam-hauled trains like the Royal Orient, Buddha Parikrama, Palace-On-Wheels and Fairy Queen are extremely popular with tourists, steam traction for special tourist segments will be continued. Trains like the Shatabdi and the Rajdhani with a special tourism and hospitality focus will be planned both for foreign and domestic tourists.

India's 7,000-km coastline and her mighty rivers will be tapped for the promotion of cruises. Care will be taken to develop world class tourism products. As the Ministry of Tourism's financial assistance to the states has not been able to have the desired impact in terms of creating of world class tourism infrastructure, the emphasis must shift to the development of specific travel circuits as internationally competitive destinations and the convergence of resources and expertise for these circuits. The availability of trained manpower is essential to achieve excellence in the tourism sector. At present, there are 21 Institutes of Hotel Management and Catering Technology (IHM&TC) and 13 Food Craft Institutes in the country.

In addition, a good number of accredited institutes also cater to the growing demand in the service sector. It is estimated that only 50 per cent of the requirement of the market is met by these institutes. Five new Institutes of hotel management would be set up in the Tenth Plan - three in the newly created states of Uttaranchal, Jharkhand and Chhattisgarh and two in the northeast. In addition, 15 more Food Craft Institutes will be set up in the Tenth Plan, and efforts will be made to take culinary crafts and training to the rural areas through mobile training units. A new scheme on capacity building to train service providers in the unorganised sector such as small hotels, dhabas, restaurants and other eating joints is also proposed.

Strategy for effective marketing

As there is fierce competition for tourists from India's source markets, India needs to change its traditional marketing approach to one that is more competitive and modern. It needs to develop a unique market position, image and brand, which cannot be held by any other competitor. India's positioning statement will capture the essence of its tourism product to convey an 'image' of the product to a potential customer. This image will be related not only to its ancient Vedic civilisation with a cultural heritage that continues to thrive especially in its rural areas but also to its essentially secular nature.

In the Tenth Plan, an extensive market research programme will be launched in the target source markets and tourism products developed to cater to the interests of each source market. An effective and ongoing market representation presence will be established with the travel trade in each source market and an Internet portal set up in various languages to provide information, description of the product and the product requirements of the target market segments.

The Internet has a great impact on the marketing of travel and tourism. It has already established itself as a channel through which tourism organisations can promote their destinations and products. Indian tourism will utilise both the Internet and other emerging interactive technologies to avail of the benefits to be gained.

Hospital Accreditation Overseas

In this age of globalisation, patients are shopping for affordable healthcare world-wide, giving rise to the phenomenon known as medical tourism. Patients who have no health insurance, or are wait-listed for procedures in their own countries under government plans, travel to developing countries to get a cardiac bypass or a hip replacement at a fraction of what it would cost them in their home countries. As an added bonus, the medical tourist gets to recuperate in style at a spa or resort as part of the vacation-cum-treatment package.

In order to attract medical tourists, investors in developing countries have built five-star hospitals staffed with expatriate doctors who are either board certified in the United States or are specialists with advanced degrees from the United Kingdom. Increasingly, such hospitals also seek accreditation because they see accreditation as a means of assuring medical tourists that they can get western quality healthcare at third world prices. Most medical tourists have no medical insurance, but insured expatriate employees who staff multinational companies in developing countries also need health care.

Hospitals in developing countries are also pursing these patients, with accredited hospitals entering into agreements with expatriates' health insurers to pay for covered procedures and treatments for the employees and their covered dependents. One West Virginia state legislator has even proposed that state employees be permitted to use accredited hospitals overseas for covered procedures under the state health plan and even be given a cash bonus for any savings that result.

In order to meet the growing demand for hospital accreditation overseas, the Joint Commission on Accreditation of Healthcare Organisations ("JCAHO") launched Joint Commission International ("JCI") to accredit hospitals world-wide. International accreditation standards for JCI were developed by an international task force and form the foundation for a regional or country model, selected with local input, to benchmark the quality of patient care and safety in a particular region or country.

The international accreditation standards focus on core aspects of patient care, including such fundamental requirements as an admissions policy that has processes in place for access to and continuity of care, with appropriate measures in place for the discharge, referral, follow-up and transfer of patients. Such policies protect the medical tourist who has at best provided a medical history consisting of on-line health questionnaires, faxed medical records and perhaps telephone communications with the doctor's office prior to actually arriving at the hospital for treatment.

The fact that accreditation standards require the hospital to identify and evaluate the healthcare needs of the patient before admission is reassuring.After treatment, there is the question of follow-up care because the typical medical tourist goes home within a week or two after the surgical procedure or medical treatment is over. At least an accredited hospital has to have a policy in place that requires the hospital to provide all patients, and therefore all medical tourists, with a complete discharge history and recommended follow-up care that they can take home to their physicians.

If the medical tourist's decision to have a procedure done at a particular hospital is based on the doctor's reputation for performing that procedure, then the fact that the hospital is also accredited assures the patient that the hospital has licensed, educated, trained and experienced medical, nursing and other professional staff to assist that doctor. After all, surgical procedures require a team of healthcare professionals, not just a single doctor.

Medical tourists who have been warned to drink only bottled water in the country they travel to for medical treatment are naturally concerned about infection control in overseas hospitals. They will find that an accredited hospital has instituted policies requiring the use of gloves, masks, soap and disinfectants, has developed infection reduction strategies, and supports programs designed to improve patient care and safety.

Similarly, even though medical tourists often select hospitals because the hospitals are known for the type of procedures the individuals seek, the medical tourists might be better off selecting an accredited hospital because such a hospital has or can arrange to have quality laboratory and radiology services for the medical tourist. An accredited hospital will be capable of monitoring the patient according to established procedures while in surgery or when anesthesia is administered prior to and during the procedure.

Medications given to medical tourists during and after their stay in the hospital may also be safer in accredited hospitals because accreditation standards require that medications be prepared, stored and dispensed according to set norms. Many medical tourists travel with a family member or friend for physical and emotional support during their medical treatment overseas. An accredited hospital will have policies in place to support such a companion by upholding their rights to information about the patient and the medical procedure(s) being provided and by allowing such persons to participate in treatment decisions.

Just as tourists ensure that they get a good hotel when they shop for a tour package, medical tourists can ensure that they get treated at a hospital that is well-maintained, is safe for patients and that has an on-going program to improve the facility. Because medical tourists research data on-line, they can be sure that the accredited hospital they select keeps accurate records, manages data well and is headed by an organisation that is responsible and accountable. Medical tourism is not without its problems, even when accredited overseas hospitals are involved. For example, medical tourists may be advised not to travel immediately after a procedure or to go to a spa or beach resort to convalesce after the procedure.

Even if medical tourists have their procedures done at accredited hospitals, patients may face problems with follow-up care at home. Patients may not have the money to go back for any required followups or check-ups. If the outcome is bad, a medical tourist may have no recourse to the courts of the country where the hospital is located. In fact, healthcare is cheaper in developing countries because there are no medical malpractice insurance costs to the doctor or hospital. On the other hand, as long as healthcare remains cheaper in the developing world, medical tourism will flourish until the west solves the problems of its uninsured and under-insured citizens.

Foreign Patients

Medical tourism is a promising new industry in Asia, offering prospects for hospitals facing saturation in patient growth. It is with a clearer view of the addressable market potential, internal strengths and limitations, as well as the level of external competition, that healthcare providers may best move forward to realise this potential. Healthcare providers may now consider the medical quality of their services, how non-medical services are key to encouraging patient access, and the various marketing options available to them.

A final consideration towards implementing such reforms would be the partnerships that stakeholders may establish. These include partnerships with universities, referring hospitals, agents, the government, accommodation and travel service providers, and even competing hospitals. A sincere commitment to these alliances allows each stakeholder to focus on his own competencies and may even alleviate the level of competition - allowing for better long run revenues throughout the entire sector.

Hospitals that are successfully attracting foreign patients enlarge their geographical footprints with representative offi ces or agencies in other countries. For example, Cromwell Hospital in the UK has represe-ntatives in India and Pakistan, while hospitals in Singapore are also setting up offi ces such as in Indonesia or the Middle-East. These agents help establish and maintain relationships such as with local hospitals, doctors, embassies, sponsor corporations, or insurers. Participating in different events also facilitates such relationships. For instance, trade shows, exhibitions or training seminars allow healthcare providers to share their medical expertise, while longer term physician exchanges may also be organised in alliance with medical universities.

7

Modern Trends in Tourism and Hospitality Services

When the ILO Governing Body created the ILO Industrial Committee for the Hotel, Restaurant and Tourism Sector, which subsequently became the Committee for the Hotel, Catering and Tourism Sector, the sector included:

(a) hotels, boarding houses, motels, tourist camps, holiday centres;

(b) restaurants, bars, cafeterias, snack bars, pubs, night clubs, and other similar establishments;

(c) establishments for the provision of meals and refreshments within the framework of industrial and institutional catering (for hospitals, factory and office canteens, schools, aircraft, ships, etc.);

(d) travel agencies and tourist guides, tourism information offices;

(e) conference and exhibition centres.

Industrial Classification of all Economic Activities (ISIC), the latest edition of which is ISIC Rev. 3. In that classification, the sectors most relevant for the ILO definition of the sector are Hotels and restaurants and Activities of travel agencies and tour operators, Tourist assistance activities. Other organizations concerned with tourism, including governments, intergovernmental organizations and NGOs, often use much broader definitions of the term than that used by the ILO. They subsume under it all services and products consumed by tourists, including transport.

In the ILO denomination of the sector, the part referring to "tourism" only covers travel agencies and tour operators. Hotels and catering, including restaurants, are considered by most organizations to belong to the "tourism characteristic industries" and therefore subsumed under tourism, although in some countries only a small part of their services is for tourists. However, the fact that the ILO definition of the sector thus differs considerably from the concept of tourism used by other organizations does not prevent most concerns about the development of tourism from being shared by those organizations.

One such concern is the sector's potential to provide employment. Nevertheless, the ILO's focus on labour issues is unique as it includes all working and employment conditions in the HCT sector. As an economic concept, tourism is defined in "demand side" terms, as it comprises all services and goods consumed by tourists as well as all investments made to satisfy that consumption. A tourist has been defined by the United Nations as a traveller or visitor. The credibility and international comparability of "tourism statistics" depend heavily on:

(1) a consensus regarding the choice of "tourism characteristic industries", i.e. those industries on which tourism demand has the most important direct impact, and an estimation of the "tourism ratio" of their output; as well as
(2) the methods used to calculate the indirect effects on the output of many other industries.

Statistical presentations differ in whether they include such indirect or induced effects in the measurement of tourism in the economy. Probably the most inclusive choice of industries is the one adopted by the World Travel and Tourism Council (WTTC), a private organization. It takes into account industries whose "tourism ratio" is low but whose products and services represent high value, such as the construction and operation of transport infrastructure.

The demand side nature of tourism is the basis of a methodology for Tourism Satellite Accounts (TSAs) developed by the World Tourism Organization and OECD and adopted by the United Nations Statistical Commission early in 2000. The ILO has been cooperating with those organizations in accordance with the mandate given to it by the Tripartite Meeting on the Effects of New Technologies on Employment and Working Conditions in the Hotel, Catering and Tourism Sector in 1997, with a view to providing a methodology for the production and presentation of tourism-relevant labour statistics to supplement the TSAs.

A proposal has been formulated by the ILO for a tourism labour accounting system (TLAS) within that framework, based on its work on a general labour accounting system. A detailed "employment module" presenting labour-related issues was already attached to the TSA by the OECD, but this module does not provide the necessary framework for linking the different units, variables and classifications used when collecting labour statistics from many different sources. Some early efforts towards TSA presentations have already been made by a number of pioneer OECD countries on the basis of figures from national accounts systems as required in the methodology adopted by the United Nations Statistical Commission in 2000.

The World Travel and Tourism Council (WTTC) has been producing Tourism Satellite Accounts using a simulation method and based on a non-systematic variety of statistical sources. The contribution of tourism activities to national GDPs, direct and indirect, varies by country and region as illustrated by the WTTC's estimates. The Caribbean is the most tourism oriented region in the world. It is estimated that in 2000, tourism employed 3.1 million people either directly or indirectly, thus accounting for 13.4 per cent of total employment.

Direct employment in the tourism characteristic industries alone amounts to 5 per cent of total employment. Visitor expenditures contributed an estimated US$17 billion, or 18.4 per cent, to export revenues. Countries whose international tourism receipts exceed 5 per cent of GDP or 10 per cent of export revenues are considered to be "tourism countries" for the purposes of the World Trade Organization.

Tourism is expanding in almost all countries including the developing countries. In fact, mass tourism involving domestic and regional travel is becoming an important phenomenon in several developing countries of Asia, Latin America, the Middle East and Africa, where the proportion of the population actively participating in domestic and regional tourism is predicted to grow considerably. In particular, regional tourism originating from China is expected to change the Asian tourism industry profoundly within the next one to two decades.

Changing Face of Tourism Industry

Mass tourism in and from the industrialized countries is a product of the late 1960s and early 1970s. Since then a number of interrelated developments in the world economy, such as overall economic growth and various other socio-economic changes, government policies, technological revolution, changes in production processes and new management practices, have converted part of the industry from mass tourism to so-called "new tourism".

The latter connotes the idea of responsible, green, soft, alternative and sustainable tourism, and basically refers to the diversification of the tourism industry and its development in targeted, niche markets.

Competition in the new tourism is increasingly based on diversification, market segmentation and diagonal integration. The identification and exploitation of niche markets has also proven to be a great source of revenue within new tourism, suggesting that further diversification and customization can be expected in the years to come. Market segmentation - as exemplified by ecotourism, cultural tourism, cruise and adventure tourism - is clearly in evidence and is experiencing great success. New niche markets are constantly being identified in an attempt to diversify the industry further. Customization has also begun to play an important role in the industry.

Tourism players are attempting to gain a competitive edge by catering for the individual needs of clients. The tourism product has thus been transformed over time from being completely dominated by mass tourism to an industry that is quite diversified and caters more to the individual needs of its participants. Today, new consumers are influencing the pace and direction of underlying changes in the industry. The "new tourists" are more experienced travellers.

Changes in consumer behaviour and values provide the fundamental driving force for the new tourism. The increased travel experience, flexibility and independent nature of the new tourists are generating demand for better quality, more value for money and greater flexibility in the travel experience. The new consumers also reflect demographic changes - the population is ageing, household size is decreasing and households have greater disposable income. Changing lifestyles of the new tourists are creating demand for more targeted and customized holidays.

A number of lifestyle segments - families, single parent households, "empty nesters" (i.e. couples whose children have left home), double-income couples without children - will become prevalent in tourism, signalling the advent of a much more differentiated approach to tourism marketing. Changing values are also generating demand for more environmentally conscious and nature-oriented holidays. Suppliers will therefore have to pay more attention to the way people think, feel and behave than they have done hitherto. In recent years the niche market has become an important factor in the tourism industry reflecting the need to diversify and customize the industry and ensure the sustainability of the product.

The main niche markets (sports travel, spas and health care, adventure and nature tourism, cultural tourism, theme parks, cruise ships, religious travel and others) hold great potential and are developing rapidly. The growth of the cruise tourism sector is an interesting case in point. Between 1980 and 1999, the cruise industry grew at an average annual rate of 7.9 per cent. The Caribbean is the most important geographic market for the cruise industry, accounting for over half of all cruises taken in 1996. Since 1984, cruise visitor arrivals have increased every year except 1987 and 1989. In addition, between 1996 and 2000, the growth rate for cruise arrivals is expected to far exceed that of stay-over arrivals.

The rapid growth and development of the cruise tourism industry opens key opportunities but also poses a number of threats to their Caribbean destinations. The environmental and economic impacts of cruise tourism are increasingly the subject of discussion. Moreover, given the pace and magnitude of its development, the cruise industry is directly competing with land-based tourism and, as a result, poses a growing threat to hotels and other land-based resorts and businesses in the Caribbean.

Impact of Globalization

The driving forces of globalization impacting upon travel, hospitality and tourism. The air transport industry, which is located mainly in the industrialized regions and in the newly industrialized countries, is a key determinant in the development of tourism. It is expanding twice as fast as the general output of the world economy, with further growth potential expected over the next two decades. In the developing countries, air transport accounts for nearly 80 per cent of international tourist arrivals. In 1998, the industry provided 28 million jobs worldwide, and by 2010 the number of people travelling by air could exceed 2.3 billion each year, with over 31 million jobs provided.

Today, liberalization of air transport largely means market access for private carriers and cabotage rights. The liberalization of air transport, traditionally pursued at the bilateral level, is now being carried to the level of multilateral trade agreements. The recent trend towards the liberalization of air transport notably through the proliferation of open skies agreements, has thus raised the issue of air transport liberalization as a discipline to be debated in the framework of the General Agreement on Trade in Services (GATS).

Multi-bilateral negotiations are already under way on an open skies agreement between the European Union and the United States. If they succeed, 70 per cent of the world's international air traffic will be covered by the agreement. It is expected in that case that the agreement will serve as a model for other international air services agreements. The formation of international alliances is an important development in the field of aviation. Airline alliances have become widespread and are still evolving, with partnership relationships becoming more intertwined and complex.

The major airlines in the Americas and Europe are the most active in securing alliance agreements. The main motivation behind such alliances is the need to minimize costs while maintaining the quality of global services and extending connections throughout the world. Alliances can take various forms including: cooperative arrangements; wide-ranging strategic alliances, most notably the so-called "mega-alliances"; groupings and concentrations at national level, as in the case of the United States; purchase or franchising of small regional companies by major operators to carry their customers to hub airports; and regional civil aviation markets.

Other trends which characterize the changes under way in the context of airline liberalization include:

— partial or full privatization and restructuring of government-owned airlines;
— partial foreign ownership of airlines;
— equity investment in foreign carriers;
— updating of airline alliances by cancelling outdated or non-performing agreements;
— airline consolidations at the national level;
— joint ventures, either between airline companies or between airline companies and equipment manufacturers or independent maintenance companies; and
— outsourcing with no provision of maintenance service.

Liberalization

Recent privatization initiatives have ended the protection of national airlines by governments in a number of developing countries. However, the possibility of the market becoming dominated by a single private company is perceived as a serious risk. In some cases, developing countries that have liberalized their air transport sectors as part of a policy to promote tourism have found themselves dominated by one or two foreign airlines.

Some bankruptcies and closures have taken place in countries where distressed national airlines were not or could not be rescued by governments. In this context, a review of the GATS annex on air transport services is intended to draw international attention to the need to design a system that enables developing countries to compete effectively in the world market for air transport. With regard to the liberalization of air transport as a whole, the trend is increasingly for each State to choose its own pace of change, using bilateral, regional or multilateral mechanisms.

In developed countries there has been a clear tightening of competition policies to prohibit governments from providing subsidies. It is well known that many bilateral agreements have resulted in inefficiency as they were based on market access restrictions, price control and protection of money-losing carriers. Full liberalization of air services as implemented in 1997 in Europe boosted the development of "low-cost" services and their integration in the European aviation scene.

Although these services still account for a rather small share of the passenger market, their marketing impact is increasingly being felt throughout the industry. It is estimated that around 25 per cent of passengers on United States domestic services use "low-cost" airlines, as compared to approximately 5 per cent in Europe. Another result of liberalization is that new route opportunities have opened up, stimulating new demands without tampering with major carriers' shares and therefore creating new opportunities for fare reductions. Some major European flag carriers have already created their own "low-cost" airline subsidiaries. The low-cost market as it stands has considerable growth potential.

Europe's low-cost airlines are finding plenty of untapped markets. Both Ryanair and easyJet have placed orders for significant numbers of additional aircraft to almost double their capacity over the next four years to meet this new demand. The challenge for low-cost carriers is to strike the right balance between maintaining low costs, low prices and high aircraft utilization and establishing a presence at a certain minimum number of airports. A further development of the concept of the low-cost airline sector has been the advent of "seat-only" sales on charter airline flights, rather than as part of a package holiday. This has resulted, for example, in the formation of the European Leisure Group (ELG), an alliance of European charter and scheduled airlines.

The General Agreement on Trade in Services (GATS) became part of the "New World Trade Order" under the aegis of the World Trade Organization as established by the Uruguay Round in 1994. The functioning of GATS is based on the interplay of fundamental standards in commercial law, procedural regulations for their implementation and specific commitments in which member States document sector-specific limitations or concessions. GATS has universal coverage and includes a comprehensive definition of trade in services comprising four "modes of supply". They are: cross-border movement of services; movement of consumers; commercial presence; and the presence of natural persons, and to these modes the three principles of liberalization enshrined in GATS.

GATS thus provides a framework for the progressive liberalization of trade in services through commitments made by the World Trade Organization member countries concerning the abovementioned principles and their applications to one or more modes of supply. Future negotiations under GATS will provide an opportunity for developing countries to address trade barriers to their services. The tourism sector had already undergone various forms of liberalization before the Uruguay Round. It is also considered to be one of the service sectors most liberalized through sector-specific commitments made by signatory States.

The number of commitments by the World Trade Organization members made so far in tourism under the GATS is rated as the highest of all sectors. Of 127 GATS signatory States, only eight have not made commitments in tourism and travel-related services. In the hotels and restaurants subsector, which offers the greatest potential for far-reaching liberalization within tourism, it is mostly low and lower-middle- income economies in Africa and Latin America that have liberalized market access for foreign investors in the "commercial presence" mode: 64 per cent of all signatory States belonging to the group of LIEs and 75 per cent of LMIEs, but only about half of the group of high-income economies (HIEs) have "no restrictions" to that mode.

On the other hand, it is not surprising that "presence of natural persons" is the least liberalized mode of supply: in 117 of the 119 countries signing commitments in travel and tourism-related services, there are restrictions on the movement of hotel staff. Sixty-eight countries refer to their non-sector-specific commitments which mostly offer only temporary stay for business visitors, intra-corporate transferees and professionals. Only an ancillary service to tourism (airline computer reservation services), is included in an annex on air transport services.

Possible impact of GATS on air traffic services, tourism services production, free movement of people, market access and labour markets. Most air traffic services are not covered by the Agreement's disciplines. The main organizations responsible for air transport are now examining ways in which the GATS could contribute to future air transport liberalization. The GATS provides a framework for negotiating temporary entry of service personnel into the territory of other parties. The movement of natural persons is a necessary condition for developing countries' participation in the world market for services.

Developing countries have given priority to making commitments under the GATS relating to the movement of natural persons, partly taking into account their competitive labour cost advantage. The World Tourism Organization, for example, is developing a range of quality standards to be applied at tourism destinations. Recognition of diplomas and professional qualifications is another precondition for the movement of natural persons abroad. This calls for the harmonization of diplomas and mutual recognition agreements between countries.

Several countries have notified mutual recognition agreements under GATS Article VII.4. It is hoped that the GATS will increase the recognition of qualifications across borders. Considerations within the framework of the GATS may also become relevant for the migration to the richer countries of persons who overstay their tourism visas and take up work. Many of them work in hotels or restaurants where in some countries they form a significant proportion of the labour force. The increased scale and diversity of global communications systems and their declining costs, which are rapidly narrowing telecommunications gaps, have helped to make international migration easier.

With regard to the movement of consumers, tourism is an example of the services sector where consumption abroad is particularly relevant. Nevertheless, the movement of tourists is in some instances constrained by the difficulties associated with the delivery of visas, hard currency regulations and insufficient availability or inadequacy of air transport services to and from tourist-receiving countries.

Specific commitments made under the GATS to encourage greater participation by developing countries in world services trade relate to three main areas:

— first, the strengthening of the domestic services capabilities of developing countries through access to technology on a commercial basis, which is normally achieved through the employment and training of local personnel in foreign-owned hotels;

— secondly, improving the access of developing countries to distribution channels and information networks.

In the tourism sector, this means access to computerized information and reservation networks managed and owned by entities in the industrialized countries; thirdly, the liberalization of market access in sectors and modes of supply of export interest to them. According to GATS Article XIX, developing countries can attach additional conditions to such access aimed at achieving the development objectives of Article IV, namely the strengthening of their domestic services capacity and improvement of their access to distribution channels and information networks.

The liberalization of services is likely to have both positive and negative impacts on the labour force in relation to wages and employment. Increased competition by better equipped hotel and restaurant companies from abroad may in the short term lead to job losses in local enterprises. However, foreign firms will employ local people, increasing local employment and contributing to a higher standard of living. The world economy is currently witnessing two distinct trends - globalization and regionalization - and within this context States as well as companies are pursuing a variety of different strategies in order to become more competitive.

Shifting patterns of production and consumption across the world are also reflected in the rise of new international tourism destinations, particularly in the East Asia and Pacific region. This has given rise to increasing regional, intra-regional and interregional competition and to new challenges in terms of investment needs and human resources development, especially with regard to training and labour mobility. The impact of trade blocs on the hotel, tourism and catering sector can be gauged by the strategies adopted to create an environment conducive to tourism development.

The European Union has launched a wide range of initiatives and activities through a variety of programmes in such broad areas as sustainable development, dissemination of information, training and enterprise promotion. The main thrust of social policy in the European Union is the improvement of labour market conditions with a special focus on those excluded from the labour market and the unemployed. European Union labour laws and social policy are having a positive impact on the tourism sector. Of importance here is the Maastricht Social Protocol which has benefited seasonal and part-time workers and small businesses.

Other policies that have proved beneficial to the development of tourism include the free movement of workers across Europe, harmonization of qualifications and tax incentives for education and training. The North American Free Trade Agreement (NAFTA) benefits the travel and tourism industry in many ways. It promotes demand for direct air and charter/tour bus travel in the region, guarantees that tourism companies will receive national treatment in all three countries and maintains high quality of tourism services by encouraging the expansion of telecommunications links between the United States and Mexico.

MERCOSUR is, in economic terms, the world's fourth largest trade bloc, covering a population of 205 million people. Economic integration, through the practice of free trade with no tariff or pre-tariff restrictions between the member States of the bloc, has led to increasing cross-border flows of labour, goods and investment. MERCOSUR's concern is to tackle labour relations, employment and social security issues and the short-term negative effects of integration on labour in the member States.

Tourism development is a priority on the agenda of the Association of South-East Asian Nations (ASEAN). Its development strategy incorporates:

— promotion of sustainable tourism development;
— preservation of cultural and environmental resources;
— provision of transportation and other infrastructure;
— simplification of immigration procedures; and
— human resources development.

A plan of action on ASEAN cooperation in tourism shows the emphasis that is being placed on investment in human resources development, with a special focus on tourism education and training with a view to upgrading the skills needed to meet the demand for improved service quality and professionalism in the tourism and travel industry and thereby sustain ASEAN's overall competitive advantage. Cooperation in tourism education and training is being intensified through the sharing of resources, skills and training facilities provided by tourism training institutions through technical assistance and experts.

Computerised Reservation System (CRSs)

Computerized reservation systems (CRSs) have been developed by large air carriers since the 1970s to process flight reservations, but have evolved and expanded over time to provide other air transport-related services. Each airline has its own CRS and they are interconnected through global distribution systems (GDSs). A huge number of Internet on-line reservation systems act as a kind of virtual agent, most of them having direct links to one or several CRS/GDS.

The CRS and GDS systems have become the main distribution and marketing tool in the international tourism trade and have greatly enhanced the efficiency of travel agents' business operations. They cater to the needs of different market segments, including management of air and land transport services, the hospitality sector and entertainment services, as well as other ancillary services which make commercial transactions and risk coverage feasible. As a result, they have become increasingly important and are extensively used by all suppliers of tourism services.

There is some concern that developing countries' suppliers may well be left out because GDSs can present major barriers to entry owing to their unfavourable access conditions. A number of African and south Asian countries are poorly represented in these systems because of structural handicaps such as the low level of tourism development in general and their underdeveloped hospitality sector. The poor representation of small service suppliers in GDSs adversely affects the dissemination of information on their tourism products, thereby holding back their sale and marketing of tourism services. This leaves such suppliers, especially SMEs, at a competitive disadvantage compared with those who are represented in the major GDSs.

GDSs in many developing countries, particularly in Africa, are established in the form of joint ventures with local partners - for example, the national carrier but operate within a de facto monopoly. This leads to excessive user fees and hinders their potential for developing tourism. Travel agents in developing countries are at a disadvantage with regard to the use of modern technology compared with their counterparts in developed countries because of poor information network infrastructure and the shortage of professionals to manage, operate and maintain the system. Human resources assume importance in the operation of GDSs and other electronic media, and this calls for staff training in mastering the systems and their application to marketing, through specific training programmes provided by both the public and private sectors.

Internet for Marketing

Deregulation, globalization and radical shifts in leisure and tourism behaviour on the demand side have driven the tourism industry towards information-oriented activities, as seen in the introduction of IT systems in a wide range of spheres in the tourism and leisure sector. The increasing use of the Internet for destination marketing, direct sales and bookings has given rise to electronic tourism markets and at present tourism is among the most important application domains in the World Wide Web.

The development of websites has made possible the direct delivery of comprehensive travel information about tourism suppliers to potential travellers. Text-based websites with photos and graphics linked to websites of tourism suppliers at the destination is another innovative approach to marketing. Developing an effective travel website has now assumed importance for obvious reasons. International tourists are increasingly using the travel websites on the Internet that were launched by most international companies in the late 1990s.

On-line sales in Europe, for example, represented only 0. 1 per cent of the European travel market, and in 1999 only 1 per cent of the world's airline tickets, hotel and other bookings were purchased over the Internet, although the proportion of airline and other ticket sales through the Internet is expected to grow sharply over the next three to four years. The Internet helps to make travel products globally accessible at much lower cost—without transaction costs and the costs of intermediaries—and has comparatively low entrance barriers with regard to financial resources and human know-how.

For many suppliers, tourism marketing efforts are increasingly focusing on Internet users. A new business environment and new ways of doing business have sprung up as a result of the accessibility and relatively low cost of the Internet which is bringing businesses and consumers, buyers and suppliers on-line. Internet and Internet protocol technology is the driving force behind the growth of e-business. The Internet will have repercussions on business in the areas of e-commerce, e-working and e-procurement.

A recent global survey of more than 500 business leaders lends support to the idea that e-business will be a key factor in competitive advantage in the future. In the sphere of air travel, attempts are frequently made to bypass traditional travel agencies by direct booking via the Internet or corporate implant offices. Customer demands are becoming more technology driven, such as the demand for professional travel and billing management in place of mere ticket issuing. Advances in technology in the hotels and tourism industry, as exemplified by readily available information to guests and employees, faster service delivery, shorter cycle times and more dynamic markets, also require prompt action from service suppliers if marketing opportunities are not to be lost.

Strategies of growth and concentration through mergers and acquisitions are becoming increasingly important from the mediators' perspective as a response to cost and performance pressures in international business travel. In addition, traditional kick-back contracts are increasingly being replaced with new performance-oriented arrangements. All aspects of business are being reshaped by the Internet and its related technologies, intranets and extranets. Hospitality enterprises will need to focus on providing customers with real-time access to rates and product information.

The Internet also provides hotels and restaurants with opportunities to redesign the way in which they interface with employees and suppliers. The high growth in global commerce accompanied by the emergence of electronic commerce driven mainly by the Internet has raised concerns about the need to regulate cyberspace by setting standards to regulate the use of the Internet for all aspects of travel and other fast-growing categories of electronic commerce. The primacy of the rules of the network economy will significantly lower transaction and communication costs, thus allowing more flexible pricing.

The regulation of the Internet through the enactment and implementation of cyber-laws and privacy standards will most probably be perceived as an encouraging initiative which will guarantee safety and security in Internet business transactions, especially in shopping and travel accommodation bookings, where the Internet is most frequently used. Hoteliers and restaurateurs have already expressed marked interest in these technologies as means of exploiting the advantages which can be derived from, for example, increased guest loyalty and market share. By using data warehousing and data mining as well as the Internet, the hotel industry can provide higher levels of personalized services and value.

The Internet is turning out to be the most sought after amenity in hotel rooms, providing communications access, information, entertainment and education. It enables more self-service oriented transactions to take place, especially in the area of reservations booking. Information technology impacts on all aspects of the hotel organization value chain and transcends all departmental and geographical boundaries. Decisions on technology-related issues need to be made at top management levels of companies, and this means that qualified information technology personnel are needed at those levels.

Another key issue is the source of investment capital required to fund information technology initiatives. Lack of capital seriously hinders the implementation of information technology and competition for fund sourcing. The Internet has brought about some very significant technological changes that enhance its capabilities and viability and its potential to drive electronic commerce. Besides introducing new and innovative business models in both the business-to-business and business-to-consumer markets, the Internet has shortened the value chain and put pressure on all players, especially intermediaries, by giving rise to the so-called "disintermediation" process, that is, the elimination of intermediary organizations such as travel agencies and global distribution systems (GDSs).

These intermediary organizations are gradually being replaced by new emerging intermediaries. On-line service and ticketless travel have significantly reduced the need for travel intermediaries, as a result of which travel agents in the United States, for example, have seen a reduction in commissions paid to them by airlines. The use of information technology in the tourism industry is determined by such factors as the scale and complexity of tourism demand and the degree of expansion and sophistication of new tourism products. Tourism plays an important role in a significant number of developing countries, many of which enjoy a competitive advantage.

There are more opportunities in the field of e-commerce than in any other existing technology which developing countries can exploit to their advantage in order to improve the marketing of their tourism products. However, in the developing countries, tourism development is constrained by a number of factors which have been summarized by UNCTAD. Computer software represents one of the largest segments of services delivered through the cross-border mode of supply, with a growing number of developing countries using the Internet both to market and to deliver these services.

In Indian software industry, electronic commerce facilitates access to new markets, as well as being cost saving and time saving. However, its effectiveness depends to a large extent on the establishment of a sound telecommunications infrastructure; in most low-income countries, that infrastructure is inadequate. A wide range of factors prevent the great majority of developing countries from accessing foreign markets through the Internet. Those factors include monopoly pricing for long-distance telephony, uncertainty about the regulatory environment, lack of human resources, lack of awareness among developing country companies of the relevance of the digital economy, and the high cost of setting up, upgrading and redesigning a significant e-commerce site.

The status of the developing countries' readiness for e-commerce is an important issue. Providers of tourism services must also have the capacity to invest in or have access to the physical infrastructure for logistics services and information technologies. The major obstacle to increased use of e-commerce in developing countries is the lack of pervasive low-cost telecommunications, broadcasting, Internet services and associated infrastructures, especially in rural areas.

At the same time there is a need to involve more hotel and tourism enterprises from developing countries in the actual use of information technologies and information networks. If African businesses fare better than consumers in terms of accessing e-commerce, they nevertheless face the same infrastructure problems, although progress has been made in the development of e-commerce activities. The shortage of IT specialists on the market, especially in the developing countries, is a serious impediment, given the rapid growth in Internet use. The demand for IT skills is increasing and the need for retraining of existing employees in both the public and private sectors in hotels, tourism and catering is clearly felt.

One solution would be for developing countries to take advantage of forthcoming GATS negotiations to ensure access for their suppliers to the most important generating markets, and they could make use of certain mechanisms provided for in the GATS which might enhance the contribution of trade in services to development. They could also seek commitments with respect to the training of personnel and access to the distribution channels which are essential to tourism exports, as provided for in Articles IV and XIX of the Agreement.

Since the mid-1990s, multinational hotel companies entering foreign markets have devised a wide range of management strategies or methods in response to competitive challenge such as the rapid development of information technology, sophisticated demands from well-informed and knowledgeable travellers and the rise of electronic business-to-business market-places and to seize the opportunities opened up by the network economy.

Within each company, core competencies are being developed and renewed through rapid information technology development, international expansion and market cooperation, relationship management, development of customer-oriented products and services, structural re-engineering, new marketing initiatives and campaigns, and quality control.

Within the context of international expansion and market cooperation, companies have had recourse to a number of competitive methods which merit attention. The growing number of alliances is changing industry structures and the level of competition has shifted from the individual company level to alliance groups level. The last five years have witnessed nine major mergers and acquisition transactions in the international hotel market-place.

There are other goals and objectives which strategic alliances can fulfil in order to assist multinational hotel firms in strengthening their market positions, improving partnership relations and supplying diversified products and quality services to their customers. These goals and objectives include:

— acquisition of new information and communication technology;
— distribution of products and cross-marketing between food-service providers and hotels;
— distribution and cross-promotion of bank credit cards and financial services between banks and hotels;
— consolidation of transportation and hotel services;
— co-promotion of hotels and films and media.

Some well established international companies provide their expertise by leasing out management teams to run local firms. The contracting company benefits from the knowledge and experience of the international company and from its reputation for quality and good service. With the evolution of the hotel industry towards a more consumer-oriented service, it is the brand rather than the company which assumes importance.

In the United Kingdom hotel industry, for example, branding has become very topical and operators are increasingly recognizing the value of brands in delivering profits. The brand is thus turning out to be a fundamental element in defining the market, so much so that it is the name of the brand under which a hotel trades that carries weight, rather than its ownership and management structure.

Vertical integration is another strategy that plays a dominant role in particular segments of the tourism industry. For a long time, tour operators have been establishing backward and forward linkages in the areas of service production. Their backward integration includes hotels and charter airlines. These operators also control all stages of distribution via far-reaching forward integration of retail distributors and travel agencies, marketing and package tours sales. This is also true of airlines which extend their level of integration far into the field of primary tourism and travel-related services via their charter airlines which have interests in tour operators, retailers and travel agencies. By contrast, hotels and hotel chains hardly pursue vertical integration strategies at all.

An expansionist strategy of diagonal integration is geared to the provision of the broadest possible array of tourism-related service markets by a company, with a view to cutting costs, making the most of synergies between individual markets and achieving systems gains. This includes, for example, the joint use of computerized reservation systems by carriers and travel agencies under the umbrella of a holding company or cooperation between credit card suppliers and tour operators or travel agencies offering the special insurance services of a holding partner.

In the accommodation industry, an impressive amount of consolidation took place in the 1980s, bringing more and more hotel brands under fewer and larger corporate umbrellas. Consolidation offers certain advantages such as cost reduction in the areas of reservation systems, loyalty programmes and staff training and other fixed costs associated with hotel management. One pertinent issue frequently referred to by the developing countries is the need to reduce the risk of "leakage" of foreign exchange earnings.

The developing countries in particular are usually unable to make the most of the economic and development potential of tourism, firstly, because of the high import content of construction materials and equipment and consumable goods needed to cater to the needs of international tourism and, secondly, because of the repatriation of income and profits earned by expatriates.

The latter is in fact a major obstacle to tourism development. Nevertheless, a number of advantages can be derived from international companies in terms of capital investment and know-how and technology, management and marketing expertise, training and consultancy. This enables countries lacking the skills base and expertise needed at all professional levels to run, develop and operate tourist establishments for an international clientele to benefit from the transfer of expertise and technology.

In a globalized economy, skills become an important determinant in competitiveness. The changing composition of the workforce and work patterns resulting from globalization processes in the industry have brought about new challenges in human resources development. Training policies in the hotel, tourism and catering sector will need to be reviewed in a new climate of empowerment and retention of staff. This is particularly the case in many parts of the world where there is an acute shortage of qualified staff to fill positions created by an expanding industry.

An internationally focused human resources policy calls for a change in personnel policies and strategies which implies, among other things, management commitment to transnational strategies, the development of IT skills and procedures to support transnational operations in a number of ways such as knowledge and information transfer, and an awareness of the different national policies on health and safety, occupational standards, dismissal, discrimination and workers' rights.

Role of ICTs

Information and communications technology (ICT) systems which integrate the power of the Internet, customer relationship management and supply chain management in a seamless, one-source destination site, allow a variety of operations - product selection, ordering, fulfilment, tracking, payment and reporting - to be performed with one easy-to-use tool. By cutting out one or more layers of the purchasing structure, these systems yield cost savings by putting the buyer in some instances into direct contact with the producer. They also have employment implications, as intermediaries find that their share of the market is shrinking, with inevitable reductions in labour requirements upstream of the HCT sector.

Technology which facilitates on-line hotel, restaurant and theatre reservations or travel arrangements will have an impact in terms of staff reductions on the front-desk hotel staff who used to perform those functions. This technology also calls for a different range of skills from employees. Although systems designers, aware of the rapid turnover among front-desk staff, are working on products that are easier to operate and thus reduce training time for new recruits, the technology is changing so fast that knowledge becomes obsolete ever more quickly. Training will therefore become a continuous need and the remaining jobs will require greater skills.

Many hotels are examining the possibility of installing personal computers in their guest rooms, and some have indeed already done so. This allows customers to use hotel rooms as their offices. Increasing numbers of business guests are also travelling with their own portable computers Hyatt International Hotels are an example of how new job profiles may be created as a result of this technology. The group has introduced "technology concierges" in their deluxe properties worldwide.

These specialist employees, known within the group as "compcierges", are trained to help guests to set up their mobile communications equipment, to explain how to use the in-room technology, hook up laptop computers, provide support in accessing e-mail or the Internet, and so on. They may also help to locate local retailers that service computers and stock software. While technological expertise is essential, the emphasis is on service; all the team members come from a hospitality background and have in addition received the training needed to become electronic troubleshooters.

ICT equipment installed in hotels also requires maintenance and planning departments, making this a new field with job creation potential, although such work may largely be subcontracted to outside operators. Swissôtel has established an ICT department employing ten people, which is now an independent, profitable element of the company. The Carlson Hospitality Group also has a knowledge technologies division, which was created to ensure the smooth operation of the reservation and customer information systems installed in the group's 600 hotels throughout the world.

The new technology is also being used by a number of companies as a means of raising skills levels. Domino's Pizza has developed interactive, learner-centred programmes to guide young employees through the steps involved in making a pizza. Computer-based coaches will soon be available to guide employees through all stages of customer relations. Companies will invest in these new techniques to fulfil their training needs.

Hotel managements are studying technologies which will reduce the attention which guests require from hotel staff. These include: electronic key cards which will open doors and act as credit cards for all on-site purchases; management systems which record the time guests are likely to check out, so that room service may be programmed more efficiently; and cleaning staff equipped with hand-held computers, linked to the hotel's property management system (PMS), so that information can be centralized and constantly updated in real time.

The Canadian Regional Office of the Hotel Employees and Restaurant Employees International Union (HEREIU) has expressed concern that such systems will allow hotel companies to computerize almost all everyday front-office operations. Where customers can make their own reservations via the Internet, they could replace switchboard operators altogether. HEREIU further maintains that new in-room technologies such as video check-out systems will replace front-line workers, while electronic keys will be able to tell the PMS exactly how long each employee has spent cleaning a room, and may thus tend to promote an aggressive productivity policy.

The International Union of Food, Agricultural, Hotel, Restaurant, Catering, Tobacco and Allied Workers' Associations (IUF) notes that placing the emphasis on time-saving and labour-saving technologies also means that the pace of work is faster, and argues that in reality, "labour-saving" and "time-saving" are inclined to mean reductions in the numbers of workers. In the IUF's view, the ultimate consequence of time-and-attendance computer software, which provides information on guest arrivals and departures so that workers can be dispatched to their duties immediately, is the dehumanization of work.

New technologies will also result in structural changes in restaurant kitchens. Use of the "sous-vide" technique, where food that has been totally or partially pre-prepared or pre-cooked is supplied directly to the restaurant, means that a large number of cooking operations can now be outsourced to independent suppliers or to centralized, chain-based kitchens New methods of food preservation, such as freezing, drying, irradiation, and vacuum and modified-atmosphere packing, enhance the shelf life of products and further reduce last minute operations. On the other hand, new types of equipment have given the baking process in restaurant kitchens a new lease of life.

Suppliers of pre-prepared dough cooperate with the manufacturers of specialized ovens so that restaurant staff are required to do nothing more than place the dough in the ovens, activate the appropriate computer programme and remove the bread when it is ready. But the tendency of these innovations is to transform restaurant kitchens into assembly lines, with fewer staff members, since both the simple repetitive tasks, such as vegetable preparation, and the more complex, last minute operations, will be outsourced. Both the HEREIU and the IUF argue that "regenerated pre-processed foods" require fewer skills of kitchen staff and result in the loss of many kinds of food preparation and cooking jobs in the industry.

The IUF also points to a devaluation in wages as a result of the deskilling of the remaining jobs. These arguments are difficult to refute, since most of these technologies provide savings in terms of staffing levels. On the other hand, the technologies could open up crucial empowerment possibilities, freeing staff to deal more attentively with customers, thus enhancing the profile of the establishment. Access to on-line booking via the Internet is causing traditional travel agents considerable problems. It will soon be possible to reserve travel tickets using new mobile phone technology, without the need for a computer.

A recent survey carried out by the International Air Transport Association (IATA) revealed that some 37 per cent of travellers worldwide had used electronic tickets, while in the United States, 50 per cent of travellers expected to use such tickets by the end of 2000. Some travel agents are responding to this situation by adopting a more entrepreneurial attitude, charging customers a fee instead of the traditional commission earned on a ticket price. However, while agents may retain business contracts, they are likely to lose individual customer business for simple trips, and this drop in trade will have an impact on employment levels in the branch. Other agencies see the future in strengthening their role as consultants capable of planning complicated trips involving numerous and varied travel means and stop-offs.

However, while the human element will not disappear, it will probably diminish with the spread of 24-hour "warehouse" travel agents which allow customers to call and make their bookings at any time. According to a 1996 survey by the European Foundation for the Improvement of Living and Working Conditions covering 15 European Union countries, working conditions within the industry included a number of potentially problematic areas, such as irregular working hours, frequent work on Sundays, wages without a fixed basic element in 25 per cent of cases, widespread absence of overtime payments and wage levels generally 20 per cent below the European Union average.

In New Orleans in the United States, the Hospitality, Hotels and Restaurant Organizing Council (HOTROC) has stated that an average hotel housekeeper earns US$5.48 an hour, which places most hotel workers and their families 20 per cent below the federal poverty level. In this connection it should be noted that hotel workers in New Orleans are the only non-unionized hospitality workers in a major United States tourist and convention destination. In Canada, average weekly earnings increased by 5 per cent in the accommodation sector between 1998 and 1999, but food and beverage earnings lag far behind, having risen by only 1.9 per cent, in line with inflation.

The average weekly wage in Canada in accommodation is Can$309.14, and in food and beverage

Can$221.30. These wages should be viewed against the national average wage of Can$582.85 a week. Basic wages reflect competitive labour markets, collective agreements and national laws. Variable pay is emerging as a way to reward employees whose performance enhances the success of an establishment. As a strategy, this idea is not yet common in the sector, but it is beginning to take hold.

In the United States, Rodeway Inn International, at Orlando, and Motel Properties, Inc. have both developed successful techniques to reward employees above their basic salaries, based on a monthly assessment scheme. Turnover figures vary from region to region within countries, but the overall picture is alarming. In the United States, according to a 1998 study, annual turnover in 1997 was running at 51.7 per cent for line-level employees, 11.9 per cent for supervisory levels, and 13.5 per cent for property managers. In Asia, rates of around 30 per cent annually are quoted, rising to more than 50 per cent in Hong Kong, China.

In the United Kingdom, a study carried out by the Institute of Personnel and Development in 1997 found a national turnover rate in the sector of 42 per cent, second only to the retail trade, with a rate of 43.5 per cent and far in advance of construction, where the rate was 25 per cent. In the fast food sector, in both Europe and the United States, turnover rates as high as 300 per cent are reported. It should be noted, however, that turnover figures do not separate out non-standard, part-time jobs from full-time posts.

Many employees, such as college students, are not interested in permanent positions. An American Hotel Foundation report puts the cost of replacement of hourly employees at between US$3,000 and US$10,000, while the average figure for restaurant employees is similar, at US$5,000. Many companies equate the cost of losing a trained manager with roughly one year's salary, allowing for the time it takes for the replacement to become fully operational.

In the United Kingdom, the 1997 report by the Institute of Personnel and Development estimated the cost of replacing a worker in the hotel and leisure industry at £1,922, and concluded that an average of ten weeks was required for training. Recent negotiations within the European Union in the context of the employer-driven search for greater flexibility at work raise the prospect of improved conditions for part-time and fixed-term contract workers.

The European Trade Union Confederation (ETUC) has made clear its position that if employers require more flexibility, then workers must have better protection. The Union of Industrial and Employers' Confederations of Europe (UNICE), which represents private-sector employers, has said that employers are prepared to discuss discrimination against agency workers, provided that the unions recognize that temporary work is an integral part of a functioning market.

The UNICE has also called for an easing of restrictions to allow shorter contracts and greater flexibility in their renewal. The ETUC has observed that temporary agency work is increasing all over the European Union. It doubled between 1996 and 1998 in Spain, while in France and Germany it increased by 30 per cent in three years. Employers' representatives generally consider that turnover in the industry should be attributed to the essentially transient nature of part of the workforce, namely students, young mothers and young people as a whole, as well as to the general difficulty in retaining staff. Employees, on the other hand, frequently cite low pay as a reason for changing employment, although lack of a career structure and benefits would appear to be of even greater importance.

In the United States, for example, even if hotels and restaurants pay US$12.00 an hour, they are in competition with such jobs as bank tellers, and restaurant work retains the stigma of being physical work. Job stability, career prospects and reasonable hours of work are all part of the equation. As long as other jobs offer equal levels of pay, but more advantageous working and employment conditions, the problem of turnover will persist in the hotel and restaurant sector, unless the industry can create equivalent conditions or compensate in other ways. The transparency provided by the Internet will only serve to highlight these factors as they become more widely known.

In France, Dégriftours, a travel agency that is 100 per cent electronically operated, has applied the 35-hour legislation in France since 1 June 2000. Teams have been increased by 10 per cent to compensate, while the working day has been reduced to 6.8 hours, with seven hours paid. The agency is open from 8 a.m. to 7 p.m., seven days a week, and operates flexibly. This system has been favourably received by staff, who can, for example, choose to work on Sundays and take Wednesdays off in order to care for children.

There is also a rotation of weekend work to ensure a fair distribution of the less social working hours. The tour operator Nouvelles Frontières has reached a different agreement after nine months of negotiation. The company has signed an agreement to increase its staff by 8 per cent with the help of state subsidies. Employees will be able to organize their working time according to one of three formulas, namely a four-day week without reduction in pay, a four-and-a-half-day week, or a five-day, 40-hour week yielding 28 extra leave days.

The employees must decide on one of the formulas for a period of one year, planned in advance with their supervisors in the services and agencies. The French fast food sector signed an agreement on 15 April 1999 effectively reducing the working week to 35 hours as of 1 November 1999. This could create between 2,000 and 3,000 new jobs in a sector that employs 80,000 people in France. A national agreement signed on 1 April 1999 also reduced the working week to 35 hours for amusement park employees, with no loss of pay.

Moreover, the 35-hour week is being implemented by some employers in the French institutional catering market. In the United Kingdom, the British Hospitality Association (BHA) claims that the new European Union Working Time Directive restricts working hours although there is no evidence that staff want them restricted. The BHA argues that the 11-hour obligatory break between shifts may cause problems for hotels with receptionists who like to see guests in at night and out in the morning, and for kitchen and restaurant staff serving dinner and breakfast.

A number of negotiated workload reductions have emerged recently in Europe and North America. In the institutional catering sector of the Netherlands, a recently negotiated national collective agreement provides for a 10 per cent annual reduction in workloads based on evaluations at the workplace. Procedures are to be established for handling workload-related grievances, and temporary contracts must now state the actual number of hours worked. The possibility of early retirement at 61 years with 80 per cent pay is included in the agreement.

While the chances of contracting or communicating HIV are minimal in the industry, training is needed to assuage personnel fears and make staff aware of the risks that do exist. In terms of employment, the disease may have an impact on three major areas of a business: productivity, employee benefits and morale. The establishment of an HIV policy within an enterprise is therefore a necessity, irrespective of the level of HIV infection in individual countries. In respect of workers who become infected, a number of good practices have come to the fore over recent years.

For example, if a worker is HIV-infected, employers should: accept a less than ideal level of performance, as long as minimum standards are met; modify the employee's job description or reassign the employee to a different job; allow more time off for health appointments; allow more sick leave or absenteeism (with or without pay); arrange a more flexible work schedule, or provide for the employee to switch to part-time work, or allow the employee to work from home.

As a means of lowering costs, a growing management trend has been to subcontract various services in the industry, such as food and beverages, housekeeping, laundry services, security and valeting. Hotels are increasingly grouping together to employ a common Internet reservation system provider, resulting in a reduction in jobs in the hotels concerned. Hotels are also leasing out their restaurants, particularly in the food and beverage market segment. This implies a severe drop in union membership if the employees of the outsourced companies are non-union members.

The New York-New York Casino in Las Vegas in the United States has outsourced virtually all its food and beverage operations to the Ark Restaurants Corporation. The nature of many jobs in the tourism industry creates an atypical employment relationship and special working conditions, such as flexible working time and temporary or part-time work. In addition, there is a general demand by enterprises for greater flexibility in working relations, so as to increase productivity in the now only a "dot-com away".

The Swiss trade journal, "Expresso", defines casual workers as those who are employed on an occasional and irregular basis in connection with specific short-term requirements. In Switzerland, the casual worker has the same legal rights as a full- or part-time worker, and the only difference lies in the fact that holidays may be paid in the form of a 10.65 per cent supplement to the hourly wage for regimes allowing five weeks' annual holiday, or an 8.33 per cent supplement for regimes of four weeks' annual holiday. A similar system prevails in France.

A hotel in London has sought to solve the problem of irregular workload peaks by employing university students on a part-time basis for a fixed number of hours annually, in this instance 500 hours, which can be used as required, with students able to exchange hours among themselves according to their individual availability.

According to the IUF, the need for labour flexibility has always given rise to problems in respect of maintenance of permanent staffing levels in the hospitality industry, and there is a very high proportion of part-time and casual work compared to other industries.

In Austria, there is a 26 per cent seasonal variation in employment in the sector; in Spain the figure is 47 per cent; in Italy it is more than 50 per cent, while in Denmark the number of employees in the sector doubles during the summer season. Part-time work has also been growing faster than full-time employment in the service sector in Australia, where its incidence is relatively high by international standards, particularly among women.

Although part-time labour has been used frequently in the Netherlands, employers have recently sought to retain more full-time personnel: the figures show a reduction of temporary and seasonal employees from 82,100 in 1995 to 67,100 in 1997, and a corresponding increase in permanent full-time contracts from 132,500 to 160,300. In the rest of Europe, the incidence of part-time employment is increasing.

In Italy, part-time contracts in restaurants have increased by 80 per cent over the same two-year period and by almost 30 per cent in hotels. The 1995 Joint ECF-IUF Declaration on Flexibility of Labour and Organization of Working Time, Part-time Work and the Creation of Jobs, while stating that the creation of full-time jobs is a priority, lists a number of advantages which part-time work may present for both employers and workers. Such employment may correspond to the needs of certain groups of workers - students, parents wishing to accommodate family responsibilities, workers in need of time for training or a flexible transition to retirement through reduced working time. It may also provide a means of reintegration into the labour market for the long-term unemployed.

On the other hand, there is the risk that such employment may lead to the creation of a kind of secondary labour market, lacking the same levels of social security cover as a result of minimum hourly thresholds for access to entitlements including training, proportionately lower pay, and the inability of these employees to participate in the collective bargaining process. Moreover, regulatory attempts by governments to create employment by reducing the charges payable on part-time labour can encourage over-reliance on such labour, to the detriment of full-time jobs.

In Australia, research in 1996 showed that casual workers accounted for over 50 per cent of employees in the industry. The unions responded by advocating the replacement of casual jobs with permanent, part-time posts, thus seeking an improvement in, rather than the elimination of, part-time work.

The rates of pay received by casual employees remained higher than those paid to permanent part-time workers, but did not include benefits such as paid holidays. Some employees enjoyed the very wide degree of flexibility offered by casual employment, while for employers it presented the advantage of allowing them to dismiss employees without a period of notice. As a result of union activity, some industry agreements were reached, containing an explicit management and union commitment to convert casual hours to permanent, part-time hours, but enforcement has remained limited.

Although hotel, restaurant and catering workers may have to work irregular hours, they reportedly have an increasing choice available to them. A law has also recently been passed according to which workers have the right under certain conditions to switch to part-time work should they choose to do so. In areas where the seasonal element of the trade is particularly marked, and where the hotels or restaurants will only function during a limited period of the year, tourist establishments are obliged to close during the low season, with many of the staff, including hotel and restaurant owners, drawing unemployment benefit.

The Scottish winter sports centre at Aviemore has made considerable headway in countering this problem by promoting itself as a centre for "green" tourism and an ideal base from which to explore the surrounding Cairngorm region. The area has undertaken this promotion in partnership with conservation societies to ensure the sustainability of the venture, and much of the business now takes place during the summer months.

8

Sustainable Tourism Development

Developing countries currently have only a minority share of the international tourism market (approximately 30 per cent) but their share is growing. International tourism arrivals in developing countries have grown by an average of 9.5 per cent per year since 1990, in aggregate across developing countries, compared to a growth of 4.6 per cent in arrivals worldwide. The tourism industry makes important contributions to the economies of developing countries, particularly to foreign exchange earnings, employment, and Gross Domestic Product (GDP). On average international tourism receipts account for around 10 per cent of export revenues of developing countries.

Tourism's contribution to GDP varies from 3-5 per cent in Nepal and Kenya to 25 per cent in Jamaica; contribution to employment is estimated at 6-7 per cent in India and South Africa. The economic significance of tourism varies greatly from country to country, with those economies most highly dependent on tourism tending to be small island states. In Fiji, for example, tourism is the largest source of foreign exchange and the most important commercial source of employment, providing over 26 per cent of export revenue and some 16 per cent of GDP.

Tourism data does not provide the full picture of its economic significance. Statistics cover the contribution of international tourism to national GDP. They hide the significance of domestic tourism (and may underestimate regional tourists travelling by land), and the importance of tourism to a local economy. For example, tourism accounts for approximately 0.8 per cent of GDP in India, but it has been estimated that tourism (domestic and international) accounts for approximately half of economic activity in the hill region of Uttar Pradesh, popular for pilgrim trails.

Tourism is clearly of great significance to developing countries. But is it important in those countries with the highest proportion of poor people? The small island economies which are most dependent on tourism tend to be middle income and contain few of the worlds' poor. Across the poorest hundred countries or so, tourism is significant in almost half of the low income countries, and virtually all the lower-middle income countries. Tourism's strong contribution to economic growth is evident. But development thinking increasingly recognises that growth is necessary but not sufficient to ensure poverty elimination. Tourism affects the livelihoods of the poor in multiple ways - economically, environmentally, socially and culturally.

Impacts on livelihoods and not just income need to be assessed along with the variety of positive and negative affects. Differential impacts between poor groups, particularly the fairly poor and the poorest, can be expected. The poor are more vulnerable to the main negative impacts, such as conflicts with other livelihood strategies through loss of natural resources, and vulnerability due to local inflation. They face the greatest barriers to seizing economic opportunities created by tourism. Therefore net direct gains are more likely to be experienced by 'the masses' than the poorest. However, in several countries and tourism areas, the masses fall below a dollar a day. Where they don't, poverty elimination according to international definitions will depend on economic links between the 'masses' and the 'poor.'

Few analyses assess the poverty status of those affected by tourism, the impacts of tourism on poverty, or the distribution of impacts between poor and less-poor local residents. Different segments and types of tourism can have substantially different impacts. Limited evidence suggests that domestic/regional tourism and independent travel can create proportionately more local economic opportunities than international packaged tourism. However, the latter can be economically significant because of its large scale. Cruises, all-inclusives and enclave tourism tend to generate fewest economic linkages, but can also limit the spread of unwanted environmental and social impacts.

'Ecotourism' and nature-based tourism are often promoted as a solution to sustainable development. While they bring development to more remote and hence poorer regions, it is not proven that they generate less damage and more benefits than mass tourism. Within the tourism industry, the informal sector is often where the poor and women can maximise benefits. Proponents argue that tourism has a number of advantages over other economic sectors in terms of its potential to generate pro-poor growth, in particular its size, labour intensity, potential for cross-sectoral linkages, and potential in countries with few other competitive exports.

On the other hand, sceptics argue that tourism, driven by foreign private sector interests is not an activity suited to poverty elimination, that economic benefits are not maximised due to high level of foreign ownership, high leakages and few linkages, and that it imposes substantial non-economic costs on the poor, in terms of displacement, lost access to resources, and cultural and social disruption. Many of the disadvantages associated with tourism are actually characteristics of growth and globalisation. Many of the negative impacts that arise as a result of tourism development would also occur with development in other sectors. For example, it is not clear from the data whether the leakage effect and the supposed high level of foreign ownership, are greater problems in tourism than in other sectors.

Similarly, while there is no doubt that tourism is vulnerable to swings in demand at country level (due to insecurity, recession or hurricanes), it is not clear that volatility is any greater than volatility in prices and demand in other exports, particularly commodity exports. It would seem therefore that many of the difference between tourism and other sectors might be perceived rather than real. Tourism can be perceived as a frivolous or elitist industry and hence is treated less seriously than other primary industries by governments and donors. The classic stereotype of tourism - the juxtaposition between the rich tourist and the poor local person - reinforces this perception. Nevertheless, there are some characteristics which do seem particularly strong, if not unique, in tourism.

Among the disadvantages, tourism requires highly sophisticated marketing, which is particularly difficult for poor producers, often involves more haphazard development than other sectors and intense competition for natural resources with local residents (particularly in coastal zones). Among the advantages:

— *Tourism is consumed at the point of production*: Because the customer comes to the product, opportunities for entrepreneurs to capitalise on linkages (e.g. tea selling) can be greater.

— *Most export industries depend on financial, productive and human capital*: Tourism depends on these but also on natural capital (e.g. wildlife) and culture, which are assets that some of the poor have, or are gaining increasing control over where decentralisation and devolution of tenure are occurring.

— *Tourism is often reported to be more labour intensive than other productive sectors*: Data from six countries with satellite tourism accounts does indicate that it is more labour intensive than non-agricultural activities, particularly manufacturing, although less labour intensive than agriculture.

— There is a greater uptake of jobs by women than in other sectors although it is not known if more jobs are taken by the poor and unskilled. The percentage of female employment varies enormously by country, ranging from over 60 per cent such as in Bolivia to under 10 per cent in some Muslim countries.

— Tourism is a much more diverse industry than many others and can build upon a wide resource base. Diversity makes it difficult to deal with a government or donor, but increases the scope for wide participation, and for the informal sector.

The potential of tourism compared to other sectors should be considered in the light of the alternative opportunities available in any location. Tourism is a traded-good, and whether it is appropriate to develop it in a particular country depends on its comparative advantage. Given that tourism is already a fact of life for many of the world's poor, the challenge is to enhance the many positive impacts and reduce costs to the poor

Natural Environment

The natural environment is an important resource for tourism. With increasing urbanisation, destinations in both industrialised and developing countries with significant natural features, scenery, cultural heritage or biodiversity are becoming increasingly popular sites for tourist destinations. Efforts to preserve and enhance the natural environment should therefore be a high priority for the industry and for governments. But the reality is not quite as clear cut.

Environments where past human interaction has been minimal are often fragile. Small islands, coastal areas, wetlands, mountains and deserts, all now popular as tourist destinations, are five of the six 'fragile ecosystems' as identified by Agenda 21 that require specific action by governments and international donors. The biophysical characteristics of these habitats often render them particularly susceptible to damage from human activities. As the scale of tourism grows, the resource use threatens to become unsustainable.

With a degraded physical environment, the destination is in danger of losing its original attraction, increasing the levels of cheaper mass tourism and forcing more "nature-based" tourism to move on to new destinations, which are likely to be even more inaccessible and fragile. Mainstream "ecotourism", as promoted after the Rio Earth Summit, hasn't always enjoyed a good reputation. Tour operators have used the concept merely as a "greenwash" marketing tool. In reality it often meant introducing unsustainable levels of tourism into fragile areas, having scant regard for either the environment or for the residents of the destination areas.

As the International Council for Local Environmental Initiatives (ICLEI) pointed out: "Tourism in natural areas, euphemistically called "ecotourism," can be a major source of degradation of local ecological, economic and social systems. The intrusion of large numbers of foreigners with high consumption and high-waste habits into natural areas, or into towns with inadequate waste management infrastructure, can produce changes to those natural areas at a rate that is far greater than imposed by local residents.

These tourism-related changes are particularly deleterious when local residents rely on those natural areas for their sustenance. Resulting economic losses can encourage socially deleterious economic activities such as prostitution, crime, and migrant and child labour". Some of the different kinds of impacts that tourism development and operational activities can have include:

— Threats to ecosystems and biodiversity - e.g loss of wildlife and rare species, habitat loss and degradation,
— Disruption of coasts - e.g shoreline erosion and pollution, impact to coral reefs and fish spawning grounds,
— Deforestation - loss of forests for fuel wood and timber by the tourist industry also impact on soil and water quality, biodiversity integrity, reducing the collection of forest products by local communities,
— Water overuse - as a result of tourism / recreational activities e.g. golf courses, swimming pools, and tourist consumption in hotels,
— Urban problems - Congestion and overcrowding, increased vehicle traffic and resultant environmental impacts, including air and noise pollution, and health impacts,
— Exacerbate climate change - from fossil fuel energy consumption for travel, hotel and recreational requirements,
— Unsustainable and inequitable resource use - Energy and water over consumption, excessive production of wastes, litter and garbage are all common impacts.

Economic Gains

Economic gains have been a major driving force for the growth of tourism in developing countries. The initial period of growth happened in the late 1960's and 1970's, when tourism was perceived as a key activity for generating foreign exchange and employment by both development institutions, such as the World Bank, as well as by governments. Despite the negative economic impacts of tourism (such as inflation; dominance by outsiders in land and property markets; inward-migration eroding economic opportunities for domestic industry including the poor) the demand for travel and tourism continues to grow.

The WTTC has estimated there was an approximate 40% cumulative growth in tourism demand between 1990 and 2000. This demand was largely driven by economic gains at all levels, including in the communities in remote, and hitherto relatively isolated, destinations. There is significant scope for enhancing the possible gains through addressing a number of issues that can help improve opportunities for entrepreneurs and the communities in the destinations, for the poorer sections within these communities, as well as at the macro level for the national economy.

Powerful transnational corporations (TNCs) continue to dominate the international tourism market. Estimates suggest that about 80% of international mass tourism is controlled by TNCs. These companies have an almost unhindered access to markets and use this to drive down the cost of supplies. The result is high levels of financial leakage, and limited levels of revenue retention in the destination or host countries.

Financial leakages tend to occur due to various factors, including importation of foreign building material, skilled labour and luxury products, and packaged travel arranged with TNCs. This is as opposed to locally sourcing the necessary resources. It has been estimated that, on average, at least 55% of tourism expenditure flows back out of the destination country, rising to 75% in certain cases e.g. the Gambia and Commonwealth Caribbean.

During the seventh UN Commission on Sustainable Development (CSD) meeting, financial leakages was identified as a key area for stakeholders to take action and work together in order to try and assess the situation, as well as seek solutions to better support local communities in host / developing countries.

The CSD called upon the UN and the World Tourism Organization, in consultation with major groups, as well as other relevant international organizations, to jointly facilitate the establishment of an ad-hoc informal open-ended working group on tourism to:

— Assess financial leakages and determine how to maximize benefits for indigenous and local communities,
— Prepare a joint initiative to improve information availability and capacity-building for participation, and
— address other matters relevant to the implementation of the international work programme on sustainable tourism development.

In most tourist destinations of developing countries, the livelihood impacts of tourism, takes various forms. Jobs and wages are only a part of livelihood gains and often not the most significant ones. Tourism can generate four different types of local cash income, involving four distinct categories of people:

— Wages from formal employment.
— Earnings from selling goods, services, or casual labour (e.g. food, crafts, building materials, guide services).
— Dividends and profits arising from locally-owned enterprises.
— Collective income: this may include profits from a community-run enterprise, dividends from a private sector partnership and land rental paid by an investor.

Waged employment can be sufficient to lift a household from an insecure to a secure footing, but it may only be available to a minority of people, and not the poor. Casual earnings may be very small, but more widely spread, and may be enough, for instance, to cover school fees for one or more children. Local participation in the industry can be categorised into three different categories; the formal sector (such as hotels), the informal sector (such as vending) and secondary enterprises that are linked to tourism (such as food retail and telecommunications).

Transport tends to fall into a grey area between formal and informal sectors. Most destinations have taxis, jeeps or other motorised forms of transport, often driven by the owners. As things expand organised associations of owners, operating on a rota system become more common. Data about employment in the formal sector is scattered and collection is often not very systematic. There are references of cases where high-status jobs in resorts typically go to non-locals, expatriate staff or foreign-trained nationals. However, there is almost no analysis of who is employed in middle and lower ranking jobs. The potential for employment of local staff seems to improve as one moves away from the luxury resorts into less established areas.

The informal sector includes activities such as vending, running stalls and collecting fuel wood for the tourist industry. The informal sector often provides an easy entry into the industry for the poor, especially for women. The incomes can be substantial but unreliable as it is often a seasonal activity. However it can still provide a substantial boost to the income of the poor. The informal sector tends to get the least attention when interventions are planned, and interventions such as planning permissions are frequently detrimental to this sector. However, there are cases where initiatives such as flexible licensing systems and cooperatives and associations have helped the sector. Causal labour and self-employment provide major opportunities for local communities to enhance their livelihood opportunities from tourism.

Unlike formal employment, self-employment tends to highlight the entrepreneurial spirit of village communities. Villagers are used to stringing together a livelihood from a diverse variety of sources, often giving them a knack for enterprise. Causal labour includes porters, cooks, guides, launderers, cleaners, caterer and entertainers. Nepal, for instance, has a well- organised labour market to employ porters, cooks and guides on a seasonal basis.

Significant gains also accrue from economic linkages between tourism and other economic sectors such as agriculture, horticulture, animal husbandry and handicrafts. There is a need for a standardised framework and guidelines for the collection and analysis of comparative data sets, to better identify the possible economic impacts for different segments of the market, as well as to develop policies which better reflect the needs of the informal as well as formal tourism ventures. Another gap in research about tourism relates to understanding how domestic tourism benefits formal and informal segments in a country and the degree to which the extreme poor gain at all from the industry.

Domestic or regional tourists are particularly important clients for self-employed sellers and owners of small establishments (the skilled poor and not-so-poor). Studies in Yogyakarta (Indonesia) and elsewhere in South East Asia show that domestic and other Asian tourists tend to buy more from local vendors than Western tourists. Budget and independent tourists, particularly backpackers are also more likely than luxury tourists to use the cheaper guest houses, home-stays, transport and eating services provided by local people. They tend to stay longer at a destination than groups of tourists and interact more with the local economy, but also spend less per day, often bargaining over prices.

Nature-based tourism (including 'ecotourism') does not necessarily provide more opportunities for the poor than 'mass tourism'. Nature tourism does offer some potential advantages however. It takes place in less developed areas, often involves smaller operators with more local commitment. It involves a higher proportion of independent travellers, and if marketed as 'ecotourism' can stimulate consumer pressure for ensuring domestic socio-economic benefits. But it remains a niche in the market, can be heavily dependent on imports, and can spread disruption to less developed areas.

Mass tourism is highly competitive, and usually dominated by large suppliers who have little commitment to a destination. They are less likely to use local suppliers. However the segment does generate jobs and negative impacts are not always spread beyond immediate localities. Some governments are trying to actively reduce this, for example the Gambian Government has recently decided to ban 'all-inclusives' in response to local demands.

The informal sector is where opportunities for small-scale enterprise or labour by the poor are maximised. For example, at Bai Chay, Ha Long Bay in Vietnam, almost a dozen local families run private hotels, but local involvement in tourism spreads far beyond this, to an estimated 70-80% of the population. Apart from those with jobs in the hotels and restaurants, local women share the running of noodle stalls, many women and children are walking vendors, and anyone with a boat or motorbike hires them out to tourists.

TOURISM AND SOCIETY DEVELOPMENTS

Tourism developments often stop people from having the right of access to land, water and natural resources. NGO's such as Tourism Concern and Rethinking Tourism have reported on examples worldwide where the articles in the UN Declaration of Human Rights are flouted, and where indigenous rights are lost or exploited. Adverse social impacts also include poor working conditions, low wages, child labour and sex tourism.

The International Labour Organisation and International Confederation Free Trade Unions (ICFTU) note that some parts of the tourist industry still degrades labour and drives workers to the lowest levels, exhibiting the worst side of unsustainable production. Fears of tourism threatening local cultures can be misplaced and many cultures have proved resilient enough to be able to take rapid changes required by tourism in their stride. However it is true that popular destinations are typically transformed at a very rapid pace. Buzzing small towns can replace sleepy one lane bazaars.

Areas where once only officials rode in motorised vehicles become a familiar site for traffic jams, and dealing with unknown faces can become a daily occurrence for people whose previous focus had been confined to a few score square kilometres to their home and work. Communities visited by tourists can adapt surprisingly quickly. For example, they rapidly adopt businesslike attitudes to maximise profits. They are creative in inventing and staging events to entertain and provide information on their culture. These attractions, while usually not explicitly developed to protect back regions (i.e. areas of a host society reserved only for local residents, where tourists are not welcome), can function to deflect the tourist gaze from private space and activities.

Host communities take specific, active measures to protect their values and customs. This can either be covert action such as private communal functions, fencing off of domesticities but also overt action such as organised protests and even aggression to protect their interests.

Tourism development in remote areas can be positive however, bringing with it infrastructure, health services and education facilities. It could be a by-product, or a result of increased incomes, or as is happening increasingly, a result of corporate and customer social responsibility. Nevertheless, rapid tourism development can come at a price and often creates its own unique problems. Tourism activities can degrade the social and natural wealth of a community.

The intrusion of large numbers of uninformed foreigners into local social systems can undermine preexisting social relationships and values. This is particularly a problem where tourism business is centred in traditional social systems, such as isolated communities or indigenous peoples. There are also examples in ecotourism segment, of communities becoming marginalised and forced out of traditional lands as protected areas and destinations become established.

Involving host and particularly local communities in all stages of tourism development, from planning right through operations, will help to alleviate some of these issues - if their needs and perspectives are properly taken into account. There is growing amount of work in this area and an expanding body of good practice examples but such approaches need to extended. In addition, programmes which aim to train and assist communities adversely affected by tourism development i.e. providing a social safety net need to be openly assessed for their suitability, and promoted where appropriate.

On the darker side to global tourism, the sex trade and drug tourism remain areas that are poorly reported or regulated, especially where it concerns children. The root causes behind these growing problems may not wholly lie with growth in tourism, but it is significant and should be a real cause for concern throughout the sector.

In recent years the industry has started to try and tackle such problems.

In 1998 it collaborated with ECPAT (End Child Prostitution and Trafficking in Children for Sexual Purposes) to draw up a Code of Conduct for tour operators in relation to child prostitution and tourism. Signatories to ECPAT's Code of Conduct commit themselves to:

— working against child exploitation in their policy documents;
— training staff on how to combat child exploitation;
— provision of information to customers;
— putting pressure on suppliers by including a clause against the commercial sexual exploitation of children in the contract (with hotels, for example);
— provision of information to key local people and organizations by creating a network in destinations to raise awareness amongst local people.

The Fritidresor Group (FRG), a subsidiary of Thomson Travel Group, has risen to the challenge by following up on this initiative in a systematic manner. Since 1999 it has designed and conducted workshops, developed an elaborate customer information programme and initiated pilot programmes in five destinations where child abuse is common. Feedback from ECPAT from one of the pilots has been positive, e.g. the number of paedophiles in Thailand is decreasing. There are concerns, however, that this is happening at the expense of other countries, especially in Central America, where ECPAT has a weaker presence.

The general picture suggests that the formal tourism industry seems to be a particularly important sector for women (46% of the workforce are women, compared to 34-40% in other general labour markets). However the proportion of women in the tourism workforce varies greatly - from as low as 2% in some countries and up to over 80% in others, depending upon the maturity of the tourism industry. For example, in countries where there is a mature industry, women generally accounted for around 50% of those employed in the industry.

Several studies have indicated, whilst this area is frequently ignored, it also tends to be a significant contributor, particularly in developing countries. Tourism was only specifically mentioned in a few sections of 1992 Rio Agenda 21, despite its huge economic significance. Agenda 21 for the Travel and Tourism Industry was written in 1996 by the World Trade Organisation, the World Travel and Tourism Council and Earth Council to try and fill this gap. It noted that with a growing standing in the world economy the tourism industry has "a moral responsibility in making the transition to sustainable development. It also has a vested interest in doing so." These and other activities have supported a growing awareness of the positive and negative impacts of tourism, including a growing realisation of the impact that a degrading environment has on the livelihoods of communities living in destination areas.

This has contributed towards the initiation of positive actions for mitigating and minimising the more negative aspects. Various different approaches have been explored, especially in the last couple of decades. Emerging from these efforts is a better recognition of the importance of the role of local communities, their valuable knowledge base and understanding of local circumstances, as well as their strong vested interest in preserving a sustainable system. Establishing partnerships with local communities is being increasingly recognised as necessary for sustainable tourism.

The trend now is moving towards more integrated approaches, which include communities working with governments. International institutions such as UNEP are working in a number of ways (often in partnership) to promote sustainable tourism. This includes a proposal by UN Economic and Social Council to the UN General Assembly to designate 2002 the "UN International Year of Ecotourism". Though facing some controversy regarding the definition and breadth of the term "ecotourism", the idea was that the year would aim to recognise tourism's potential benefit as both a tool for environmental protection and development.

For example the World Tourism Organisation has produced a "Global Code of Ethics for Tourism in 1999 (an extension of the WTO "Manila Declaration on the Social Impacts of Tourism" 1997), as well as a "Compilation of good practices in sustainable tourism", and a practical guide for the development and application of indicators of sustainable tourism, "What Tourism Managers Need to Know".

The Rio Earth Summit 1992 was a major turning point for the tourism industry. Environmental issues subsequently became an important part of the agenda for the industry. However, the approach has not yet generally been an integrating one. Instead the focus has been on minimising environmental impacts that the industry is directly responsible for.

There is growing support by lead companies throughout the private sector to implement principles of Corporate Social Responsibility (CSR), Environmental Management and Auditing Systems (EMAS), "Triple Bottom Line" accounting procedures (Environment, Society and Economics) and Sustainability Reporting. Measures are predominately based on adopting a voluntary approach to tackling impacts rather than having regulations/ legislation imposed on business by governments. The action plan for the industry, "Agenda 21 for the Travel & Tourism Industry: Towards Environmentally Sustainable

Development" contains a number of priority areas for action and suggested steps to achieve them.

The importance of partnerships between government, industry and NGOs is stressed, along with the enormous benefits that will be obtained by making the tourism industry more sustainable. However it also makes it clear that the long-term costs of inaction will far outweigh those for starting to act now. Companies are encouraged to set up systems and procedures to incorporate sustainable development issues into core management functions and to identify actions needed to bring sustainable tourism into being.

A long-term communications programme was initiated after the document launch to increase awareness and promote regional implementation (WTTC). The 10 priority areas for action are:

- Waste minimization, re-use and recycling
- Energy efficiency, conservation and management
- Management of freshwater resources
- Waste water treatment
- Hazardous substances
- Transport
- Land-use planning and management
- Involving staff, customers and communities in environmental issues
- Design for sustainability
- Partnerships for sustainability

Another major voluntary activity highlighted by many companies is the use of codes of conduct and certification. However, even the voluntary codes lag far behind activities for environmental performance in the area of social responsibility. The World Tourism Organisation recently produced a study "Voluntary Initiatives for

Sustainable Tourism" examining 104 schemes worldwide and gives recommendations to improve the conditions for voluntary initiatives and achieve better effectiveness in the operation and support of voluntary initiatives.

Industry surveys have identified the need for establishing mandatory regulations, making it compulsory for everyone to meet the same standards and thereby incur similar costs. Legal and fiscal regulation of corporate sector includes market-based tools such as carbon trading, as supported through the Kyoto Protocol of the UN Framework Convention for Climate Change. Also environmental standards legislated by governments on water quality and waste management, labelling standards, are growing but need to be more widely implemented and effectively enforced. NGOs are increasingly engaging with the travel sector.

They have been playing an active role in addressing problems such as financial leakages and in trying to encourage greater corporate responsibility. Key activities involve consumer education about the potential impacts of tourism and about how local communities might benefit more from the industry. They actively lobby policy-makers on associated issues of trade liberalisation, fair trade and globalisation. There has also been a concerted effort to set up common certification standards, independent of the industry, along the lines of Fair Trade certification or eco-labelling.

During the 1990's a number of initiatives emerged which aimed to help communities in destination countries make the most from opportunities provided by tourism. Many have been self initiated, locally and have continued to expand under their own steam, sometimes attracting external technical and/or financial assistance on their own terms. In others, external agents have acted as catalysts. The nature of the activities have been broad, ranging from small one-village initiatives for organising handicrafts production to building powerful networks of small accommodation providers and creating a marketing network for them. Over time, and by learning from experience and sharing knowledge, these initiatives have tended to become more complex and inclusive.

Effective multi-stakeholder processes have evolved from the ground. Backed with success and experience at the ground level and on a significant scale, lessons learnt here have the potential for wide and rapid replication. A World Tourism Organisation report on the role of local authorities noted that local authorities have a key role to play in many aspects of tourism development and operations. As countries becomes more decentralised, they are taking on more in this area and realising that the sector may assist local areas in achieving development.

Community involvement is referred to as a key part of this process - ensuring participation in planning and development, therefore increasing the possibility of achieving more local benefits from tourism e.g. employment, income, establishing tourism related enterprises. The report notes that many local authorities lack in experience for planning, nurturing and developing tourism however. This can result in wasted resources and opportunities. The report states that proper planning, efficient implementation and effective management are all essential to optimise the benefits of tourism (WTO 1998).

The statement by the International Council for Local Environmental Initiatives (ICLEI) during the seventh session of the CSD said that "in addition to their direct roles in the development process, perhaps the most important role that local authorities can play in a global economy is that of facilitator among the diverse interests seeking to influence the direction of local development". ICLEI also stated that "solutions to adverse tourism impacts are to be found in the shared interest of local communities, tourism businesses, and tourism consumers to maintain the natural wealth and social heritage of the tourist destination". Thus a major challenge for "sustainable tourism" will be the creation of tangible and working local partnerships.

One way to approach this will be through the principles espoused in Local Agenda 21. These principles should be applied, through partnerships, to evaluate and improve efforts to address sensitive tourism development issues, including:

— Inequitable distribution of tourism revenues and "financial leakages"

— Displacement of pre-existing local settlements by tourism developments

— Equal access to local coastal and recreational resources

— Conflict over use and long-term protection of those areas

— Concerns related to lack of foreign tourist sensitivity to cultural traditions and sites

A study for the European Union made some useful recommendations for governments to take action in support of sustainable tourism. In addition, it recommends production of regional and national tourism strategies, as well as the development and exchange of knowledge through regional networks on sustainable tourism, engaging stakeholders as well as government ministries.

Pro-Poor Tourism (PPT) is an approach that gaining recognition by national governments and local authorities. Although PPT is still relatively new and has not been widely applied in practice, existing case studies reveal a number of lessons. These include:

— Diverse activities - beyond community tourism it includes product development, marketing, planning, policy, and investment.

— A lead advocate for PPT is useful, but involving other stake-holders is critical. PPT can be incorporated into the tourism development strategies of government or business.

— Location: PPT works best where the wider destination is developing well.

— PPT strategies often involve development of new products, particularly products linked to local culture. These products should be integrated with mainstream markets where possible.

— Ensuring commercial viability is a priority. This requires understanding demand, product quality, marketing, investment in business skills, and involving the private sector.

— Economic measures should expand both formal and casual earning opportunities.

— Non-financial benefits (e.g. increased community participation, access to assets) can reduce market vulnerability.

— PPT is a long-term investment. Expectations must be prudent and opportunities for short-term benefits investigated.

— External funding may be necessary to cover substantial transaction costs of establishing partnerships, developing skills, and revising policies.

Environmental Impacts of the Tourism Industry

Environmental management in the United States over the past several decades has focused on regulating production industries, such as manufacturing and mining. However, there has been increasing interest in the environmental effects of the service industry. Generally speaking, a service is as an activity done for others. A perhaps even broader definition of a service is anything sold in trade that cannot be dropped on your foot. The service industry therefore comprises a variety of activities, from restaurants to hospitals to financial institutions. It accounts for 75% of the U.S. gross domestic product and 80% of U.S. employment.

The service industry merits attention because of its large size and consequently its potential for environmental impacts (both negative and positive). The tourism industry is one of the largest components of the service sector, and has considerable ability to influence environmental quality. Travel and tourism contributed $91 billion in revenue into the U.S. economy in 1998, supporting 16.2 million jobs directly and indirectly. Over forty-three million tourists visited the United States in 1998. Furthermore, the tourism industry is projected to be the largest U.S. private employer by 2000, and now represents 10% of the national private gross domestic product.

Tourist destinations tend to be places of the highest amenities, whether the amenities are social, cultural, or natural. These destinations, due in part to their high quality, are often in short supply relative to demand. This scarcity leads to the potential for degradation of tourist areas, as they reach and in some cases exceed their carrying capacity. The tourism industry is complex; being fragmented into several industries that, taken together, constitute what is commonly referred to as the travel and tourism industry. It comprises components of other industries that do not cater exclusively to tourists.

Sectors of the tourism industry include transportation (e.g., airlines, buses, automobiles), lodging, restaurants, the cruise industry, amusement parks and resorts, and general retail and merchandise stores. Included in the definition of the tourism industry is the associated development (e.g., tourist infrastructure) of tourist destinations, and tourist activities. We have identified impacts from tourist-related transportation, tourist-related development, tourist activities including some recreational activities such as boating, and direct impacts of the lodging and cruise industries.

The degree of environmental impact varies, depending on the type of tourist and the intensity of site use. There are day tourists, who visit a destination for a day and then leave; summer residents who are in effect tourists for a season; and tourists on bus tours and other trips that may visit a location for a few minutes or a number of days. Day tourists have an impact on the environment through their transportation to their destination as well as their activities once there. This is true for summer residents, but these tourists also have a cumulative impact, as they are in one place for a longer period of time.

For example, nutrients leaching from the septic systems of tourists' waterfront homes can accelerate eutrophication and contribute to depletion of dissolved oxygen supply of the adjacent water body. On the other hand, summer residents often are an important force in preserving the natural beauty of an area (e.g., the Adirondacks). Tourists who visit an area for longer than a day and choose to stay in hotels contribute to the impacts that the lodging industry has on the environment. In addition to the length of stay, tourist impacts depend on the type of activity undertaken. Passive activities such as birdwatching have different impacts than more active pursuits, such as snowmobiling or boating.

There are environmental impacts from the travel to a destination, the tourist activities in and of themselves at that destination, such as hiking or boating, and from the creation, operation, and maintenance of facilities that cater to the tourist, such as hotels. In 1995, twenty percent of U.S. commercial air travel was attributed to leisure, including rest and relaxation, sightseeing, and outdoor recreation. Aircraft emit the most carbon monoxide of any of the five listed air pollutants, but it is a small amount relative to other modes of transportation.

In total, aircraft are responsible for approximately one percent of the total ground-level emissions from mobile sources; therefore tourism-related air travel is responsible for only .2% of total ground-level emissions. Furthermore, tourism-related air travel contributes less than 1% of total U.S. emissions of each of the listed criteria pollutants. Although aircraft contribute only a small amount to total air pollution, emissions from this source is increasing. Between 1970 and1995, hydrocarbon and no emissions from aircraft sources have grown 53%. Projections to 2010 indicate that aircraft emissions will continue to increase. Aircraft emissions in nonattainment areas with large airport facilities in particular are projected to represent a growing percentage of regional sources of air pollutants.

The projections indicate an increase in the aircraft component of total regional emissions between 1990 and 2010 in ten metropolitan regions (nine of which are currently not in attainment of the National Ambient Air Quality Standards (NAAQS) for ozone; the tenth city has attained the ozone standard, but is considered an ozone 'maintenance' area). The 2010 percentages are still relatively low, ranging from 0.2% volatile organic compounds (VOC) in Philadelphia to 5.1% VOC in Charlotte; and 1.8% NOin Philadelphia to 7.6% in Charlotte.

The percentages are higher in Charlotte in part because other sources contribute less. The EPA has had regulations for smoke and hydrocarbon emissions from aircraft engines in place since 1984. In 1997, the agency promulgated new emission standards for nitrogen oxides and carbon monoxide. This rule was adopted to codify the existing voluntary emission standards of the United Nations International Civil Aviation Organization (ICAO).

Noise Pollution

In addition to air pollution, aircraft contribute to noise pollution. The FAA is responsible for addressing the noise abatement issue. The 1990 Airport Noise and Capacity Act authorized the FAA to reduce aircraft noise by requiring replacement of louder planes with quieter aircraft. In fact, airlines have spent billions of dollars to address this problem. There are also noise impacts from air tour operators, such as those that take 800,000 passengers a year on scenic overflights of the Grand Canyon.

In an effort to reduce unnatural noise, the FAA proposed new rules in August 1999 that would cap the number of overflights in the Grand Canyon. However, again, as tourism-related travel represents only 20% of commercial air travel, and airplanes are only one source of noise pollution, tourism's contribution to total noise pollution is minor. Much of the tourism-related air pollution comes from automobiles. Thirty-five percent of people traveling for leisure in 1995 used personal automobiles as their means of travel. Four-hundred million leisure trips are taken in automobiles per year in the United States; 80% of those trips are 250 miles or less. In 1997, light duty vehicles emitted an average of 1.53 grams of exhaust hydrocarbons per mile, 19.86 grams of carbon monoxide per mile, and 1.51 grams of nitrogen oxide per mile.

Automobiles emit by far the most carbon monoxide, nitrogen oxide, and volatile organic compounds in comparison to other transportation. Personal automobiles emit 32% percent of the total national carbon monoxide emissions, and 12% of total national nitrogen oxide emissions. However, it is difficult to separate the amount of tourismrelated automobile travel from all automobile travel. One area where it is possible to distinguish between tourism-related automobile travel and other travel is within national parks. Exhaust from tourists' cars affects air quality and vegetation in some national parks.

Adverse impacts on vegetation have been attributed to automobile exhausts in Yosemite. Almost three-quarters of n national park superintendents surveyed cited exhaust from tourists' cars as a significant factor affecting air quality within the parks. Tour buses have an impact on air quality as well. Often referred to as the motorcoach industry, the tour bus industry includes 3,000 companies and 25,000 vehicles. Companies are classified as inter-city or charter-tour. The latter constitutes more than 50% of the market. Charter-tour bus trips have increased, while inter-city trips have declined.

Specific emissions data on tour buses are not available, but most tour buses belong in the category of heavy-duty diesel vehicles. In 1997, these vehicles emitted 1.468 million short tons (mst) of carbon monoxide, and 1.886 mst of nitrogen oxide. Another form of ground transportation that has grown in the past twenty years is the recreational vehicle (RV) and off-road recreational vehicle (ORV) sector. These non-road recreational vehicles do not include sport utility vehicles, or SUVs. These data suggest that this segment of tourism-related transportation does not contribute significantly to air quality problems, as land recreational vehicles contribute less than 1% of U.S. total emissions of each listed pollutant.

Ground transportation can also have an impact on natural habitat. This impact occurs primarily through road construction. However, some vehicles such as ORVs can have a direct impact. As noted earlier, the distinction between tourism and recreation is a difficult one to make. While ORVs can be considered to be primarily recreational, some ORV users travel significant distances to participate in a recreational activity. When ORV use occurs during a trip away from home (as part of a larger tourist trip), it can be considered a tourist activity as well as a recreational one.

Off-road vehicles have damaged dune systems and salt marshes in Barnstable, and Provincetown, Massachusetts. Only 50 passes of an ORV at the foot of dunes halted growth of beach grass that stabilizes the dune. This causes erosion of the dunes, which in turn increases the risk of damage from flooding, as dunes provide natural flood protection. In addition, the use of ORVs by tourists has proven destructive to wildlife in some areas. Cape Cod National Seashore has had to initiate seasonal and spatial permits for ORV users to protect Piping Plovers during their nesting period. An ORV race across the deserts of California and Nevada has been permanently cancelled as a result of the damage the vehicles were doing to the desert tortoise populations.

For example, recreational boaters who take their boats to Block Island from the coast of Connecticut can be considered tourists (because they are visiting a destination away from home). The impact of this activity occurs in transit to a tourist destination. Recreational marine vehicles, can, therefore, affect air quality during transit to a destination and while their owners boat in and around that destination. Recreational marine vehicles do not emit as much carbon monoxide as automobiles, but they do emit significantly more of it than recreational land vehicles (such as off-road vehicles) and aircraft.

The EPA found that nonroad hydrocarbon emissions represent 10% of urban summertime HC emissions. Recreational marine engines were responsible for 30% of the nonroad engine emissions. In addition, two-stroke engines, such as those found on personal watercraft, are rather inefficient and typically release 25-30% of oil and gas into the surrounding water. However, emissions from marine recreational vehicles represent only a small percentage of total national emissions; therefore their effects are less pronounced than with automobiles. The Clean Air Act Amendments of 1990 gave the EPA authority for the first time to regulate emissions from nonroad engines and vehicles.

The EPA set emissions standards for new spark-ignition gasoline marine engines in 1996, including outboard engines, personal watercraft engines, and jet boat engines. These are designed to reduce hydrocarbon emissions from these types of engines 75% by 2025. These emissions standards do not apply to inboard motors, as they emit fewer pollutants, but they do apply to outboard engines sold starting in 1998, and to personal watercraft (such as jetskis) engines sold starting in 1999.

The environmental impacts of the construction and development of facilities needed to support the industry are both immediate and gradual. Development associated with tourism includes accommodations, roads, retail stores and restaurants, tourist attractions, tourists seasonal waterfront homes, water supplies, and waste disposal facilities. Cumulative effects over time are particularly problematic because the developer in question is often out of the picture before impacts become obvious. An example of a gradual impact is the leaching of nutrients from septic systems of tourists' waterfront homes into the waterbody, accelerating eutrophication and depleting dissolved oxygen supplies.

Tourist infrastructure can also adversely impact water quality because more wastewater is created in one place and reduced someplace else, putting more pressure on sewage treatment plants or septic systems in the tourist destination. When a sewage treatment plant receives more effluent than it can treat, the excess can flow directly into water bodies untreated, creating a potential health hazard. The sewage problem with tourist facilities is further exacerbated by the seasonal nature of many tourist areas. An area which off-season may have the capacity (either through septic systems or treatment plants) to properly treat sewage may be overburdened during the tourist season.

Sewage effluent can damage coral reefs because it stimulates the growth of algae, which cover the filter-feeding corals, hampering their ability to get food. Furthermore, the algae impede the transmission of sunlight to the plant cells (zooxanthellae) living within the corals' tissue, hindering their ability to grow and provide the coral with needed nutrition. Tourist facilities increase the amount of impervious surfaces, causing more runoff to reach water bodies. This runoff contains nutrients, suspended particles, and oil and gas. Excess nutrients added to a water body can accelerate the process of eutrophication, causing an overgrowth of algae, which in turn uses up excess dissolved oxygen as the algae decays, causing fish kills.

The overgrowth of algae is also a nuisance to swimmers. Furthermore, if masses of algae wash up on shore, they can create a foul-smelling area and a breeding ground for biting flies. A relevant example is the accelerated eutrophication of Lake Tahoe since the 1950s. Increased development to accommodate tourism and recreation contributed to the degradation of water quality for two primary reasons:

i) the increase of impervious surface, which in turn led to increased runoff of nutrients into the lake, and

ii) the destruction of wetlands needed to filter those pollutants. Construction of facilities supporting the tourism industry can damage wetlands, mangroves, coral reefs, and estuaries.

Wetlands have been destroyed to make way for roads, airports, marinas, sewage treatment plants, and recreational facilities. This destruction is problematic because wetlands provide many crucial functions, including acting as a nursery ground for a diverse aquatic community, and helping to buffer the impacts of pollutants to the water body.

In Cancun, Mexico, the natural environment of mangrove wetlands was almost completely destroyed by the development of tourist hotels and their associated infrastructure. Similarly, in Jamaica over 700 acres of wetlands have been destroyed since the 1960s for tourism development. In the Rocky Mountain National Park, the construction of a high-level road increasing human accessibility led to the destruction of 95% of the vegetation cover in some areas close to the road.

Although tourism has been the impetus for much destructive development, it has also been the motivation for preserving sensitive ecosystems. Some of this motivation stems from economic benefits, as natural parks serve as attractions for tourists. An example on an international level is the Parc des Volcans in Rwanda, which provides ecological benefits through protection of the local watershed, and economic benefits, as it is the country's third largest source of foreign exchange.

Everglades National Park in Florida is a domestic example of a sensitive wetland and estuarine environment where tourism has spurred preservation efforts. Tourism with an emphasis on cultural and historic sites has been called 'heritage' or 'cultural' tourism, and is one of the fastest growing trends in the industry. Heritage tourism focuses on sharing the historical and cultural resources of an area with travelers, while still maintaining the integrity of each site.

This type of tourism has been the impetus for the rehabilitation of existing historic sites, buildings, and monuments, such as the facelift that historic houses, lighthouses, and piers received on Cape Cod in the name of tourism. Similarly, the 18century capital of the former

British colony of Virginia, Williamsburg, has been transformed from ruins to a thriving historic site and tourist destination.

Renovations to the Custer House at Fort Abraham Lincoln State Park in North Dakota were completed in part to attract additional tourists. A final example where heritage tourism has been the catalyst for improvement is the rural, somewhat neglected farm town of Fort Benton, Montana. It was transformed into an international tourist attraction because of several historic sites that were restored, including a Lewis and Clark memorial, the Museum of the Northern Great Plains, and the Museum of the Upper Missouri.

A related benefit of tourism can be the revitalization of derelict urban areas. Another benefit of tourism development is its role in fostering an appreciation and understanding of nature. Tourism development can facilitate an increasing awareness and appreciation of the natural world. Development undertaken to cater to tourists in coastal areas can have adverse impacts. Jetties and breakwaters built to create artificial harbors can increase erosion of those areas on the downstream side of the littoral drift (i.e., the movement of sand along the nearshore underwater propelled by the prevailing current).

In addition to their physical impacts, these structures can detract from the aesthetics of an area. The construction of marinas can alter water levels and nutrient concentrations, as well as destroy habitat. However, tourism-related development can benefit a coastal zone as well as harm it. Public access, for example, often increases with tourism development, as some states have legislation requiring developers to maintain some public access with development. Furthermore, tourism injects the resources along a coast and adjacent waters with political and economic value, helping to ensure their protection.

The political value stems from the significant constituency of summer residents and day tourists who want to maintain their recreation area. Slightly more obvious are the economic benefits from fostering tourism along the coast, as revenue is generated from entrance, parking, and other fees, as well as from sales and employment. Tourism-related development has an impact on wildlife, also. Development in the lower elevations of mountain resorts (where it usually is located) restricts the migratory winter range of certain wildlife.

Impacts on wildlife associated with tourist development can be indirect as well as direct. For example, automobile headlights, streetlights, and resort illumination on beachside roads can disorient marine turtles. This disorientation causes them to head inland instead of towards the sea. The growth of tourist communities can affect wildlife habitat.

Communities adjacent to national parks that cater to tourists are called 'gateway communities.' Development of these areas is often undertaken without consideration of the natural landscape. Indiscriminate and scattered development tends to detract from the local character of such areas and homogenizes the experience for the visitor. It is important to note that development adjacent to national parks is a trade-off for less development within the parks. If it is a question of one or the other, then it is preferable to develop outside of the parks.

However, there is no reason why areas adjacent to the parks cannot be developed in accordance with the natural environment and local character. There are positive economic impacts associated with tourism in gateway communities and host communities. More visitors can mean increased employment opportunities and an improved standard of living. Other economic benefits of tourism studies in the literature include improvement of public utilities and transport infrastructure, and an increase in tax revenues.

Air Pollution

The cruise industry has the potential to affect air quality through engine emissions. Most marine fuels are residual fuels with higher concentrations of contaminants such as sulfur. Recent studies have suggested that ocean-going vessels have the potential to affect air quality in coastal regions, port areas, and heavily traveled trade routes where annual sulfur emissions from ships equal or exceed land-based emissions. However, passenger vessels (cruise ships) contribute only 5% of nitrogen emissions from ships and 6% of sulfur emissions from ships.

The cruise industry contributes the least of all categories of ocean-going vessels to total nitrogen and sulfur emissions. The IMO approved global emission limits in September 1997, with no regulations applying to new ships or major ship conversions after January 1, 2000. Sulfur fuel levels are currently limited to 4.5% of the total fuel mixture. Cruise ships also produce toxic chemicals and hazardous waste from dry-cleaning procedures, used batteries, and paint waste from brush cleaning.

Waste oil is produced from normal leakage from the main engines and generators, the cleaning of fuel filters, losses during maintenance, and leaks from hydraulic systems. In 1997 passenger vessels (cruise ships) had 136 oil spills in U.S. waters, totaling 1,778 gallons. This amount represents only 1.6% of the total oil spills in the United States that year. The introduction of non-native species through discharge of ballast water is another potential environmental impact of the cruise industry.

The Council on Environmental Quality found that over 130 non-native species have been introduced to the Great Lakes since 1800, with almost a third thought to have been carried by ships. It is impossible, however, to distinguish how many of those ships were cruise ships. Introduced species cause problems because they can disrupt the food web of the ecosystem and clog the intake pipes of power plants and water treatment facilities. The International Maritime Organization has recognized these problems, and promulgated guidelines to minimize transfer of organisms.

Tourist Activities

Many tourist activities occur in fragile ecosystems, such as coral reefs. While snorkeling and diving in and of themselves do not cause much damage, inadvertent related activities, such as stepping on coral do cause damage. With such activities, it is the cumulative nature of the damage that is most problematic. One or two tourists may not cause much harm, but hundreds of them over time can do considerable damage to an ecosystem. Coral reefs are also affected by tourism as a result of the market for souvenirs. Tourists break off pieces of coral themselves, or the reef is dynamited by locals to sell the pieces.

The cumulative effect is relevant here as well, as one tourist may not understand her impact when aggregated with other tourists. Damage to coral reefs from tourists in the above-mentioned manners has occurred in Tanzania, Kenya, and Madagascar, among other places. Tourists hiking along mountain ranges can harm the ecosystem by littering and by trampling vegetation. The greatest impact of tourists on vegetation usually occurs during initial contact with an area, with the most sensitive species affected first.

The cumulative impact of tourists on vegetation gradually shifts species composition, because only the most resilient plants can survive in an area under constant pressure from tourist activities. Excessive hiking on trails has caused damage to the sequoia redwoods in California. Increased visitation at Arches National Park has contributed to the deterioration of the soil there, which can take up to 250 years to recover after being trampled. Alpine tundra in the Rocky Mountain National Park also has been damaged by human trampling. Hiking on the soil can also damage wildlife habitat.

Constant pressure can damage or destroy the burrows of reptiles, mammals, and underground-nesting birds. Tourists' use of trees for firewood and tent poles has diminished tree populations, altering the age structure of the plant community. In addition, fires started by tourists for camping have caused major damage in the forests of California. Littering not only contributes to visual pollution, but can also change the nutrient composition of soils and prevent light from reaching plants.

Furthermore, tourists have unwittingly carried exotic species to ecosystems, thereby upsetting their balance. Littering by tourists has caused wildlife, such as bears, to frequent the garbage area of campsites to scrounge for food. As animals become accustomed to human food, their behavior becomes more aggressive and can be potentially dangerous to humans. When Glacier National Park implemented management plans to restore normal feeding patterns for bears, there was a decrease in injuries to tourists.

Problems with Ecotourism

The numerous names and definitions make it difficult to ascertain how environmentally responsible ecotourism is. There are important distinctions among nature tourism, adventure travel, and ecotourism. Nature tourism implies enjoyment and appreciation of nature, yet it often does not include protection of the environment. Adventure travel utilizes local resources often without consideration of impacts. Ecotourism, as the above definition suggests, is concerned with the concurrent enjoyment and preservation of the natural environment. Aside from the uncertainty and discrepancies surrounding the labels, there are also problems with the term ecotourism itself.

It is possible that some travel suppliers that call themselves "eco" are only paying lip service to a marketable concept that is gaining popularity. Some travel outfitters use the label "eco" for short-term economic gain without truly abiding by environmental principles. One tour operator suggested in a survey that the label 'eco-tour' should be given only to those tour operators that directly benefit the culture or environment; otherwise they should be known as adventure travel operators. The development of industry standards or regulations about the definition of ecotourism would be a productive first step in differentiating these groups.

The Ecotourism Society (TES) established guidelines in 1993, which are fairly comprehensive and can be used as a starting point for developing an industry standard. These guidelines include educating travelers to minimize impact, ensuring that the tour company minimizes impact by example, and contributing to the economy of the region visited. The guidelines are voluntary and are therefore not monitored or enforced. One study suggested that tour operator compliance with the TES guidelines is strongly influenced by whether or not they can gain economically from them. Therefore, emphasizing the potential for economic gain from abiding by these ecotourism guidelines would increase compliance with them.

An accepted industry standard such as the TES guidelines can help identify the tour operators that conduct truly environmentally friendly tours. This identification would in turn aid travel agents in recommending qualified groups to interested tourists. Ecotourism can adversely impact the environment in the same way as traditional, mass tourism. Two examples are the destruction of coral reefs in the Caribbean and the disturbance of breeding habits of birds in Antarctica. In January of 1988 an Argentine naval vessel carrying paying tourists ran aground off the coast of Antarctica, spilling 250,000 gallons of fuel, damaging rookeries of 24,000 penguins.

A less dramatic type of damage is the disruption of wildlife when ecotour operators get too close to their habitat. The Virginia EcoTourism Association suggests that educating tour operators is the first step in preventing this type of damage. To that end, they are in the process of developing a guide certification system. Another problem with ecotourism is that it is often exclusive because eco-trips are usually more expensive. Therefore the 'mass' tourist is less likely to participate.

Bibliography

Adams, T. B.. "The Power of Perceptions: Measuring Wellness in a Globally Acceptable, Philosophically Consistent Way". *Wellness Management*. 2003. www.hedir.org Accessed on 20 September 2005.

Barnes PM, Powell-Griner E, McFann K, Nahin RL. "Complementary and alternative medicine use among adults: United States, 2002". *CDC Advance Data Report #343*. 2004.

Bhatt AD. "Clinical research on Ayurvedic therapies: myths, realities, and challenges". *Journal of the Associated Physicians of India*. 2001;49:558-562.

Chopra A, Doiphode VV. "Ayurvedic medicine—core-concept, therapeutic principles, and current relevance". *Medical Clinics of North America*. 2002;86(1):75-88.

Dash B, Kashyap L. *Basic Principles of Ayurveda Based on Ayurveda Saukhyam of Todarananda*. Concept Publishing Company. New Delhi.1980.

Dunn, H. L. "High-level Wellness for man and society", in: *American Journal of Public Health* 49 (6), S. 786-792.1959.

Gogtay NJ, Bhatt HA, Dalvi SS, et al. "The use and safety of non-allopathic Indian medicines". *Drug Safety*. 2002;25(14):1005-1019.

International trade in health services: difficulties and opportunities for developing countries.Geneva: United Nations Conference on Trade and Development; 1997. Background note by UNCTAD Secretariat, TD/B/COM.1/EM.1/2.

Janjaroen W, Supakankunti S. *International trade in health services in the millenium: a case of Thailand*. Bangkok: Centre for Health Economics; 2000.

Lodha R, Bagga A. "Traditional Indian systems of medicine". *Annals of the Academy of Medicine, Singapore*. 2000;29(1):37-41.

Manning, T., "Indicators of tourism sustainability", *Tourism Management*, 1999.

McCarthy, John, "Are Sweet Dreams made of this *Tourism in Bali and East Indonesia*", IRIP, 1995.

Mishra L, Singh BB, Dagenais S. "Healthcare and disease management in Ayurveda". *Alternative Therapies in Health and Medicine.* 2001;7(2):44-50.

Morgan, Derek. "Medical Tourism: Ethical Baggage and Legal Currencies." *Medical Ethics Tomorrow* 63.1 (2003):1-5.

Newson, Carey, "Tourism without traffic: a good practice guide", Transport 2000, London. Oversize G155, 2001.

Ormond, Meghann. "First World Treatment at Third World Prices." *Online posting*, 12

Pizam, Abraham & Mansfield, Yoel, "Consumer Behavior in Travel and Tourism", The Haworth Hospitality Press, Binghampton, New York, 1999.

Sen Gupta KN. 1984. *The Ayurvedic System of Medicine*. 1906, Reprint. Logos Press. New Delhi

Shankar K, Liao LP. "Traditional systems of medicine". *Physical Medicine and Rehabilitation Clinics of North America*. 2004;15:725-747.

Solomon, Jay. "A Hospital Empire Grows." *The Wall Street Journal*. 26 Apr. 2004.

Taylor, Gordon D, "Tourism and Sustainability - Impossible Dream or essential objective?", *Travel and Tourism Research Assocation*, Canada, 1991.

WTTC, World Tourism Organisation (WTO) & Earth Council, "Agenda 21 for the Travel and Tourism Industry: Towards environmentally sustainable tourism", *WTO*, Madrid, 1996.

Index

Acoustical environment 84
Acoustical treatment 87
Analogous harmony 77
Audible environment 87

Beverage department 95

Casual dining 100
Catering company 101
Catering facilities 95
Catering functions 96
Climate control 88, 89
Colour sensations 75
Community-based ecotourism 167
Community-Based Tourism Planning (CBTP) 146
Complementary harmony 77
Comprehensive planning 142
Cultural tourism 18

Dense materials 86
Dining area 89
Direct employment 213
Domestic market 160

Ecotourism 164
Emotional responses 76
Exhaust systems 89
Exterior design 92

Fluorescent tubes 82
Foodservice facilities 79
Foodservice lighting levels 83
Foodservice operations 109
Formal tourism plan 142

General Agreement on Trade in Services (GATS) 216
Global Distribution Systems (GDSs) 224
Globalized economy 234
Green tourism 18
Guest houses 156
Guiding Elements 152

High-Income Economies (HIEs) 220
Hong Kong Tourist Association (HKTA) 34
Hotel catering services 97
Hotel employment 2
Hotel managements 236
Hotel reservations 156

Industrial Classification of all Economic Activities (ISIC) 210

Information and Communications Technology (ICT) 235
Intelligent development 5

International Air Transport Association (IATA) 238

Kitchen areas 86

Leave Travel Concession (LTC) 161
Local capacity building 155

Market research technique 143
Marketing plan 174
Mass tourism 213
Meal plans 100
Mechanical equipment 86
Monochromatic harmony 77
Multi-bilateral negotiations 216

National policy plans 145
Natural environment 171
Nonmetropolitan regions 5

Organisational development 155

Periodic community assessment process 148
Primary colours 77
Professional literature 3
Property Management System (PMS) 237

Recreational areas 95
Refrigeration system 107
Relative humidity 89
Reverberant sound levels 85
Rural communities 154

Scramble serving line system 111
Sound-absorbing materials 85
Stakeholder experience 153
Straight-line configurations 110
Successful tourism planning 144
Sustainable tourism 17

Table settings 91
Targeted tourists 143
Thermodynamic comfort 88
Total serving capacity 111
Tourism industry 159
Tourism Labour Accounting System (TLAS) 212
Tourism planning 141
Tourism Satellite Accounts (TSAs) 212
Tourism Sector 210
Tourist industry 4
Travel management 157
Triad harmony 78

United Nations Conference on the Environment and Development (UNCED) 16

World Travel and Tourism Council (WTTC) 212

Notes